Cartouches

Field Guide
and
Identification Key

Identify and Read
Ancient Egyptian Royal Names

John R. Sharp

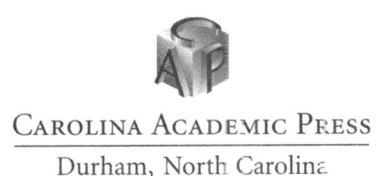

CAROLINA ACADEMIC PRESS
Durham, North Carolina

LCCN 2021947455
ISBN 978-1-5310-2267-9
e-ISBN 978-1-5310-2268-6

Inquiries:
EgyptFieldGuides@gmail.com
EgyptFieldGuides.com

Carolina Academic Press
700 Kent Street
Durham, North Carolina 27701
(919) 489-7486
www.cap-press.com

Printed in the United States of America

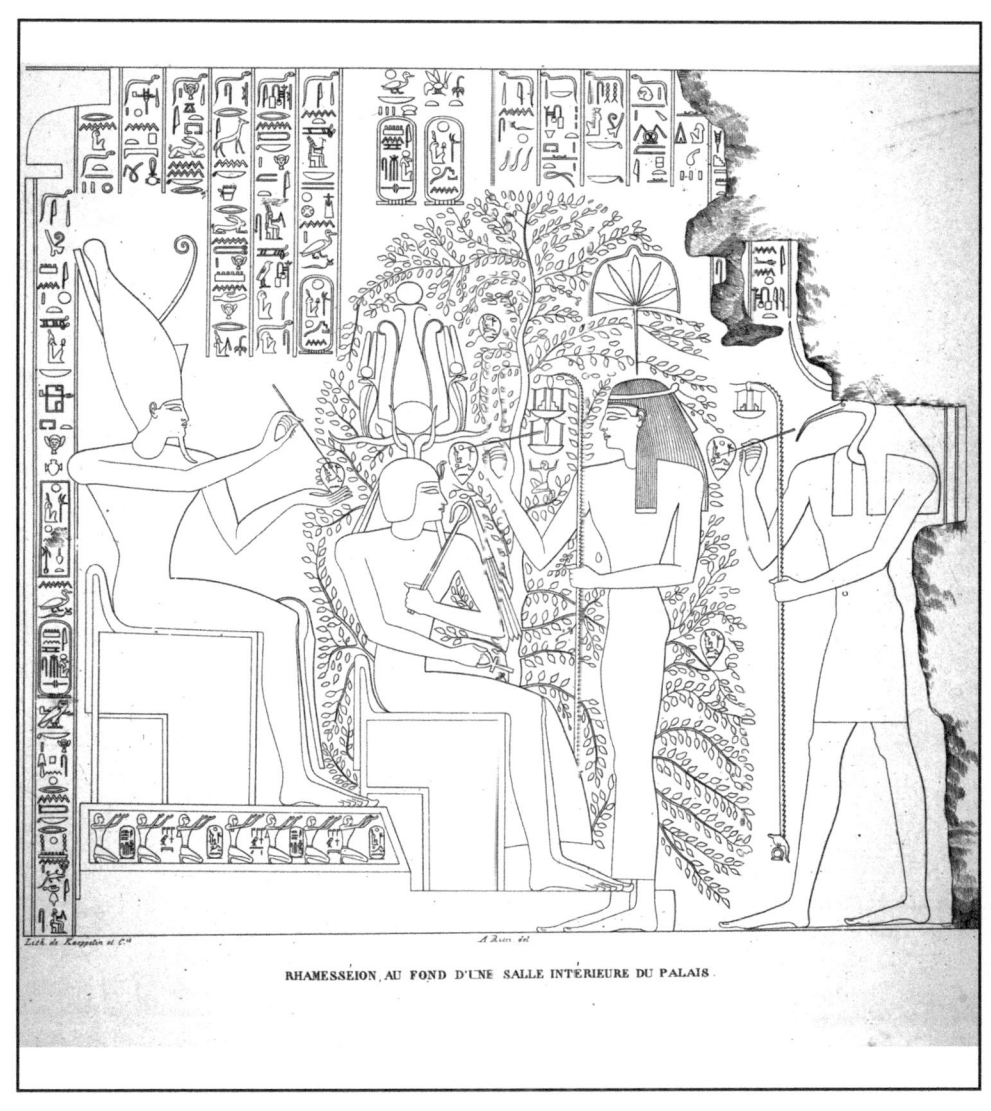

RHAMESSEION, AU FOND D'UNE SALLE INTÉRIEURE DU PALAIS.

Deities write the name of Ramses III on leaves of the Tree of Life

Cartouches

Field Guide
and
Identification Key

Dedication

To my loving, long-suffering wife, Janet

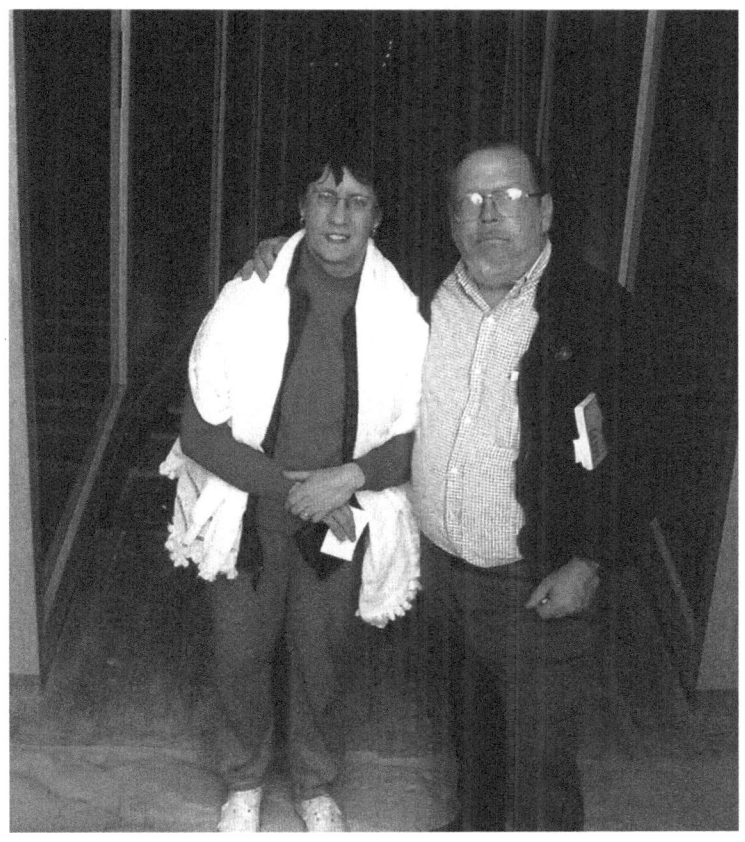

In front of a royal tomb, Valley of the Kings

Contents

Introduction and Acknowledgments

Reading royal names from ancient monuments and inscriptions is extremely satisfying and fun. What if, on a visit to Egypt, you accidentally put your foot through the ceiling of an undiscovered tomb? You'd want to know whose tomb it was in time for your press conference, wouldn't you? If you have visited ancient Egyptian sites, admit it, this possibility has crossed your mind! It wouldn't be the first time it has happened, either.

My introduction to Egyptology happened in 1974, when I was in Cairo to study the Arabic language at the American University in Cairo (AUC). The university was kind enough to send us on some field trips to ancient sites as well as contemporary points of interest. At the time, my knowledge of Egyptology was limited to what I had learned in Sunday School and the classic movie *The Ten Commandments*.

Inside the tombs and temples, every surface was covered with enough hieroglyphs and strange images to make your head swim. The Egyptian Museum was even worse—as my eyes got used to the dim interior I felt like Howard Carter when he first peered into Tutankhamen's tomb by candlelight: "(I see) wonderful things!" even though I had not yet come across that quote. The museum's atrium and corridors were piled with exquisite artifacts, any one of which could form the centerpiece of a lesser museum's collection, but here was seemingly shoved into a dark corner to make room for something even more exquisite. Unfortunately, at the time, many of the best items were unlabeled, or the original label, probably handwritten in Arabic or French over a century ago, had dried up and fluttered to the floor decades earlier.

As the year wore on, when I needed a break from studying Arabic, which was often, I would escape the hot dorm room or the even hotter classroom and take refuge in the lobby of the Nile Hilton on Tahrir Square, kitty-corner from the Egyptian Museum in Cairo. The Hilton was amazing. First, I would spend some time in the sumptuously appointed rest room, where I would stuff my pockets with soft American toilet tissue, then spend some of my meager savings on a book about Egyptology from the small bookshop. I read it in one of the soft chairs in the air conditioned lobby. Egypt was just getting over the 1973 War, you must remember, and things were tough, at least outside the Hilton.

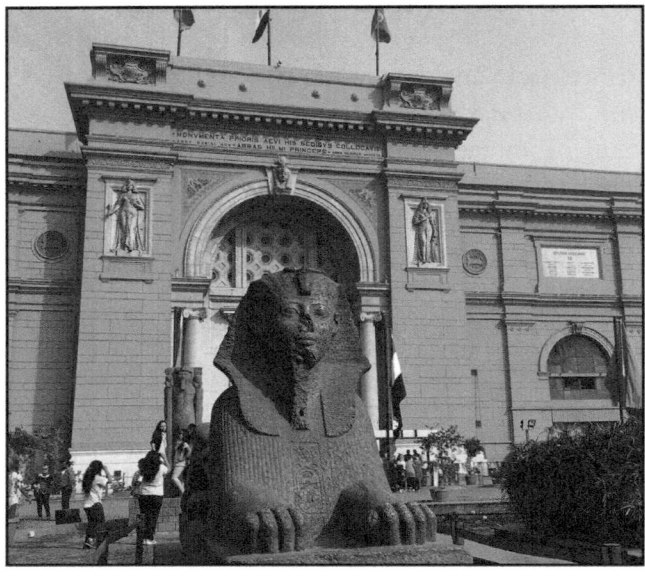

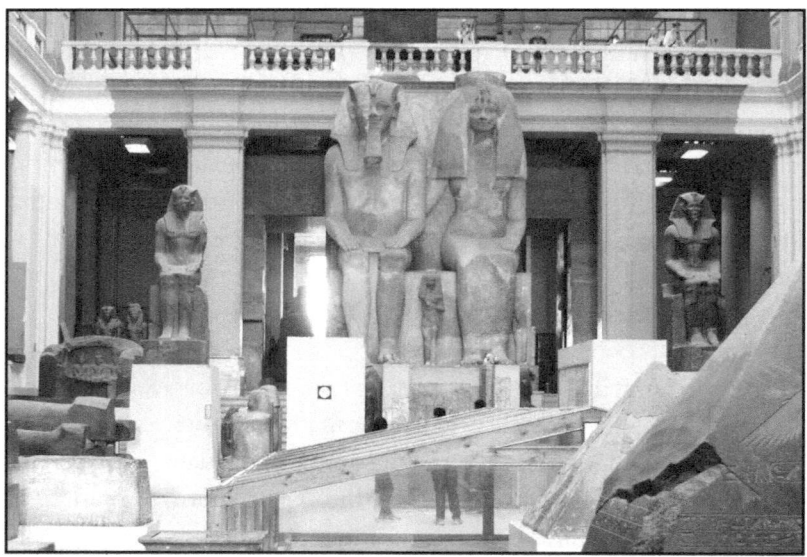

Egyptian Museum, Cairo

I was able to pick up some excellent guidebooks to the antiquities, including a series of pocket-sized site-specific books by JILL KAMEL. As wonderful as these books are, they share a characteristic with most Egyptology books of the day, namely that some of the vocabulary used is incomprehensible to the novice. For one thing, many of the authors grew up in a school system where Latin and Greek language classes were mandatory. The pronunciation of some of our guides at the ancient sites reinforced my confusion. I vividly remember looking forward to seeing the *hippo-style hall* at one of the temples. I thought hippos would be interesting, but knew that *hippopotamus* meant *river horse*, so I figured the *hall* might have something to do with horses, maybe some kind of Ben Hur-type chariot race track. Actually, it was just a columned courtyard. It took me years, actually, to realize that the term was *hypostyle hall*, (*hypo* = *under*, *stylos* = *pillar*). Other words we were assumed to understand were STELE, MODIUS, URAEUS, and the French SCARABÉE. (GLOSSARY TERMS AND BIBLIOGRAPHIC REFERENCES ARE IN BOLD).

I have always loved languages and writing systems. The constant stream of *aha!* moments exhilarates me. One of my earliest memories, circa 1956, is of seven-year-old me crouching next to a library shelf, browsing through *Long is a Dragon* by PEGGY GOLDSTEIN. The problem with this memory is that as near as I can tell, *Long is a Dragon* was published in 1992! It must have been a similar book. It explained the origin of Chinese characters through clever illustrations and calligraphy. The book, whatever its title, was burned into my memory because while I was looking at it, the siren of the volunteer fire department went off just on the other side of the wall, literally knocking me onto my rear.

Although I love languages and have studied and even taught several, they do not come easily to me—I just work harder on languages than many other people do. But I have a passion for making difficult things easy (or easier) for *me* to understand, then repackaging what I have learned to help others.

I was particularly interested in the accounts in the books of how Jean-François Champollion and others, using the ROSETTA STONE, obtained a toehold into the HIEROGLYPHIC code by focusing first on the CARTOUCHES, the names of ancient Egyptian royalty inscribed in oval frames on the stone. This slab was inscribed in Greek, known to any scholar at the time, and two versions of ancient Egyptian. The decipherment story has been told hundreds of times and I will not repeat it here, except to say that once it was surmised that the cartouches contained royal names, it was "easy" to compare the hieroglyphs with the known Greek versions of the names of the royal figures mentioned, Ptolemy and Cleopatra, and solve for the phonetic values representing the sounds P, T, O, L, E, M, Y, S, Q, A, T, and R. Champollion's knowledge of **COPTIC**, the latest form of Egyptian language written in a known alphabet, eventually led to success in deciphering the hieroglyphs.

I wanted to learn to read the royal names for myself. I was excited to find *How to Read Hieroglyphs*, a 20-page pamphlet published by Lehnert & Landrock in 1974, at a souvenir stand in the courtyard of the Egyptian Museum. This booklet contains the names, in cartouches, of 35 well-known **PHARAOHS**, and parses out each hieroglyph for 15 of them. I had fun with the book in the museum and at ancient sites, but was continually frustrated because 35 names provided no more than a taste of the cartouches out there.

It is my nature to want to understand "everything," and for me, that comes with organization of knowledge. I am a life-long user, proponent of and contributor to dictionaries. At AUC we were required to read 2000 pages of Arabic literature over one school year, so we spent a *lot* of time searching for words in the dictionary. In my own mind, at least, I hold the world land speed record for looking up words in the 1300-page **HANS WEHR** *A Dictionary of Modern Written Arabic*, no mean feat in that language. I wanted a complete "dictionary" of cartouches, and it looked like I would have to create it myself.

I took to copying down royal names from any and all books or artifacts wherever I found them, trying to make a complete, searchable list.

I started this in our apartment in Maadi, a suburb of Cairo, overlooking Muhammad Ali's citadel to the north and the Dahshur pyramids to the southwest. I sat on the floor surrounded by tiny cut-out slips of paper, each bearing a name and cartouche of a pharaoh. I had spent hours sorting them into categories, using a glue stick to paste them into a spiral notebook, hoping in vain that my slips would not be scattered by our large dog or the ceiling fan.

A lecturer at the Egypt Exploration Society pointed me to the oversized, multi-volume *Le Livre des Rois de Égypte* (1907) by **HENRI GAUTHIER**. I spent years prowling through used bookstores in Cairo and elsewhere to complete my set (you can get it now online). Although fascinating, the series is unwieldy, and, of course, dated. And in French, sprinkled with Greek.

In 1990, STEPHEN QUIRKE's *Who were the Pharaohs? A History of their Names with a List of Cartouches* was published by the British Museum Press. Quirke gives cartouches of 146 pharaohs with historical notes. The cartouches were drawn by Dr. Richard Parkinson. This was the book that I photocopied and dismembered, trying to cobble together an index of cartouches.

I finally came up with a usable prototype of the *Field Guide* in the early 90s. I tested it on a group of fourth grade students for ease of use. It worked well, but was not as complete or as nice-looking as I would have liked.

More resources meant more work for me. The following works were published or were discovered by me since my original preliminary booklet.

Who were the Pharaohs? was followed by a gold mine in the publication in 1994 of PETER A. CLAYTON's *Chronicle of the Pharaohs, the Reign-by-Reign Record of the Rulers and Dynasties of Ancient Egypt.* Clayton performed the herculean task of translating each pharaoh's names, insofar as they are translatable. A companion volume by the very prolific Egyptologist JOYCE TYLDESLEY, *Chronicle of the Queens of Egypt, from Early Dynastic Times to the Death of Cleopatra,* followed in 2006.

Most recently, in 2011, Museum Tours Press published *The Names of the Kings of Egypt* by KEVIN L. JOHNSON and BILL PETTY. This book is the most complete of the recent publications from the standpoint of number of cartouches shown. It is notable for the variations listed, with 20 or more versions each of Ramses the Great's BIRTH and THRONE NAMES. It also shows representative HORUS NAMES (see below) for each. It provides an index where you can find every cartouche containing a given hieroglyph.

I must mention SIR ALAN GARDINER's *Egyptian Grammar* (1927). He categorized the bulk of known hieroglyphs and gave them standardized numbers that are still used. I refer to them in the *Field Guide* as GARDINER NUMBERS.

These latest sources' bibliographies also led me to JÜRGEN VON BECKERATH's ·*Handbuch der ägyptischen Königsnamen* (1984).

With these reference materials and better resources in the form of the Adobe suite of tools (Photoshop, Illustrator, and InDesign), along with extra time in retirement, I am finally ready to make the *Field Guide* available.

What is a Cartouche?

The five names of the Egyptian kings

Throughout most of ancient Egyptian history, reigning pharaohs bore five names, the so-called **FIVE-FOLD TITULARY**:

- The **HORUS NAME**, written inside a **SEREKH**, surmounted by an image of the god Horus in the form of a hawk.
- The **TWO LADIES** (or **NEBTY**) name, associated with goddesses represented as a vulture and a cobra sitting atop baskets. You could consider each of the 750 hieroglyphs in **GARDINER'S** sign list and be hard pressed to find two more unlikely candidates for *ladies* than the vulture and the cobra!
- **HORUS OF GOLD**, with the Horus falcon sitting on top of the symbol for gold.
- The **BIRTH NAME** (the personal name or **NOMEN**)
- The **THRONE NAME** (**PRENOMEN**).

As might be expected, in theory at least, the **BIRTH NAME** is what the tiny pharaoh-to-be was called from birth, the name we know him or her by today. It is preceded by the hieroglyphs for Son of (the sun god) Ra.

The **THRONE NAME** was the new name adopted by the pharaoh at his (or her!) coronation. This practice is echoed today when popes and some secular monarchs take new names upon their investiture.

Of these five names, the *Field Guide* deals exclusively with the last two, the **BIRTH NAME** and the **THRONE NAME**. I can never remember which is which, **PRENOMEN** or **NOMEN**. Why use those terms when we have perfectly descriptive terms in English? I won't use them again.

Both of these names are written inside the frames known as **CARTOUCHES**, the subject of this book. Note that at certain periods, the names of queens as well as royal children were also written in cartouches. The cartouche is an oval frame, often depicted as twisted rope or cord, bound together at one end with more rope. It resembles the old-fashioned quoits, rope rings that were thrown at a stake in a game like horseshoes. The oval is an elongated form of the SHEN RING (GARDINER sign number V9), which has been said to mean *to encircle*. "...it seems not unlikely that the idea was to represent the king as ruler of all that which is encircled by the sun." (GARDINER P 74).

The cartouche was of profound importance to the ancient Egyptians. Individuals are shown adoring the cartouche as if it were the Pharaoh himself; some tombs and SARCOPHAGI are shaped like cartouches.

Virtually every book or article on Egyptian hieroglyphs claims that Napoleon's soldiers in Egypt (1798–1801) saw a resemblance between the pharaohs' cartouches and the cartridges (French, *cartouche*) they used in their muskets, and that Napoleon's team of SAVANTS took the term from them. I submit that it is more likely that the scholars, well educated in art, architecture and cartography, simply called the cartouche a cartouche because that is what it was, a decorative frame or label, like that on a map, or a plaque above the door of a building, enclosing a name, number, heraldic device or other image. Since at least the 16th Century the term *cartouche* has been used in relation to maps, as in the illustration on page 9. It makes more sense to me that the soldiers would borrow the term from the scholars than vice versa. *A Visual Dictionary of Architecture,* (FRANCIS D.K. CHING, P 183) defines a cartouche as "an oval or oblong design with a slightly convex surface, typically edged with ornamental scroll work. It is used to hold a painted or low relief design." See examples on the next page.

While a pharaoh's cartouche may resemble a *modern* ammunition cartridge, one from the time of Napoleon looked more like a paper-wrapped bonbon or a hand-rolled cigarette with the paper twisted at the top (illustration next page). A cartridge *á la Française* in the 18th century consisted of a greased paper sleeve containing a ball at one end, tied off with string. The rest of the sleeve was filled with black powder, the paper serving as wadding. The soldier bit off the end of the paper, poured the powder down the muzzle of his firearm, and rammed home the ball and paper with a ramrod. Our word *cartridge*, referring to ammunition, derives from medieval Latin *carta*, meaning *paper* or *card*. You can still buy *cartridge paper,* a heavy drawing paper, similar to that once used to make cartridges for firearms.

Five-Fold Titulary
(Five Names of a Pharoah)

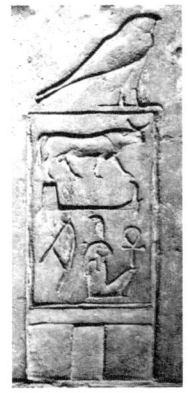

Horus Name

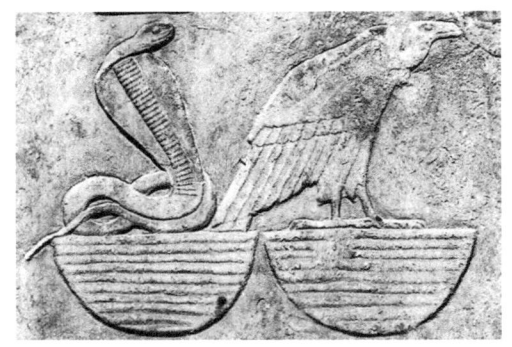

Two Ladies or Nebty

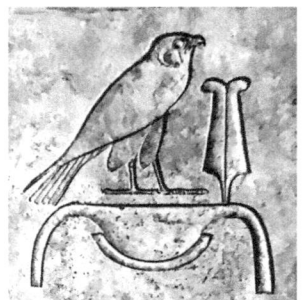

Horus of Gold

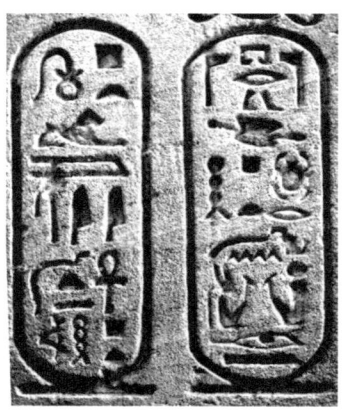

Birth   Throne
Name   Name

The Cartouche
Maps, Art, Architecture

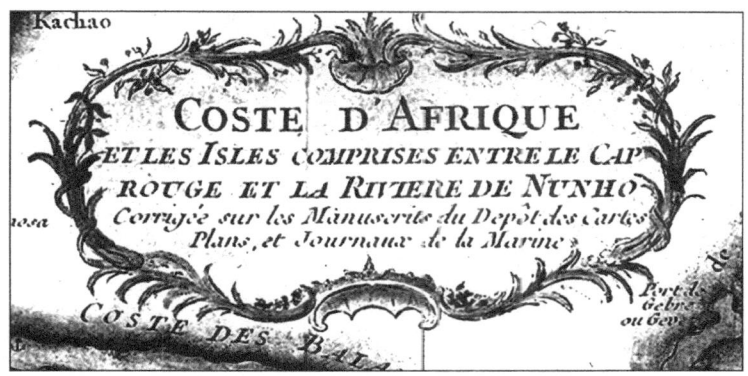

Cartouche from map, 1747

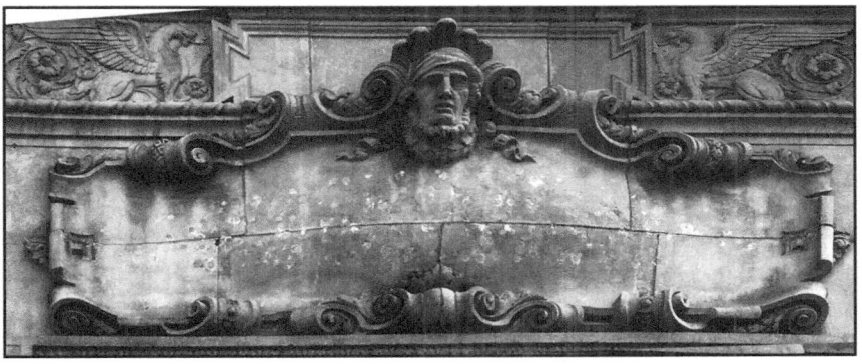

Architectural cartouche, downtown Honolulu

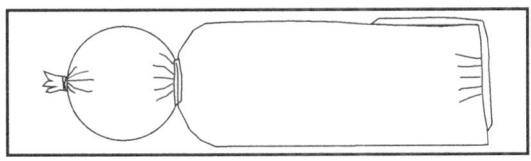

A paper cartridge, *Cartouche papier à poudre noire á la française du XVIIIᵉ siècle*

Why Study Cartouches?

First, cartouches are easy to pick out from an inscription: It can be dizzying to visit or view an ancient Egyptian archaeological site or artifact where every surface is densely covered with human, animal and unidentified figures. Where to begin? How can you ever understand what you are looking at? Where do words begin and end? There are no spaces between words, no paragraphs, and no punctuation!

As mentioned before, the Egyptians put the names of their royalty inside cartouches. An untrained individual cannot comprehend a wall covered with inscriptions, but anyone can easily pick out the cartouches.

Compare the top illustration on the opposite page with the one below it. It is a copy of an inscription at Abu Simbel made by Jean François Champollion.

The top inscription is completely daunting. Focusing on the names in the cartouches in the bottom illustration provides a toehold toward understanding the whole text. The supposition that the cartouches on the **ROSETTA STONE** contained personal names, names already known to history, as well as providing word breaks in the text, allowed Champollion and others to finally crack the hieroglyphic writing system, an endeavor which had occupied scholars and mystics for hundreds of years.

With the *Field Guide*, visitors to ancient sites and museums can zero in on the cartouches even if advanced points of grammar are still out of their reach.

Second, cartouches are a good introduction to the ancient Egyptian writing system. It's not the only way to start your study of Egyptian, and probably not the best way, but one that can bring immediate satisfaction.

Third, it's fun! Impress your friends and fellow tourists! For a minute or two, anyway.

By the way, since this book is about ancient Egyptian texts, I'll dispense with the adjective *ancient* from now on. *Ancient Egyptian* will be assumed.

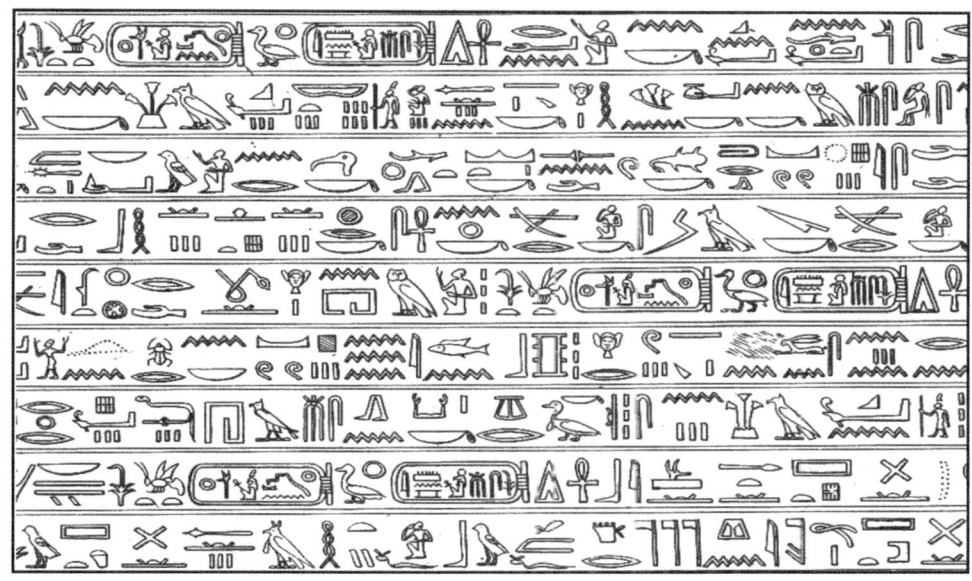

Why photos and drawings?

All the reference books cited in the *Field Guide* make use of the very usable and clear HIEROGLYPHIC fonts that are available, or standardized handwritten SIGNS. When typing hieroglyphs I use *LaserHIEROGLYPHICS*™ by PHILIP BARTON PAYNE from Linguist's Software, Inc.

So why would I go to the trouble of reproducing drawings and photographs of cartouches and hieroglyphs in the *Field Guide*? For me a large part of the fun of studying hieroglyphic inscriptions is just the art. I take pleasure in the perfectly proportioned, highly detailed miniature works of art that many hieroglyphs are. I equally enjoy the more naïve or rustic art you see on low-budget monuments and coffins.

SIR ALAN GARDINER (P 438), in his milestone work *Egyptian Grammar*, states:

"It must never be forgotten that in the eyes of the old Egyptians the hieroglyphic writing always remained a system of pictorial representation as well as a script. Hence the capricious variety exhibited in the more elaborate inscriptions. To take but one example, the sign for 'statue' (A22) is apt to change sex, head-gear, dress and accouterments according to the context or the scribe's fancy may dictate. This is the principal reason why the printing of hieroglyphic texts is so unsatisfactory. No fount of type is sufficiently rich or sufficiently adaptable to do justice to the Egyptian originals. Indeed, there is only one wholly satisfactory method of publishing hieroglyphic texts, namely reproduction in facsimile. Two possibilities here present themselves, facsimile by hand and facsimile by photography."

"...There is only one wholly satisfactory method of publishing hieroglyphic texts, namely reproduction in facsimile...by hand and facsimile by photography."

Sir Alan Gardiner

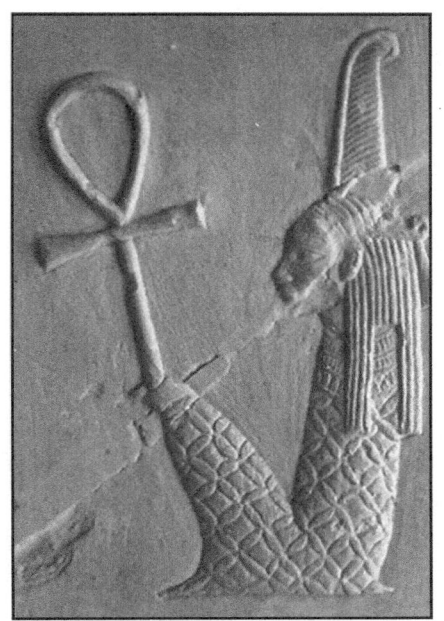

Elegant Maat   Rustic Maat

Compare these two depictions of Maat, goddess of Truth. The first has exquisite detail, right down to beaded lozenge pattern on her dress and the striations on her feather headdress and wig. Even the lines around her eyes and details of her ears are shown.

The cartouche on the right, Ramses II's **THRONE NAME**, shows a rudimentary Maat, her signature feather and **ANKH** barely recognizable. Figuring out what this is for the first time is one of those "aha!" moments that are so exciting.

If you were an enthusiast of ancient coins, you would want your coin catalogue to show you what the coins look like. What fun, or use, would it be if the guide showed only typed out versions of the inscriptions?

Students need to get used to reading cartouches of every quality and in every direction.

How the Field Guide is organized

This book includes royal cartouches covering the entire period they were used, from approximately 2544 BC through the Roman emperors, ending about 305 AD.

Section I, Cartouches of Ancient Egyptian Royalty, illustrates the names of the major royal personages, including Roman emperors, in approximate chronological order, introducing each hieroglyph as it comes up in the list. Seldom-seen hieroglyphs will be identified but not explained. Some royal titles are included. Although no effort is made to explain how to read Egyptian texts, this section can serve as an introduction to Egyptian hieroglyphs and language.

Section II, Cartouche Identification Key, helps anyone quickly identify almost any cartouche to be found on a monument or statue. Prototypes of the *Key* have been tested successfully on several groups, from first graders to adults. No prior knowledge of hieroglyphs is needed. Note that this section includes some variations not cited in Section I.

The *Key* is patterned after a nature field guide, a guide to trees, flowers, or birds. In a field guide to trees, for example, the first page asks you to determine, with the aid of illustrations, whether a tree bears cones and needles, scales, or leaves. If you choose *leaves*, then it next asks you whether the leaves are simple, compound, or fan-shaped. If you choose *fan-shaped*, the guide states that your tree is a ginkgo (https://www.arborday.org/trees/whattree/). Even with no botanical knowledge, you have identified your tree in two steps. Other trees will take more steps, as you narrow down whether compound leaves, for instance, are *opposite* or *alternate*, and so on.

In the *Key*, you will be asked whether the cartouche in question contains a given hieroglyph or combination of hieroglyphs. If you find a hieroglyph that matches, you will be directed to a subset of those cartouches, and so on. More instructions and examples will be provided later

Appendices include lists of all hieroglyphs in the book according to GARDINER'S sign list as well as alphabetically, in "English" TRANSLITERATION, and a list of the royal names treated in the *Field Guide*. Words in BOLD are explained in the glossary, and this font is used for BIBLIOGRAPHY ENTRIES.

Notes and caveats

I said it would be fun, not that it would be simple. Keep in mind that the scope of Egyptian civilization is huge, both chronologically and geographically. From Meroë, Sudan to the Nile Delta is 1500 miles, and from First Dynasty King Aha to Roman Emperor Diocletian is 3,200 years!

Some dynasties are not well attested. Certain periods had competing pharaohs whose reigns overlapped; some of them may not even have existed! The order of kings in a particular dynasty is not a given in many cases.

Dates: I will use the dates cited by CLAYTON, which are in turn taken from *The Penguin Guide to Ancient Egypt*.

Scope: The cartouches chosen for this book mirror those illustrated by Quirke and Clayton. Since their books do not include many queens except those who reigned as "king," some of the major names from TYLDESLEY's *Chronicles of the Queens of Egypt* have been included as well. I've tried to illustrate the cartouches most likely to be seen by a visitor to a museum or ancient site.

Although Pharaohs from the earliest dynasties had not yet adopted cartouches, sometimes their names were retroactively enclosed in cartouches by later scribes. I do not include these. I do, however, include a few cartouches besides those of kings and reigning queens, namely those of some minor queens and royal children.

Pronunciation and spelling of names: We do not really know how Egyptian was pronounced. Scholars take clues from COPTIC, as well as from renditions of Egyptian royalty and place names taken from other ancient languages. Of course, we don't know exactly how *those* languages were pronounced, either! All languages change over time and distance, so sound systems, "spellings" and conventions change. The miracle is that the names and writing system stayed so remarkably consistent through the entire period.

The really bad news about Egyptian royal names:

Today there are two main versions (*always* with other spelling variations) of
most pharaohs' names:

1. A spelling which more or less represents the pronunciation of the name, or
at least the Egyptian spelling, as far as we can reconstruct it. I'll call it this *The
Egyptian version*. As scholarship advances the accepted readings can change.

2. A greekified version of that name, taken from **MANETHO**'s **DYNASTY** list,
where the names are so distorted they often bear little resemblance to the
original name. This is outrageous and annoying, until we realize that we do the
same thing when we call *Al-Qahira, Cairo*, or *Yangon, Rangoon.*

Examples:

Egyptian Version	The Greek Version
Khufu	Cheops
Khafra	Chefren
Amenhotep	Amenophis
Djedefra	Ratoises

I smugly use the *Egyptian* version of the name, with one important exception:
in those which include the name of one or more gods, by convention
"everyone" uses the Greek form of the god's name, or a form closer to the
Greek than to the Egyptian. To do otherwise woulds make the pharaohs'
names incomprehensible: *Djehutimes* becomes Thutmose; *Imnhetep* becomes
Amenhotep, because we tend to call the god *Djehuti, Thoth*; the god *Imn* is
usually called *Amen* or *Amun.*

So in **TRANSLITERATIONS**, or renderings of pharaohs' names in Latin letters,
variations in spelling are seemingly infinite. You just have to get used to it and
be flexible. Don't come running to me looking for consistency!

In transcribing Egyptian texts, English-speaking scholars have at least two
scientific transliteration systems which prevent ambiguity. I have chosen not to
use those systems, but to stick with a more phonetic style, more suited to non-
specialists.

How Egyptian works

I will not go into too much detail here about the origins or characteristics of the hieroglyphic system of writing. Egyptian uses several types of symbols (I use the terms **HIEROGLYPHS**, **GLYPHS** and **SIGNS** interchangeably) based on pictures. We still do not know what all the symbols represent.

Types of symbols used. Examples of each of these will be given as they appear in the chronological list of names.

    1. Logograms: These signs represent meaning. Sometimes the meaning is obvious from the object depicted. In other cases, we have no idea why they assigned a given meaning to a particular sign.

    2. Phonetic symbols: In addition to logograms, you need a way to spell names of people and places which are difficult to express in pictures: foreign words and names, for instance. Also, Egyptian, like most languages familiar to us, contains features like verb endings and pronouns. *I go, he goes; tango, tienes, tiene, tenemos, tienen; ich habe, du hast, er hat, wir haben* and so on, that must be represented phonetically.

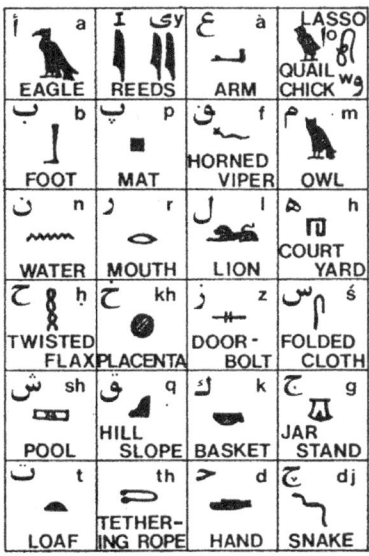

Souvenir card of
phonetic hieroglyphs

a. Single sound signs: The simplest class of hieroglyphs, to our minds, is that of the phonetic characters, where one hieroglyph stands for one sound. These are based on the *A is for apple, B is for ball* system we learned in kindergarten. Jewelers and T-shirt hawkers in Egypt, and even some popular children's books, tell you that that's all there is, that "Each symbol stood for a sound, just like our own letters" **(COLE P 34)**. There are also myriad websites aimed at elementary students where you can "write your name in hieroglyphics!" As you will see, the system is immensely more complicated than that.

No need to memorize these phonetic symbols now. I'll introduce them one by one as they appear chronologically. Variations on these phonetic symbols became more common during the **PTOLEMAIC** and Roman eras, when temple overseers and craftsmen had to figure out how to convert the barbaric sounds of Egypt's new foreign overlords' names into hieroglyphs and jam them into cartouches. Those variations will be introduced as they show up in the list.

b. Two or three-sound signs: Some signs, while still phonetic, represent syllables of two or three consonants. Also, one sign could represent the sound of a god's or goddess's name.

Remember, we are talking about *sounds* here, not English spelling. One English letter can have more than one sound (*go, germ*); also, some sounds in English are represented by two letters (*ch, sh*). The *een* syllable in *Charlene, queen, Jean and Christine* would be written the same way in Egyptian. Except when it wasn't.

3. Determinatives: Sometimes an unpronounced sign is added to the end of a word to clarify the meaning of the word. For instance, if we had figured out a way to spell out the word *bark* phonetically, (say, *Ball, Apple, Rabbit, King*) we could add a little picture of a dog, a tree, or even a boat after *bark* to clarify which of the meanings was intended. These are rare in cartouches, but we will see some.

What! No vowels!? I don't want to name names, but all the best Egyptian language books for novices insist that the ancient Egyptians did not write vowels. An example is usually given along the lines of "If written English did not use vowels, *car, core* and *acre* would all be written the same!" Arabic and Hebrew "do not write vowels" either, but neither would ever spell *car, core and acre* the same. Consonants called *semi-vowels* or *weak consonants* are routinely called to stand in for initial, final and some internal vowels and diphthongs, usually taking care of any ambiguity.

For our purposes, "If it quacks like a vowel, it's a vowel."

We write the letter *e* to fill in for vowels not explicitly written, to make it easier for us to say the words. See an example under Pharaoh Sneferu in **DYNASTY** Four.

A note on Ra and Amen. I follow Stephen Quirke, Flinders Petrie and the British Museum in spelling the sun god's name *Ra* instead of the more common *Re*. A final *e* implies that we have no indication as to what, if any, vowel follows a particular consonant. *Ra*, the sun god, is actually a syllable of two consonants, the second being *ayn*. We spell *Maat* with *aa* rather than *e* to acknowledge the presence of this consonant pronounced in the back of the throat. (*Maat* actually has two "silent" consonants in a row, even though no one pronounces them in English). When I was studying Arabic it took me years to master *ayn* , which could be why I'm obsessive about it. Read more about *ayn* at the end of Dynasty 13.

As for *Amen/Amun*, even Quirke varies on this: he and most others write *Amen*emhat and *Amen*hotep; but Tutankh*amun* and "the god *Amun*." My old pal Flinders Petrie and I will stick with *Amen* in all cases unless quoting a source.

Not surprisingly, right after putting my foot down regarding the spelling of Amen/Amun, I discovered plenty of other spelling inconsistencies in the *Field Guide*. Oh well. Don't say I didn't warn you.

How to use this book:

Each **PHARAOH'S** name is presented like this:

Aa1	G43	I9	G43
Kh	**U**	**F**	**U**

This is what I call the **BREAKOUT**. It lists each hieroglyph in the name in *pronunciation order* (you will see later that the order of the signs can vary within the cartouche). The top row tells you the **GARDINER NUMBER**, a standardized number taken from **SIR ALAN GARDINER'S** *Egyptian Grammar*.

The second row includes the hieroglyphs themselves.

The third row gives the pronunciation of each sign. Some signs may be in parentheses—these are usually redundant or not pronounced.

Read the name from row three out loud. Don't worry about "correct" pronunciation, just wing it.

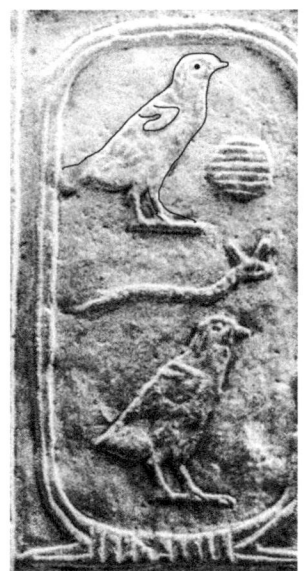

Next, look at the photograph of the cartouche (here, Khufu, of the Fourth **DYNASTY**) and try to find and read the signs, again out loud, in the order given in the breakout. Although the arrangements of signs inside actual cartouches is not set in stone...um, you know what I mean... the breakout is always read from left to right.

Instead of trying to memorize the hieroglyphs, you can look in the back of the book at any time to see the details of each and where it is introduced in the *Field Guide*. They are listed by GARDINER NUMBER and according to the English alphabet. Memorization of the most common signs will come automatically.

Please go through each cartouche in this section in order–don't skip around. The individual hieroglyphs are introduced sequentially.

Write out the names. It is very useful, not to mention fun, to copy out the names. You will learn the signs and combinations much faster if you copy them down. As with the pronunciation, don't worry about your hieroglyphic penmanship! As long as *you* can distinguish one sign from the other, that's fine.

The main sources for the *Field Guide,* QUIRKE, CLAYTON, VON BECKERATH and ROSE, feature handwritten hieroglyphs. They vary from writer to writer, and some, frankly, are not entirely legible for the novice. The level of calligraphy and style even among ancient Egyptian sculptors and scribes varies greatly. Compare these two examples, the Country Duck and the City Duck, if you will.

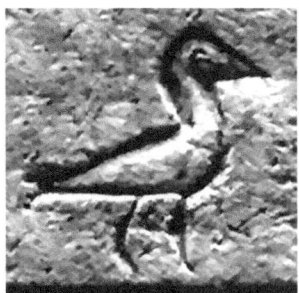
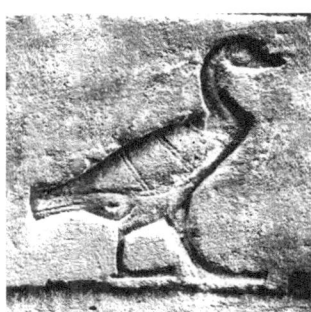

I enjoy the rustic and quaint as much as or more than the elegant and suave.

A note on the photographs: Virtually all the photos are my own. Many were taken up to 40 years ago with a hand-held film camera, mostly in dark tombs, museums or eroded temples. Moreover, more cartouches than not were situated high above my head, distorting the image. Finally, a limestone-gray image on a limestone-gray background does not make for a prize-winning photograph. I have unapologetically used Photoshop to boost contrast, sharpen and "undistort" the images, and I have darkened some lines where necessary. I have chosen readability over aesthetics. I beg your indulgence.

I have typed out important cartouches for which I have no photographs of my own, using the LaserHIEROGLYPHICS™ fonts, writing from left to right. Where my photographs are legible to me but are too poor to include, I have traced them or typed them in the original format, right to left, left to right, or vertically, as appropriate.

I have had great fun producing the *Field Guide*. The process has taught me a lot, and each time I read through it I find more things that can be corrected or improved, or more points to research. Let me acknowledge here that all errors are mine and mine alone. I welcome comments and suggestions. Please send them to

EgyptFieldGuides@gmail.com

Section I
Cartouches of Ancient Egyptian Royalty
Chronological List

Chronological is a relative term. The exact dates, or even the existence, of many pharaohs is in dispute. I will follow the order and dates given in QUIRKE and CLAYTON, and make arbitrary decisions where their lists differ.

Each cartouche will be given a one-up *reference number*, such as D5:2, meaning Dynasty 5, pharaoh number 2. The letters *T* and *B* refer to the THRONE NAME and BIRTH NAME respectively, as in D20:5T. Please note that these sequential numbers are taken from VON BECKERATH's *Handbuch der ägyptischen Königsnamen*.

I do not include every pharaoh, only those whose names students will be most likely to encounter, chosen, entirely egocentrically, based on those that I myself have encountered and photographed over several decades of collecting.

Underneath each cartouche the hieroglyphs are listed in what I call a BREAKOUT, mentioned earlier, in supposed pronunciation order, along with their GARDINER INDEX NUMBERS and pronunciations. The most important signs are highlighted and explained. (See the Appendices for all hieroglyphs introduced in this book.) Hyphens or spaces are added to help make sense of the longer names.

 Important principles to help you read cartouches and hieroglyphic texts in general are marked with this icon, and are recapped in an Appendix starting on page 280.

Old Kingdom
Dynasties 3-6

> Names in this small font are either Greek renditions of the names, or just alternate spellings you may see elsewhere.

→

D4:1 Sneferu
Snefru, Snofru, Soris

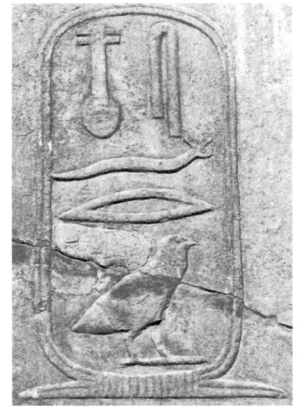

S29	F35	I9	D21	G43
⌐	☥	～	⬭	🐦
S	**Nefer**	**(F**	**R)**	**U**

There are a lot of interesting points about this cartouche. I'll introduce each hieroglyph first. (Letters inside slashes (/) indicate pronunciation).

 This is a single consonant sound /S/. It can mean *person*. (**CLAYTON (p 42)** translates Sneferu as *He of beauty*.). The sign represents a folded *piece of cloth*.

 /Nefer/ means *good*, or *beautiful*. It is not a musical instrument, but, believe it or not, an *esophagus and heart*.

 The single consonant /F/. In some contexts it means *his*. This is not a cute cartoon of a garden slug, but rather a deadly *horned viper*.

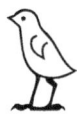 /R/ a *human mouth*.

This is a *quail chick* (the early Egyptians didn't have chickens). It represents a long /U/ or /O/ vowel, or the consonant /W/.

Arrangement of Hieroglyphs: The Egyptians liked to fill the space in a pleasing way. They wrote hieroglyphs so they would fill an imaginary rectangle. In Sneferu's name, two tall, vertical signs fit neatly on top or to the side of the low, horizontal ones. The tall, diagonal quail chick can fill the space on its own.

The e: When a vowel isn't explicitly written in Egyptian, we insert an *e* to make it easier to pronounce. The consonantal skeleton of /Nefer/ is NFR. We supply the *e* so we can comfortably say it. We don't know what the original vowels were exactly.

Phonetic complements: That sign that looks like a banjo expresses the word /Nefer/. Often the Egyptians would add a redundant consonant or two to a word just for clarity. We don't pronounce the extra *f* and *r*, so the whole word, in this case, is just /Nefer/. These extra consonants are called **phonetic complements**.

u-nefer-S

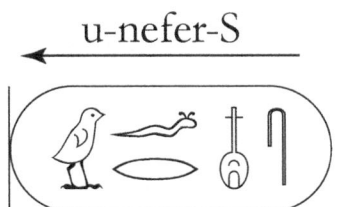

S-nefer-u

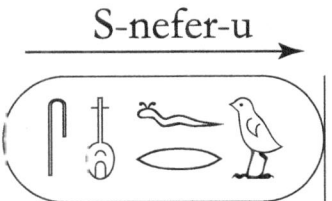

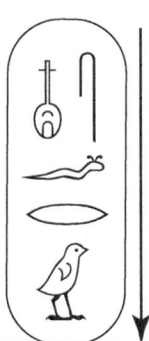

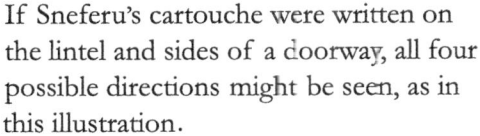

Hieroglyphs can be read from left to right, right to left or top to bottom. Always read toward the animals' or persons' faces. It would be rude to approach them from the rear!

Of course, in a cartouche, you always read toward the straight line at the base or end of the cartouche.

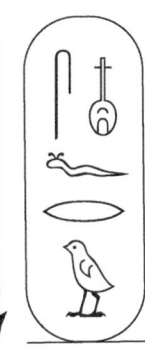

If Sneferu's cartouche were written on the lintel and sides of a doorway, all four possible directions might be seen, as in this illustration.

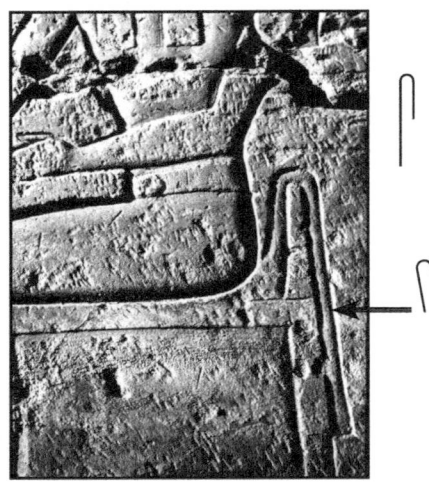

/S/ (S29) a *piece of cloth*, is illustrated draped over the back of virtually every depiction of a throne

A nice example of the /W/ or /U/ sign (G43), showing the markings of the *quail chick*.

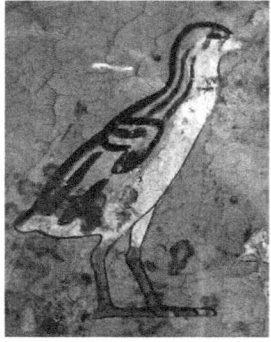

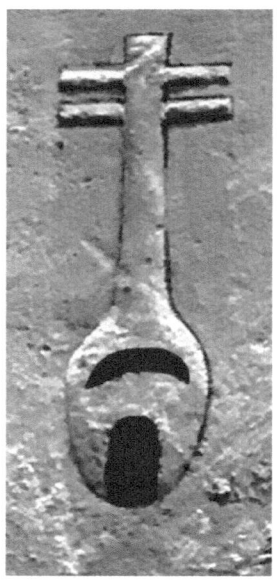

Here is /Nefer/ (F35), where certain anatomical features of the heart are emphasized.

D4:2 Khufu
Cheops, Suphis

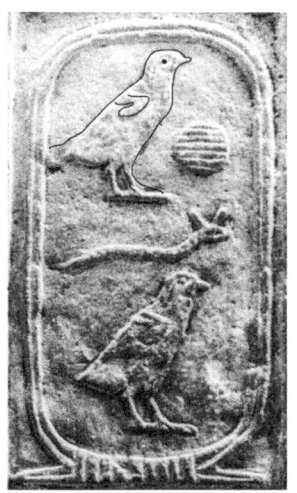

Aa1	G43	I9	G43
⊜	🐦	🐍	🐦
Kh	**U**	**F**	**U**

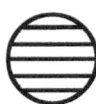

/Kh/ is the only new hieroglyph here. It has been said to represent a *human placenta*. GARDINER questions that definition and lists it under the "unclassified" signs. The /KH/ is a raspy sound made in the back of the throat, like the *j* in Spanish *juan*.

D4:3 Djedefra
Ratoises, Radjedef

R11	I9	N5
𓊽	𓆑	𓇳
Djed	**(e)F**	**Rᴀ**

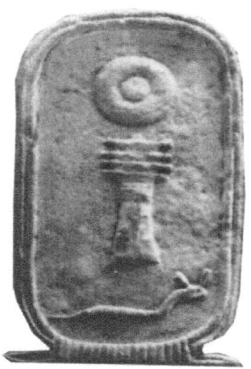

𓇳 /Ra/ is the *sun god.* This is the most common hieroglyph in the entire corpus of pharaohs' names. Be sure to distinguish the /Ra/*sun disk* (below left), from /Kh/ the so-called *placenta* (below right). The /Ra/ sign does *not* always have a dot or circle in the center.

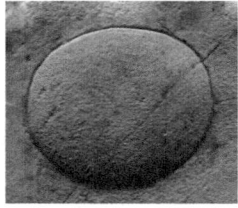   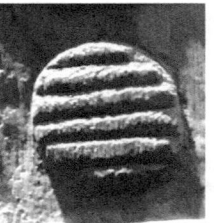

Ra   Kh

 /Djed/ is another mysterious symbol. **Gᴀʀᴅɪɴᴇʀ (ᴘ 502)** says it is a *column imitating a bundle of stalks tied togethe*r. It has also been said to represent Osiris himself, or the latter's backbone. Regardless of the origin of the sign, the basic meaning is *stability.*

Cʟᴀʏᴛᴏɴ (ᴘ 50) translates Dedefra's name as *Enduring like Re.*

Wait! Something's wrong! The signs are out of order!

If you've been paying attention, you will have noticed that although the last king is called *Djed-ef-Ra,* the actual hieroglyphs in the photograph are written in a different order: *Ra-Djed-ef.*

Honorific Transposition: When a cartouche contains the name of a god, the Egyptians always "bump the god up to first class", the front of the cartouche, regardless of where the god's name is mentioned in the cartouche.

Hence, here, the name is read *Djedefra*.

D4:4 Khafra
Chefren, Suphis II

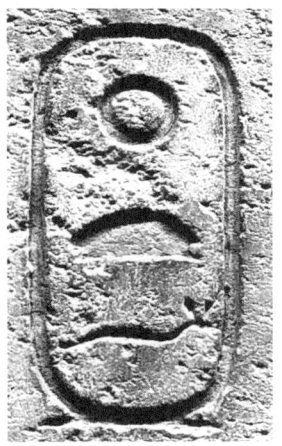

N28	I9	N5
⌢	⌇	☉
Kha	**F**	**R**ᴀ

/Kha/ represents the rays of the rising sun appearing from behind a hill. The rays of the sun can be quite understated, as the photo on the left, or exaggerated, rainbow-colored affairs, as at right. I know it's black and white here--trust me about the colors.

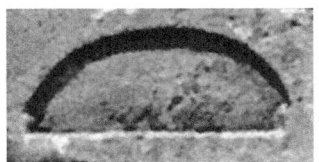

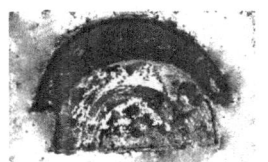

D4:6 Menkaura
Mycerinus, Mencheres

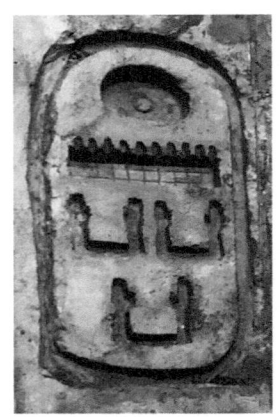

Y5	D28	N5
	⎵⎵⎵	⊙
Men	**Ka-u**	**Ra**

As promised, some of the lesser-known pharaohs are omitted from the *Field Guide*. We jumped from D4:4, the fourth Pharaoh of the Fourth Dynasty, to D4:6, the sixth.

This cartouche introduces two very important signs:

/Men/. This is a *board game* like chess, complete with playing pieces. The meaning is *to be firm, to be established, eternal*. It is extremely common in the royal names, and is part of the name of the god *Amen*, which will be introduced later.

/Ka/ *soul* or *spirit*. Two human arms raised. In Egyptological literature the word *Ka* is usually left untranslated. Here the plural form, the sign repeated three times, refers to the *souls* of Ra (CLAYTON P 56).

Plurals: In Egyptian, three signs together denote plural. Phonetically, a /U/ sound is added to the word. Thus, /Ka-u/, written with three /Ka/s, is *spirits*.

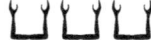

D4:7 Shepseskaf
Bicheres

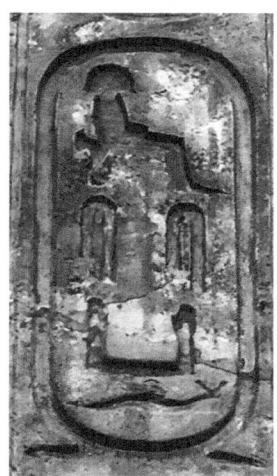

A50	S29	S29	D28	I9
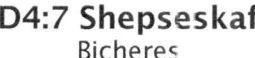				
Sheps	**(Se)**	**S**	**Ka**	**F**

 /Sheps/ means *noble person.*

/S/ is the *piece of cloth* used in Sneferu's name, D4:1.

D5:1 Userkaf
Usercheres

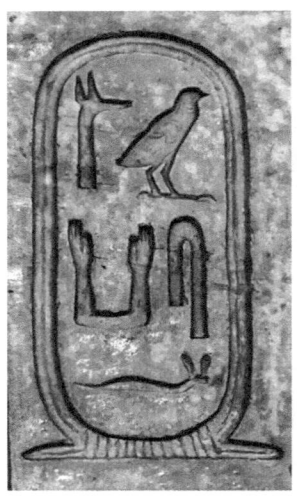

G43	F12	S29	D28	I9
🐦	🪶	∩	⊔	⌒
(U)	**User**	**(S)**	**Ka**	**F**

/User/ (say "oo-sir") means *powerful, wealthy*. It seems to be a ceremonial staff with the head of a canine (jackal?).

The leading /U/ and the /S/ that follow /User/ are both **PHONETIC COMPLEMENTS**. Leading with a phonetic complement is rather unusual—they usually *follow* the hieroglyph being complemented.

In later cartouches, /User/ usually stands on its own with no need for phonetic complements.

D5:2 Sahura
Sepheres

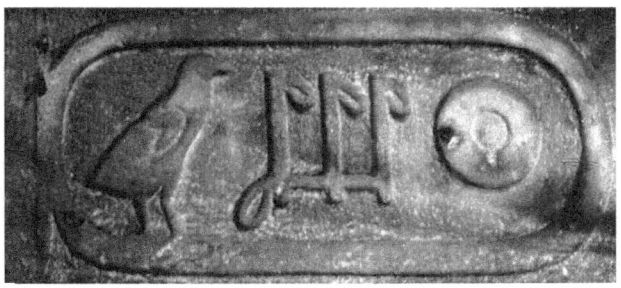

D61	G43	N5
𓄿𓄿𓄿	𓅱	☉
Sah	**U**	**Rᴀ**

/Sah/ represents, believe it or not, *toes,* seemingly in the sense of *approaching (on tip toe?) or being close (to the sun god, Ra)* (ꜱᴇᴇ **Cʟᴀʏᴛᴏɴ ᴘ 61**). I don't think anyone knows what was going through the original scribe's mind when he invented this sign.

D5:3B Kakai
D5:3T Neferirkara
Nephercheres

This is the first of our pharaohs to have two cartouches, the **BIRTH NAME**, Kakai, and the **THRONE NAME**, Neferirkara, the name he took when he became king.

Remember that the *B* and *T* in the number designations (B5:3*B*, D5:3*T*) show which is the **BIRTH NAME** and which the **THRONE NAME**.

D28	D28	M17
⊔	⊔	↑
Ka	Ka	I

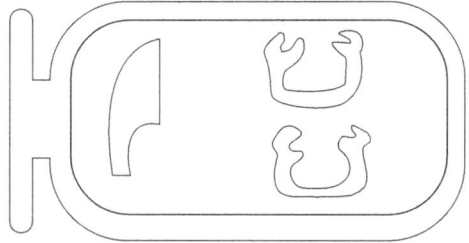

/I/ is a *reed*, like the canes that grow on the banks of a river or canal. Bulrushes, if you will, but the ones that have tassels on top, not cattails. This is *not* a feather. We'll come across the sign for feather later on.

Here is an offering table covered with reeds, symbolizing the bounty provided by the Nile. Note the striations representing the tassels blowing in the breeze.

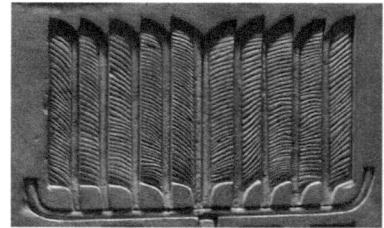

F35	D4	D28	N5
Nefer	**Ir**	**Ka**	**R**A

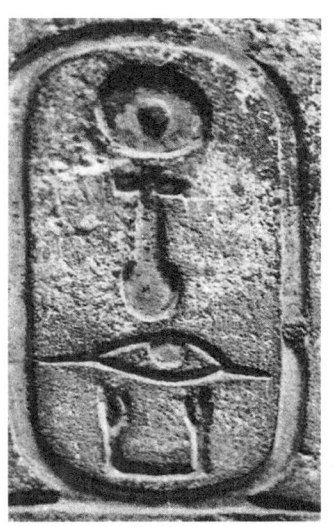

/Ir/ is obviously a human *eye*. The meaning here is *to do, make.*

D5:6B Ini
D5:6T Niuserra
Rathures

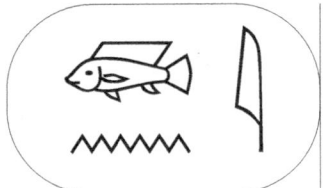

K1	N35	M17
🐟	〰️	𓏤
In	**(N)**	**I**

🐟 /In/ *tilapia* fish, probably used for its phonetic value only.

〰️ /N/ *water*. Here it is a **PHONETIC COMPLEMENT** for the /N/ in /In/. It is redundant and not necessary to the pronunciation.

 /I/ Explained under D5:3B

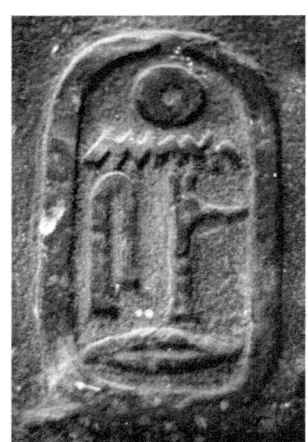

N35	F12	S29	D21	N5
〰️	🐕	𓎛	⬯	☉
N(i)	**User**	**(Se**	**R)**	**RA**

𓎛 and ⬯ are **PHONETIC COMPLEMENTS** for /User/. 🐕

D5:7B Kaiu
D5:7T Menkauhor
Mencheres

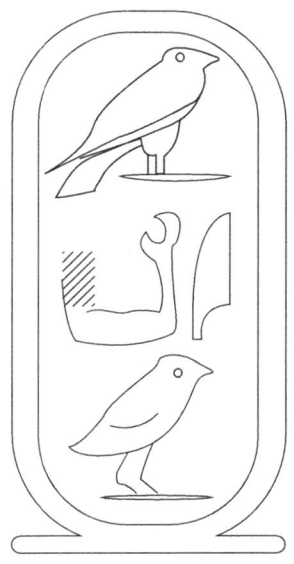

G5	D28	M17	G43
(🦅)	⊔	𝄖	🐦
(HOR)	Ka	I	U

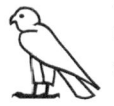 /Hor/ is the *falcon god, Horus,* optional in the **THRONE NAME** but always found in the **BIRTH NAME**. This is a departure from the emphasis on the sun god Ra seen in almost all other pharaohs' **THRONE NAMES.**

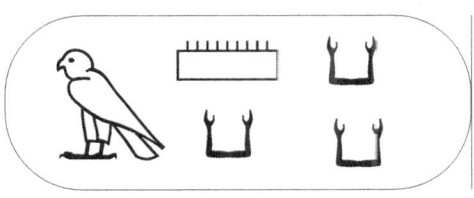

Y5	D28	G5
⊡	⊔⊔⊔	🦅
Men	Ka-u	HOR

D5:8B Isesi
D5:8T Djedkara
Tancheres

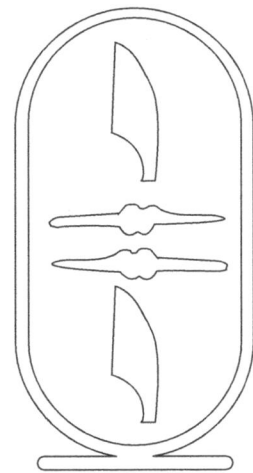

M17	O34	M17
	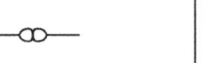	
I	S(e)S	I

/S/ is a *door bolt*. It can often be used interchangeably with the *piece of cloth* sign, right, below.

Here are some actual ancient door bolts, the type used on both doors and boxes and cabinets. A string attached to the door was wrapped and tied around the slot in the center, then sealed with clay and stamped. Any subsequent tampering with the door would be evident.

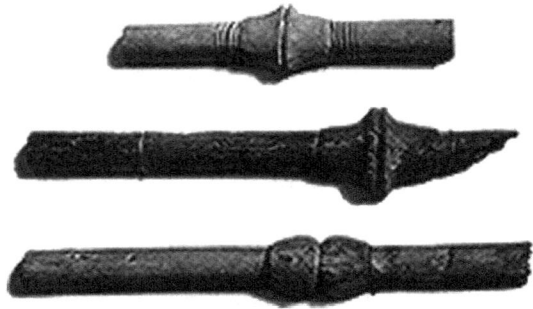

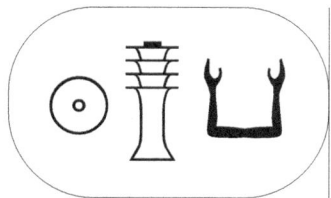

R11	D28	N5
Djed	Ka	Ra

D5:9B Unas
Wenis, Onnos

Only one cartouche for Unas.

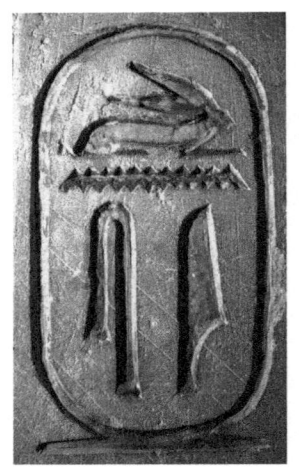

E34	N35	M17	S29
	∿∿∿	◖	◗
Un	**(N)**	**A**	**S**

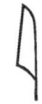 has a phonetic value of /un/ or /wen/. It is shows a *desert hare*.

◖ although usually transliterated /I/, gives an /A/ sound in this case.

Here is another cartouche of Unas (D5:9B), which contains an important royal title:

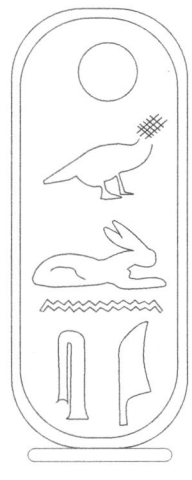

G39	N5	E34	N35	M17	S29
Sa	RA	Un	(N)	A	S

/Sa/ is obviously a duck, a *pintail duck*, to be specific. Phonetically its name, /Sa/, sounds like the Egyptian word for *son* and is used to express that concept.

/Sa Ra/ means *Son of Ra*. It usually written with the sun tucked behind the duck's back, for the sake of symmetry, as illustrated below. This title is usually found immediately in front of a pharaoh's **BIRTH NAME**, *outside the cartouche,* but in the earlier dynasties you may find it enclosed within the cartouche, as in the Unas example, above left.

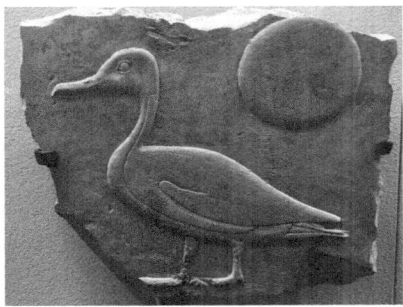

Due to space considerations, I will not generally include the *Son of Ra* title from here on out, unless it is written inside the cartouche, or happens to be in an interesting style.

D6:1 Teti
Othoes

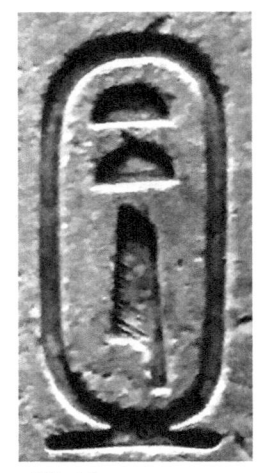
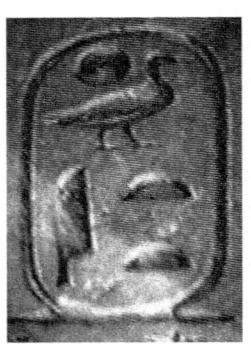

X1	M17
T(e)t	I

Both photos are the same name (Teti has no **THRONE NAME**), but just to make a point, in the second photo he shares his cartouche with the *Son of Ra* title.

/T/ is a bread loaf. While the Egyptians had many types and shapes of bread, this is the default sign for it.

It is important to note that while a pharaoh's cartouche may be seen on the wall of a tomb or sarcophagus, that does *not* mean that the tomb or object belonged to that king. An official who worked under one or more pharaohs usually included the names of those monarchs in their résumés on his tomb wall. Furthermore, officials tended to include pharaohs' names, inside cartouches, in their children's names.

In his tomb at Saqqara, Mereruka, Vizier to and son-in-law of Teti, depicts his son, Meri-Teti. The son's name contains Teti's cartouche:

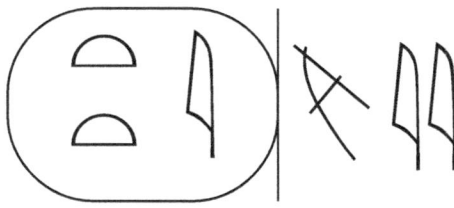

/Mer/ (U6) is a *hoe*, which sounds like and is used for *love* in Egyptian.

 /I or Y/ is obviously based on /I/, the single *reed*. The *double reed* shown here is one sign. It is a grammatical ending that goes with the *hoe* to mean *beloved*. In other words, *Beloved of Teti*.

Note that Teti's cartouche is written before the other two signs. Remember honorific transposition? It would be rude to put the king's name anywhere but first in the child's name. Remember that we read toward the faces of people and animals and toward the vertical bar at the end of a cartouche.

Here is a portrait of Meryteti, showing his name. He is dwarfed by his father's leg and foot. Although he is depicted as a child, with the side lock of youth and holding a pet bird, he was most likely an adult when Mereruka's tomb was finished. His tiny stature and childish attributes represent his status compared to that of his father.

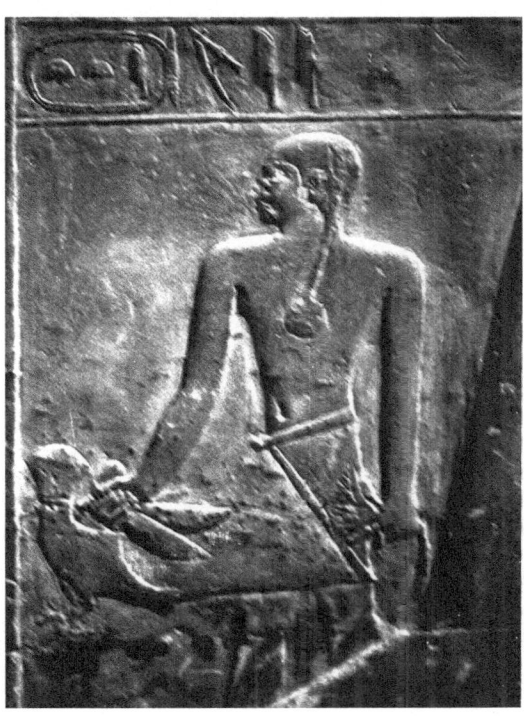

D6:3B Pepy I
D6:3T Meryra
Pepi, Phiops, Phios

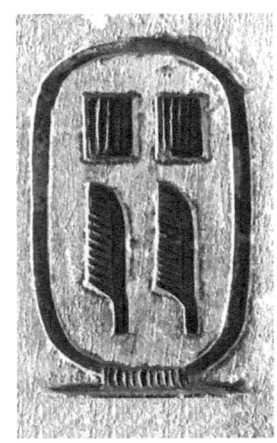

Q3	M17a
▢▢	𓇌
Pep	**Y**

U6	M17a	N5
⟋	𓇌	⊙
Mer	**Y**	**R**A

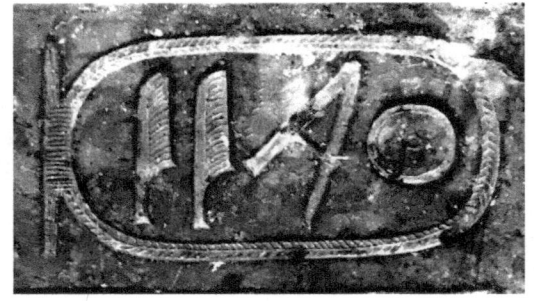

/P/ probably depicts the woven top of a *stool*. On the left, below, is a detailed stool hieroglyph from Mereruka's tomb; on the right is an ancient stool with a top woven of rushes.

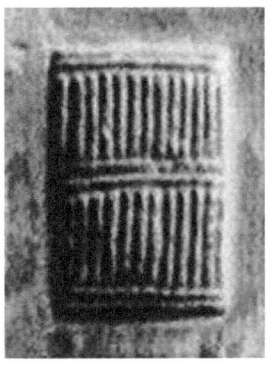

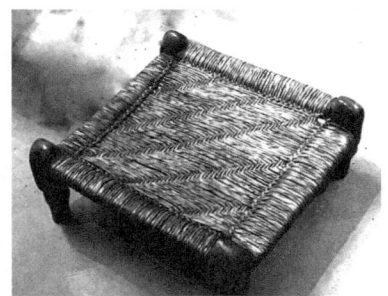

D6:5B Pepy II
D6:5T Neferkara
Pepi II, Phiops II

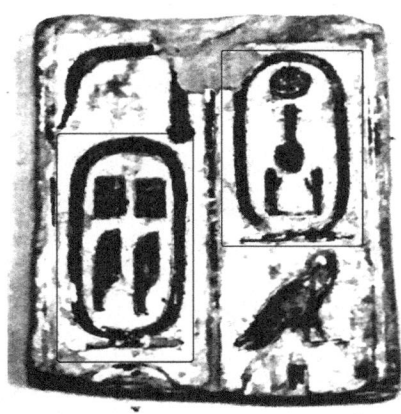

Q3	M17a
□□	ᐊᐊ
Pep	**Y**

F35	D28	N5
☦	⊔	⊙
Nefer	**Ka**	**Ra**

Oh oh, we have another Pepy, Pepy II. How can we tell them apart? If all you have is the Pepy cartouche, the sad truth is that you *can't*.

Both cartouches may be required for positive identification:
For pharaohs with duplicate names, you need to see *both* the **THRONE NAME** *and* **BIRTH NAME** to be sure who is whc. The small ceramic tablet illustrated here shows both of Pepi II's cartouches, so we can be sure it is him. There are several other Neferkara names in other dynasties, so in this case both cartouches are needed.

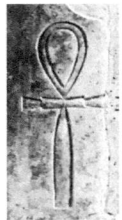

D6 Queen Ankhnespepy

S34	N35	Aa1	N35	S29	Q3	M17a
♀	ᴡᴡᴡ	⊜	ᴡᴡᴡ	⌐	☐☐	⫽⫽
Ankh	**(N**	**Kh)**	**N(e)**	**S**	**Pep**	**Y**

 /Ankh/ means *life* or *to live*. The following /N/ and /Kh/ are **PHONETIC COMPLEMENTS**. It probably represents a *sacred knot*.

Speaking of duplicate names, there were four royal women of the 6th Dynasty named Ankhnespepy. **Tyldesley (p 59)** notes that Pepy I married "two sisters.... most appropriately, and most confusingly, named Ankhnespepi ('She lives for King Pepi I')." One bore a son who became Pharaoh Nemtyemsaf Merenra, not listed in the *Field Guide*; the other bore Pepy II Neferkara. The other ladies were less important. An inscription and portrait of one of the Ankhnespepys gives us a chance to read an inscription outside of a cartouche, but using only hieroglyphs we have seen.

Follow along with me here (left-hand photo on page 47):

 /Sa/ is *son*.

 /T/ is a **FEMININE GRAMMATICAL ENDING**, so /Sa-t/ is *daughter*. This is basically the same /T/ as in *Bat (Mitzvah)*, "*Daughter (of the Commandment)."*

 /(e)F/ Way back at Sneferu D4:1, we learned that /F/ can mean "his." Consequently…

 I9 horned viper/Satef/ means *his daughter*.

 /Mer/ is *love*. Can you figure out the meaning of this phrase?

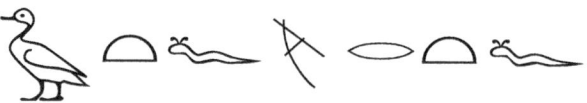

Right! *His beloved (daughter).* (The /R/ is a phonetic complement for /Mer/). *Beloved*, here, also takes a feminine ending

Below is the inscription and a portrait of one of the Ankhnespepys, here again dwarfed by the walking stick of her husband.

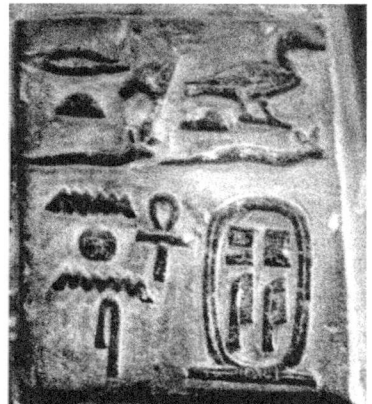 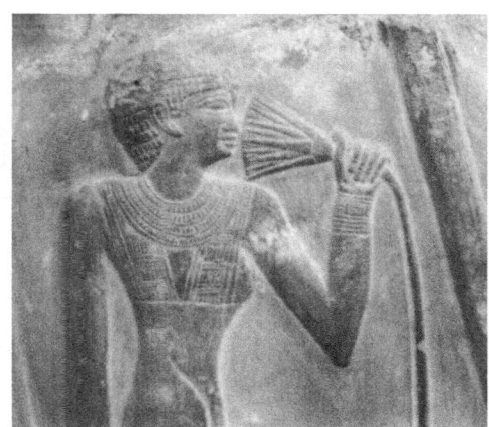

His beloved daughter, Ankhnespepy

First Intermediate Period
Dynasties 7-10

The history of Dynasties 7 through 10 is extremely murky. They mark the beginning of the First Intermediate Period, a period of chaos and disruption. The rulers during this time are not well attested. The *Field Guide* will ignore them.

Middle Kingdom
Dynasties 11–12

D11:2 Intef I
Inyotef, Antef

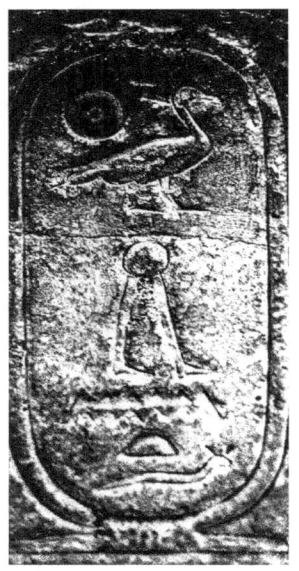

G39	N5	W25	N35	X1	I9
![Sa]	![Ra]	![In]	![N]	![Te]	![F]
Sa	**R**_A	**In**	**(N)**	**T(e)**	**F**

/In/ A *pot with legs*: meaning *to bring or fetch*.

There are several Intefs in the Eleventh and later dynasties. They tended to include *Son of Ra* in their cartouches. As many do not have **THRONE NAMES**, it is impossible to tell them apart from their cartouches alone, except for Intef II, D11:3, who added *the Great* to his name. (They have distinct Horus names, but those are beyond the scope of the *Field Guide*.

D11:3 Intef II
Inyotef, Antef

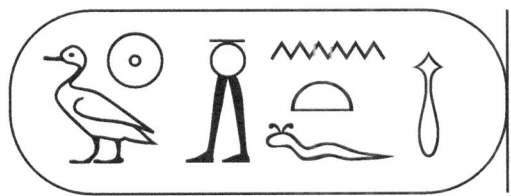

G39	N5	W25	N35	X1	I9	O29
🦆	⊙	𓊮	∿∿∿	◠	𓆑	𓊽
Sa	**R**A	**In**	**(N)**	**T(e)**	**F**	**Aa**

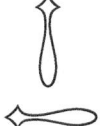 /Aa/, represents a *column*, in the architectural sense, and means *great*.

D11:5B Mentuhotep II
D11:5T Nebhepetra
Mentuhotpe, Montuhotep

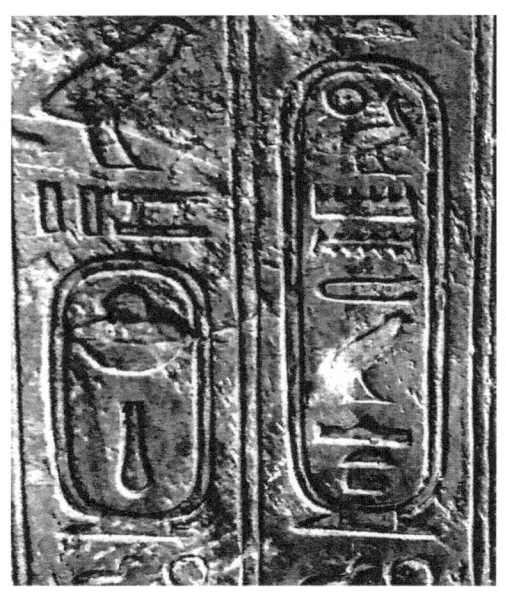

Mentuhotep means *the God Montu is Content* (CLAYTON P 72). Mentu, or Montu, is a falcon war god. There are several Mentuhoteps and the numbers (Metuhotep I, II), etc. are disputed, or at least not standardized. QUIRKE doesn't assign numbers; CLAYTON calls this one Mentuhotep I, while others give number I to a NOMARCH (provincial governor) early in the 11th Dynasty.

Cartouche, right

G39	N5	Y5	N35	V13	G43	R4	X1	Q3
🦆	⊙	𓏠	〰	⊶	🐦	△	⌒	□
Sa	R_A	M_EN	(N)	T	U	Hotep	(Te	P)

 /Men/ or /Mon/ a *game board* with playing pieces, was introduced with Pharaoh number D4:6, Menkaura. This sign almost always takes the phonetic complement /N/.

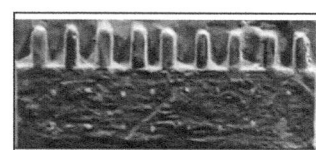

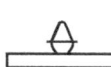 /T/ a *tether* for cattle, may have been pronounced like the /ch/ in *cheese*. As the usual transliteration of this pharaoh's **BIRTH NAME** is Mentuhotep, we'll just use a /T/ in the *Field Guide*.

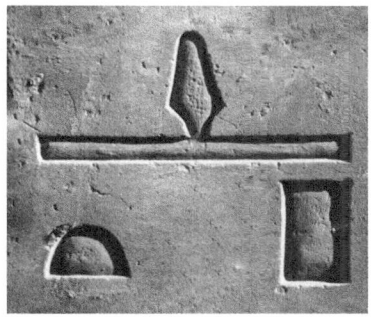 /Hotep/ or /Hetep/ is a *loaf on a reed mat*, intended as an offering. It carries the meaning of *to be pleased or satisfied*. The final /T/ and /P/ are optional phonetic complements.

Like /Men/, /Hotep/ is usually written with its phonetic complements inside an invisible rectangle, for symmetry's sake, like this:

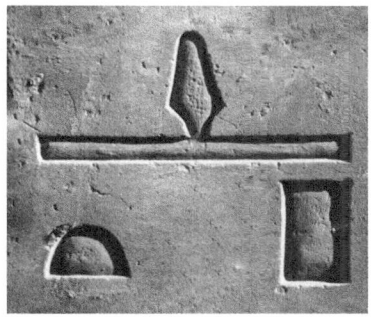

Cartouche, left, previous page

V30	P8	N5
⌣	𓏏	⊙
Neb	**Hepet**	**RA**

 /Hepet/ (*not* /Hotep/) is an *oar*, and signifies *voice*.

 /Neb/ is a *basket* and means either *lord* or *all*. In cartouches, this is often translated as *Lord* or *Master (of)*.

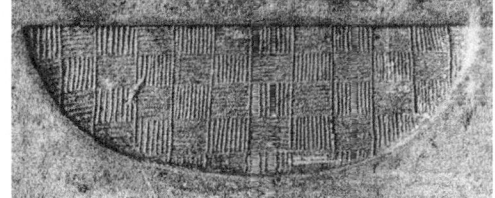

D11:6B Mentuhotep III
D11:6T Sankhkara
Montuhotep, Mentuhotpe

Cartouche, right

Y5	N35	V13	G43	R4	X1	Q3
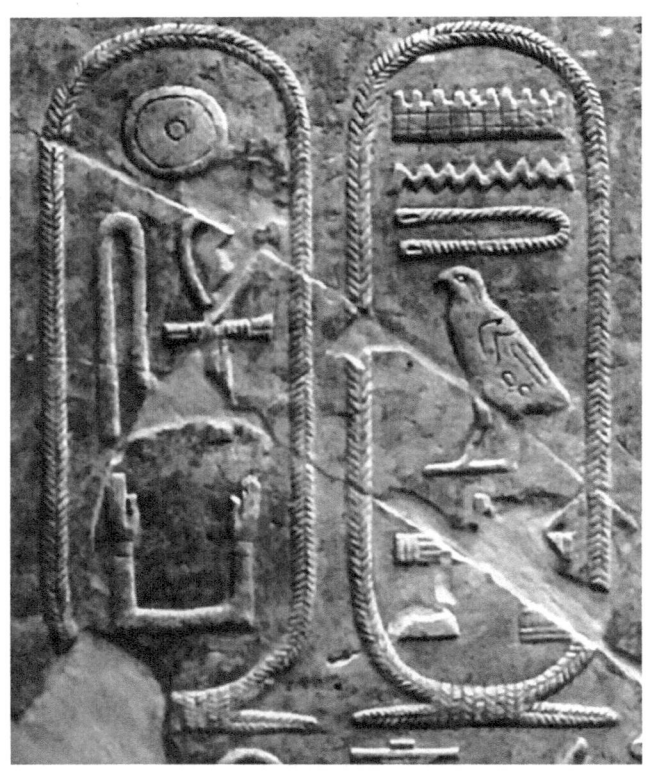						
Men	**(N)**	**T**	**U**	**Hotep**	**(Te**	**P)**

Cartouche, left

S29	S34	D28	N5
S	**Ankh**	**Ka**	**R**A

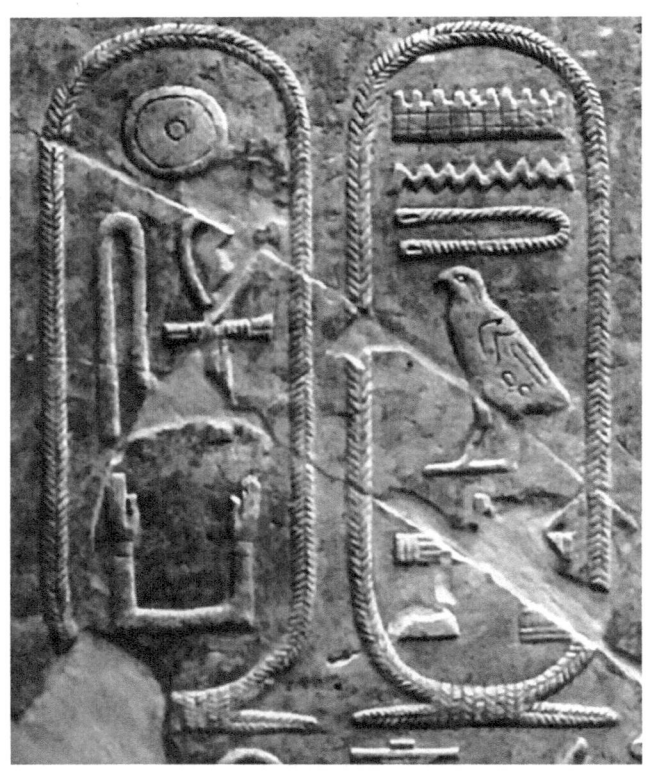

Even though they are damaged, I love the detail in these cartouches. The little hands and even cuffs or bracelets on the *Ka*; the markings on the *quail chick*; the *game board* /Men/ and its pieces; the sacred *Ankh* knot; the *twisted rope* on the /T/ *tether*; the details of the woven wicker on the /P/ *stool top* and the /Hotep/ *offering mat*. The SHEN RINGS themselves, encircling the hieroglyphs to form the cartouches, show details of the twisted or braided ropes they are made from.

We've seen all these signs before. You can find them in the sign index and see with which ruler they were introduced, and go back and read any notes on a given sign.

D12:1B Amenemhat I
D12:1T Sehetepibra
Ammanemes

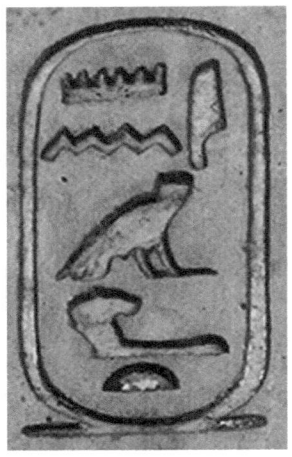 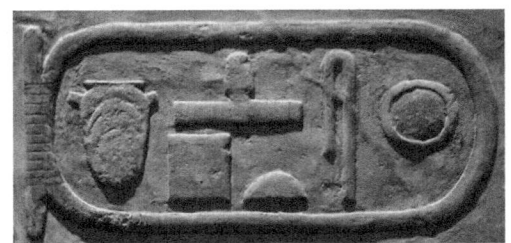

Cartouche, left

M17	Y5	N35	G17	F4	X1
(M17 sign)	(Y5 sign)	(N35 sign)	(G17 sign)	(F4 sign)	(X1 sign)
A	MEN	(N)	(e)M	Hat	(T)

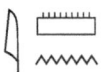 We've seen /A/, /Men/ and /N/ separately, but this combination will be one of the most commonly found in the cartouches: /Amen/ *the god Amen*. In the name **BREAKOUTS** I will write that combination of signs as one group from now on.

 /M/ is quite obviously an *owl*, one of the few hieroglyphic animal or bird signs that face the viewer.

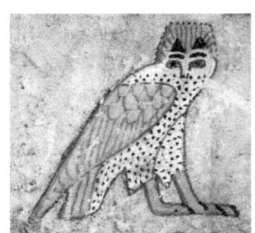

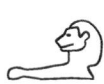 /Hat/ the head and *forequarters of a recumbent lion*, meaning *front*. Consequently, Amenemhat means something like *Amen is number one!* or *Amen's out in front*. The final /T/ is a phonetic complement for /Hat/.

Wikipedia lists eight pharaohs named Amenemhat, plus a number of princes and other officials. Not all of the Amenemhat pharaohs will make the cut for the *Field Guide* (I'll apologize when I see them next).

Cartouche, right, facing page

S29	R4	X1	Q3	F34	N5
∩	△	⌒	□	⊽	⊙
S(e)	Hetep	(Te)	P)	Ib	Rᴀ

 /ib/ is not a jar, as it would appear, but is a bull's *heart*. The meaning is *heart*, with some of the same connotations we use now relating to *joy*, *stout-heartedness*, etc. **CLAYTON (P78)** translates Sehetepibra as *Satisfied is the Heart of Re*.

How they can tell that this heart belongs to a bull or cow and not to a human is beyond me, but it is accepted that internal organs and bones (ribs, uterus, intestine, tongue and so on) are usually represented in hieroglyphs as those of animals, specifically cattle, even when referring to human organs.

Like the name of the god Amen, /Hetep/ or /Hotep/, *to be pleased* or *satisfied*, is extremely common.

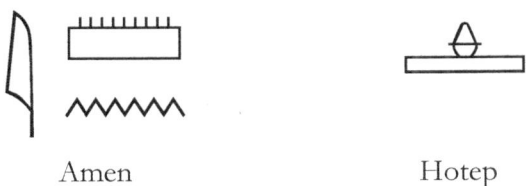

Amen   Hotep

D12:2B Senusret I
D12:2T Kheperkara
Senwosre, Sesostris, Userten

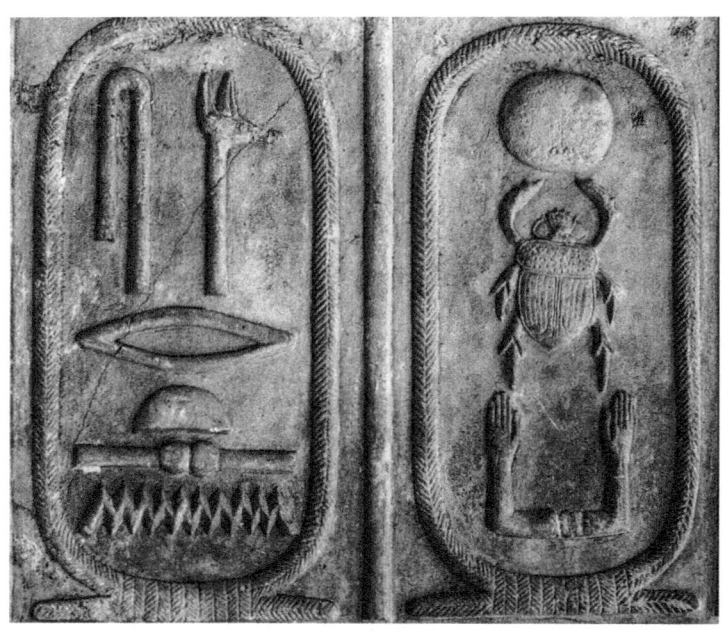

O34	N35	F12	S29	D21	X1
—∞—	⌇⌇⌇	🦊	⎮	⬭	◠
S(e)	N	Uꜱᴇʀ	(S	Rᴇ)	T

L1	D28	N5
🪲	Ш	⊙
Kheper	Ka	Rᴀ

The order of the signs in Senusret can be confusing. /User/, the canine head on a staff, with the **PHONETIC COMPLEMENTS** /SR/ means *powerful*. We encountered /User/ in D5:6B. But with the addition of the feminine ending /T/, it becomes the name of the Theban goddess *Wosret*. As a goddess, her name moves to the front of the queue in the cartouche.

/Kheper/ the *dung beetle*, carries the idea of *becoming, coming into being,* or *shape*. It can also represent the god Khepri, the rising sun.

I love the detail on this beetle.

There are three Senusrets, all in Dynasty 12.

Just for fun, take a look at this **COMBINED CARTOUCHE**, below, which includes both the **BIRTH NAME** and **THRONE NAME** of Senusret I Kheperkara, plus a lot of titles and attributes that normally go outside the cartouche. Can you find each name? (Combining both names into one cartouche is unusual, but obviously not unknown.) Here the individual names are typed out as reminders.

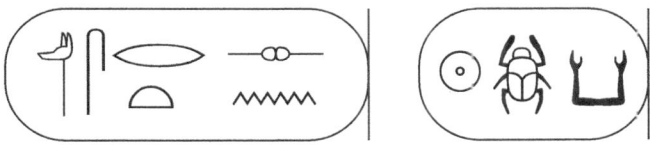

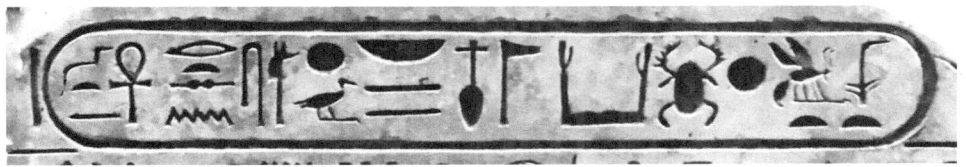

There are 23 total hieroglyphic signs in this cartouche. Of these, there are only five or six that are new.

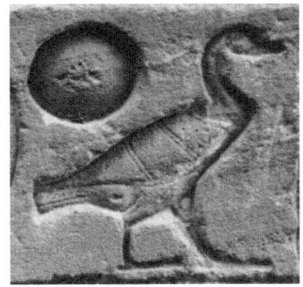

/Sa Ra/ (G39, N5), as you know, is *Son of Ra*, which always precedes the **BIRTH NAME**, usually *outside* the cartouche. In this instance, the **BIRTH NAME** is Senusret, introduced earlier.

Note the fashionable wig worn by the /User/ (canine-headed) staff in *Senusret*, above.

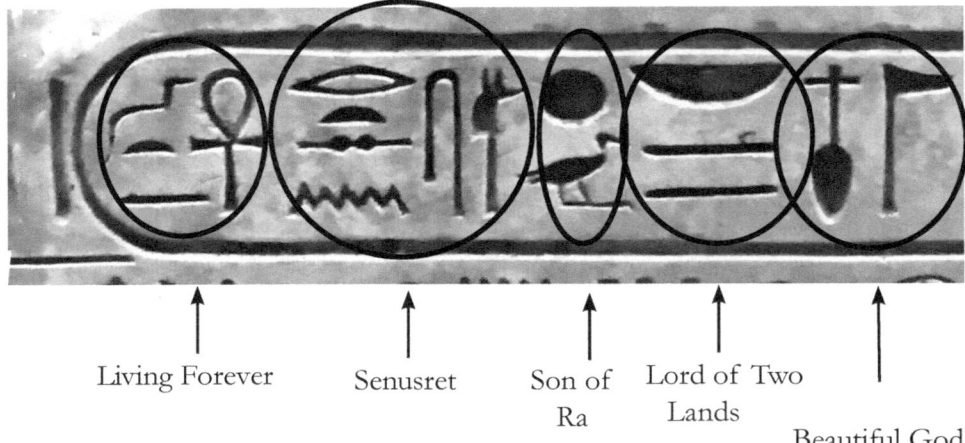

Living Forever   Senusret   Son of   Lord of Two
                                          Ra   Lands
                                                                    Beautiful God

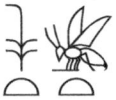 The first new title we encounter introduces the **THRONE NAME** of a pharaoh, /Nesu-Bit/ *He of the Sedge and the Bee.*

 /Su/ (M23) *Sedge* plant. Traditionally, *King of Upper Egypt.*

 /Bit/ (L2) *Bee.* Traditionally, *King of Lower Egypt.*

This is a very ancient title. According to **GARDINER (P 482),** the (unwritten) /N/ sound at the beginning of this compound phrase means *belonging to (the sedge plant.)*

The combined title used to be interpreted as *King of Upper and Lower Egypt,* but more recent scholarship indicates that the meaning is not so simple. A closer translation might be *Two-Aspected King* **DODSON (P 11)** referring to the dual nature of the Land of Egypt, perhaps the green, cultivated part contrasted with the uninviting desert.

Moving on, the first thing after the **THRONE NAME** (Kheperkara) is this pair of signs, one of which, /Nefer/, we saw way back in the Fourth Dynasty:

/Nefer/(F35), a *heart and windpipe*, means *good, beautiful, perfect.*

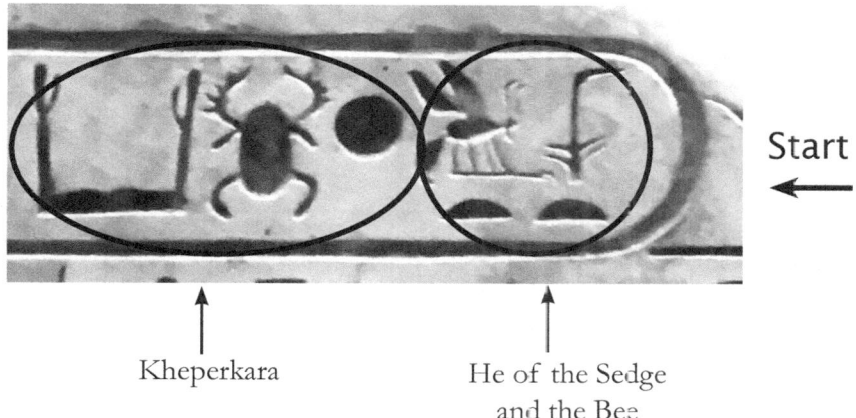

Kheperkara

He of the Sedge
and the Bee

Start ←

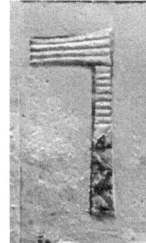

 /Netjer /(R8) is said to be a *banner* or *flag*, the kind that flew from masts outside the **PYLONS** of temples. The sign means *god*, or *divine*. /Netjer Nefer/, then, is *the good, beautiful, perfect god*.

We know ⌣ /Neb/ (V30) as *lord*. Here, it is combined with ⎐ /Tawy/ (N19). **GARDINER (P 487)** calls a single one of these bars *a sandy tract*. Doubled, they refer to *the Two Lands*, the double nature of Egypt mentioned earlier. /Nebtawy/, *Ruler of the Two Lands*, can replace or be combined with *He of the Sedge and the Bee*. **(GAUTHIER VOL 6 P 3).**

 /Ankh/ (S34) is next, denoting *life, to live*.

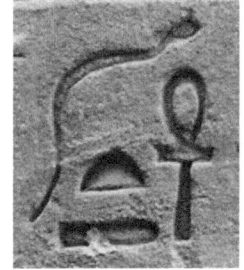

(I10) /Dj/ an extended *cobra*, combined with /T/ (X1) and a single *sandy tract* (N17) sign means *forever, eternal*, pronounced /Djet/. The combination means *living forever*.

D12:4B Senusret II
D12:4T Khakheperra
Senwosre, Sesostris, Userten

O34	N35	F12	S29	D21	X1
—∞—	∿∿∿∿	𓄹	𓏤	⬭	⌂
S(e)	N	USER	(S	RE)	T

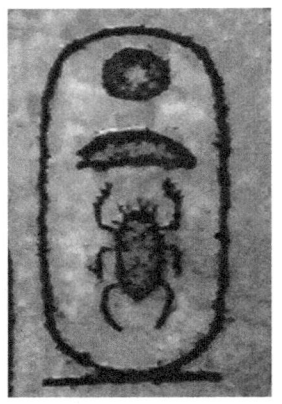

N28	L1	N5
⌢	🪲	⊙
Kha	Kheper	RA

No new hieroglyphs here. We saw ⌢/Kha/, *the rising sun*, in Khafra's cartouche, D4:4.

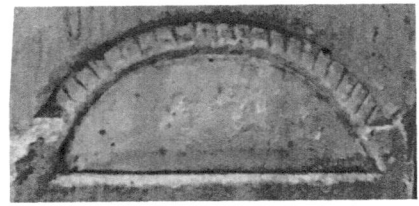

D12:5B Senusret III
D12:5T Khakaura
Senwosre, Sesostris, Userzen

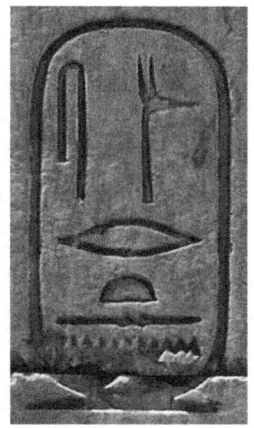 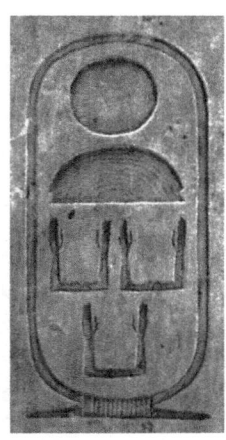

O34	N35	F12	S29	D21	X1
—∞—	∿∿∿∿			⬯	△
S(e)	N	User	(S	Re)	T

N28	D28	N5
⌒	⊔⊔⊔	⊙
Kha	Kau	Ra

Nothing really new in either of these cartouches. Remember that the three-fold repetition of a sign makes it plural. So /Ka-u/ is *spirits, souls*.

Even though the names are not novel, the actual carving is wonderful. Look at the delicate thumbs on /Ka/, the *upraised arms*. The *rising sun* /Kha/ shows concentric rings of glory appearing above the hill (right-hand cartouche).

D12:6B Amenemhat III
D12:6T Nimaatra
Ammenemes

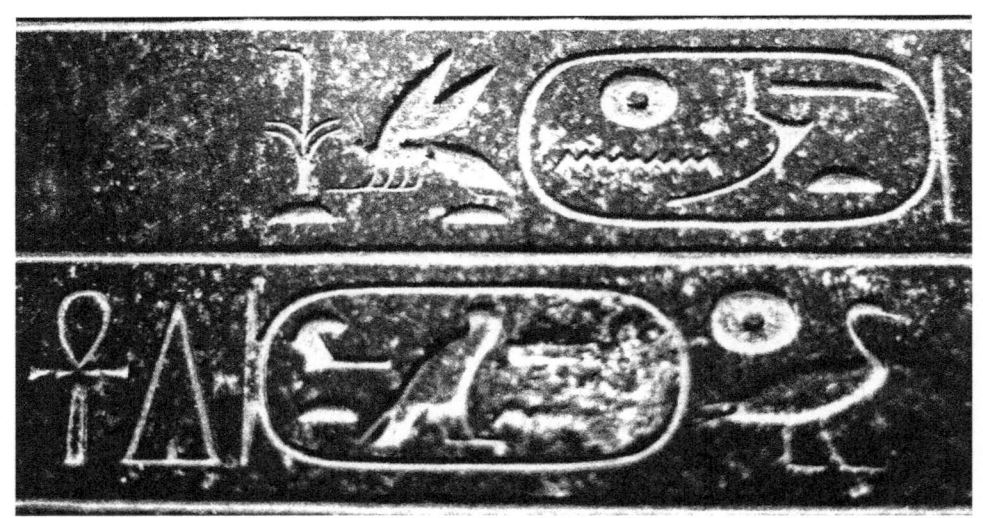

Bottom Cartouche

M17	Y5	N35	G17	F4	X1
A	Men	(N)	(e)M	Hat	(T)

Top Cartouche

N35	U1	Aa11	X1	N5
N(i)	Maa	(Maa)	T	Ra

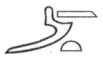 /Maat/ *truth, order, justice*, is a word combining three signs:

 /Maa/ (U1) is a *sickle* for harvesting grain. It is made of wood, and the inside curve is studded with sharp teeth of stone or other material.

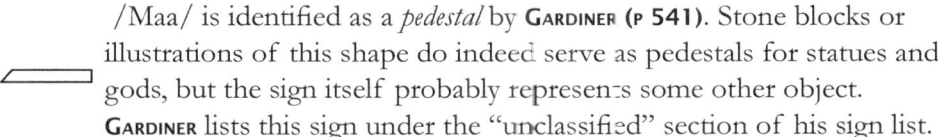 /Maa/ is identified as a *pedestal* by GARDINER (P 541). Stone blocks or illustrations of this shape do indeed serve as pedestals for statues and gods, but the sign itself probably represents some other object. GARDINER lists this sign under the "unclassified" section of his sign list.

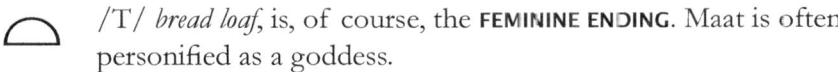 /T/ *bread loaf*, is, of course, the FEMININE ENDING. Maat is often personified as a goddess.

You just have to learn /Maat/ as a "sight word," without worrying too much about why it is written the way it is.

The inscription illustrated is very interesting. The top register, or row, is read from left to right; the bottom row, from right to left. Remember to approach each sign from the front. In other words, read toward the faces of any animals or people (or insects!).

You should recognize the *Sedge and the Bee*, identifying the following name as *King of the Dual Land (of Egypt)*. Likewise, the *duck* and *sun*, labeling the following name as *Son of Ra*. See D12:2

After *Son of Ra* comes the name Amenemhat, with the /Amen/ portion of the name purposely mutilated. During the time of Akhenaten, the cult of Amen was forbidden, and the god's name was hacked out of monuments throughout Egypt. In later dynasties, this same treatment was inflicted on others, notably the god Set and Queen Hatshepsut. One's name was an essential part of an Egyptian's identity. Having one's name repeated by priests or descendants (or by anyone, for that matter) ensured eternal life.

The attackers (hackers?) never found all instances of a name during their campaign of destruction. There are examples where an intact name can be found on the back side of a statue. The chiselers were either careless or too lazy to check every side.

After the mutilated Amenemhat cartouche is /Ankh/, *life*, preceded by a triangular sign.

/Di/ (X8) is a conical *loaf of bread*. The meaning is *to give*. So the entire inscriptions reads, *King of the Dual Land (of Egypt), Son of Ra Amenemhat, Given Life.*

D12 Princess Neferuptah

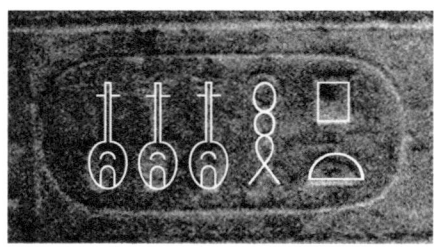

F35	
(F35 glyphs)	(PTAH glyphs)
Nefer-u	**P**TAH

Neferuptah was a daughter of Amenemhat III. Again, the triple /Nefer/ denotes plural *beauties.*

 /H/ (V28) is a *twisted wick of flax fibers.*

/Ptah/ is a god associated with the city of Memphis, near modern Cairo. His name is usually spelled out, as it is here.

Second Intermediate Period
Dynasties 13-17

D13:7B Ameny Intef Amenemhat VI
D13:7T Sankhibra

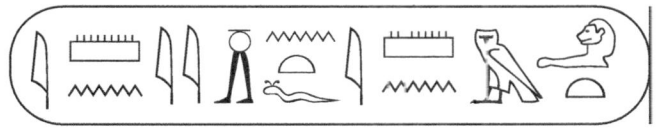

	M17a			G17	F4	X1
AMEN	Y	Intef	AMEN	(e)M	Hat	(T)

S29	S34	F34	N5
S	Ankh	Ib	RA

Nothing original about this king's names: He. or his mother, (whoever named him) combined Intef, from the the Eleventh Dynasty, and Amenemhat, from the Twelfth, with the given name Ameny (derived from the god Amen). His **THRONE NAME**, Sankhibra, *is* unique, using /Ankh/ *life*, and /Ib/ *heart*.

He is known as Amenemhat VI, for short.

D13:12B Sobekhotep I or II
D13:12T Khaankhra
Sebekhotpe

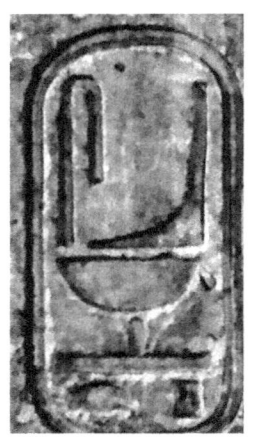 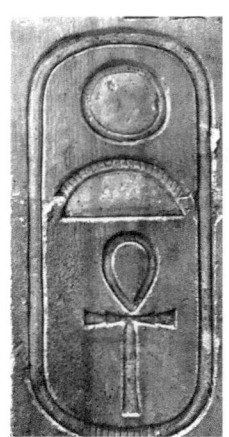

S29	D58	V31	R4
S(o)	B(e)	K	Hotep

N28	S34	N5
Kha	Ankh	Rᴀ

We encounter two new phonetic signs in this pharaoh's **BIRTH NAME**:

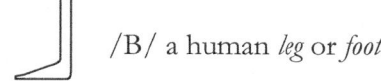 /B/ a human *leg* or *foot*.

/K/ a *basket with a handle*, not to be confused with /Neb/, a *basket without a handle*, meaning *lord*.

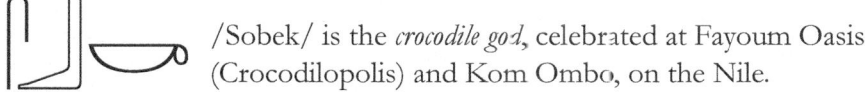 /Sobek/ is the *crocodile god*, celebrated at Fayoum Oasis (Crocodilopolis) and Kom Ombo, on the Nile.

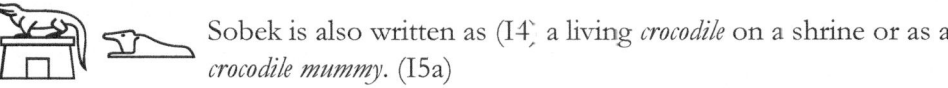 Sobek is also written as (I4) a living *crocodile* on a shrine or as a *crocodile mummy*. (I5a)

There were up to nine Sobekhoteps in this dynasty, most of whom will not be mentioned in the *Field Guide*. There is great disagreement about their numbers (I, II and so forth).

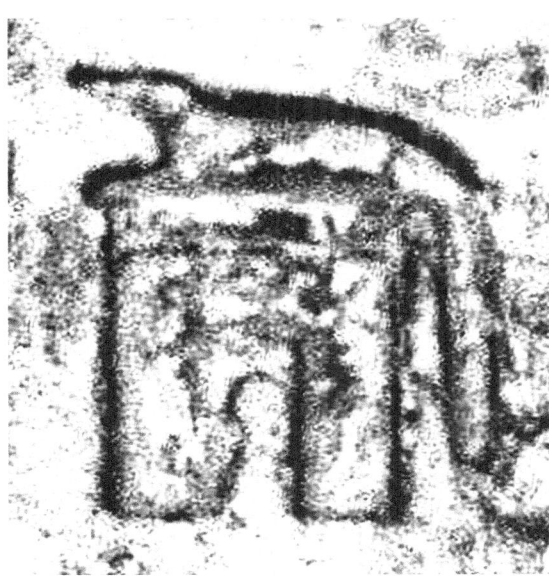

D13:21B Sobekhotep III
D13:21T Sekhemra sewadjtawy
Sebekhotpe

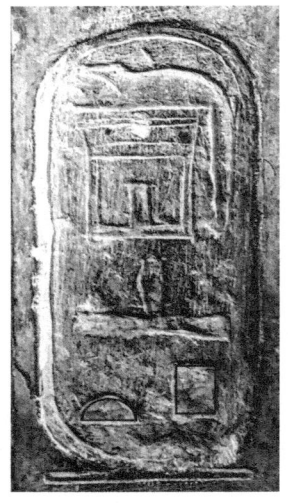

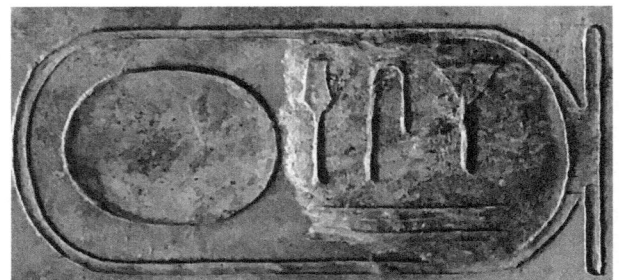

I4	R4
Sobek	Hotep

S42	N5	S29	M13	N19
Sekhem	**Ra**	**S(e)**	**Wadj**	**Tawy**

 /Sekhem/ one of the many scepters held by Egyptian rulers. It represents *power, authority.*

 /Wadj/ a *papyrus stalk and umbel.* Besides meaning a **PAPYRUS**-shaped architectural column, it means *green, flourishing,* so this name means *Powerful Ra, who makes the Two Lands Flourish.* (See **Clayton, p 90**).

Effaced names, usurped monuments: We saw how some pharaohs, or at least their supporters, hacked out the names of gods who were out of favor, or removed other pharaohs or gods' cartouches entirely. They also *added* their names to those of existing pharaohs, on temples and sarcophagi. At left we see two examples of where lovely, convex inscriptions of the cartouches were crudely hacked out and replacement signs were even more crudely scratched into the cartouche frames.

In spite of the rough surface, you can see that in the cartouche on the right the /Ra/ *sun*, is quite out of proportion to the following three signs, a dead giveaway that someone has meddled with the cartouche.

D13:pB Seshib
D13-14:?T Menkhaura
Sena'a-ib

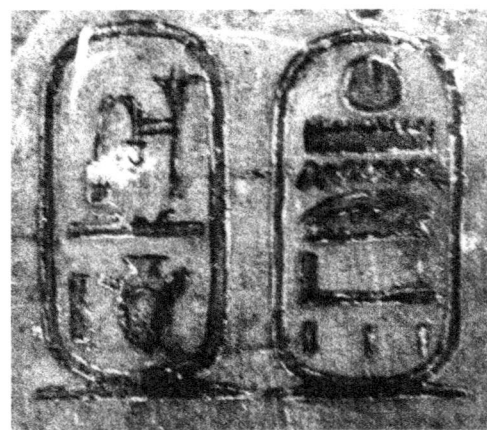

Let me show you one of my rarest and most prized butterflies, er, pharaohs. This cartouche, in the Egyptian Museum, Cairo, taunted me for years. I eventually found him in my references, but even they don't agree as to whether Seshib ruled in the 13th or 14th Dynasty. GAUTHIER (DYNASTIES VOL 2 P 63) calls him Seshib; VON BECKERATH, (P 210) calls him Sena'a-ib.

Y3	Y1	F34	Z1
Sesh	-	Ib	-

 /Sesh/ *scribe*. It represents the scribe's kit of a reed pen, water jar, and a wooden "watercolor palette" with depressions holding red and black ink, all tied together with a cord.

Seshib's **BIRTH NAME** also contains a silent **DETERMINATIVE**:

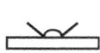 /silent/ a papyrus scroll, signifies *abstract ideas*. The roll is wrapped and tied with a string and sealed with a daub of clay and the impression of a signet. This sign is a **DETERMINATIVE**,: not pronounced, but clarifying the meaning. See the entry under D17:5T, the next pharaoh in the Field Guide.

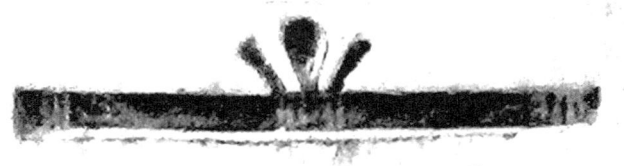

| /Silent/ (Z1). This vertical mark indicates that the picture of the item, as used above with the *heart* sign, actually represents the item itself, and not an abstract concept.

 for instance, can be the *sun god* /Ra/, but if you add the stroke, it means the actual *sun*, not referring to the god.

Y5	N35	N28	D36	Z2	N5
⬓	∿∿∿	⌒	()	‖ ‖	☉
Men	**(N)**	**Kha**	**(A)**	**U**	**RA**

/A/ human *arm*. This is the phonetic symbol for a sound we don't have in the western languages, the *Ayn*, or *Ayin*, a *guttural* sound that exists in Arabic and Hebrew. At least this sound exists in all versions of Arabic except Maltese (https://www.omniglot.com/writing/maltese.htm). The Ayn still exists as a letter in the Hebrew alphabet, but is not pronounced as a consonant by most speakers. The Ayn is the second consonant in many of the syllables you see in the royal names which end in /A/, although it is not usually written. Examples are /Ra/ and here, /Kha/.

Arabic Ayn

Hebrew Ayin

 **Plurals:** The three vertical strokes make this sign plural—quicker than repeating the entire sign three times, as seen in earlier names. The three strokes take an /U/ sound, the same spoken plural marker as when the sign itself is repeated three times.

| | |

D17:15B Kamose
D17:15T Wadjkheperra

D28	D52	F31	S29	A24

Ka	-	Mos	S	-

Determinatives: Kamose's BIRTH NAME shows some interesting features. For one thing, it has two DETERMINATIVES—signs that clarify the meaning of other signs or groups of signs whose sense may be ambiguous—but which do not affect the pronunciation of the word or name.

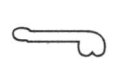

D52, *male genitals*, denoting that the pharaoh is a real man. What a stud! This sign is traditionally called *phallus*, a Victorian way to avoid modern explicit sexual terminology, to my mind. I'll temper squeamishness with accuracy and call it *male genitals*.

Kamose's name does not always have this determinative.

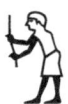

A24 The next determinative, also not pronounced, is a man striking with a stick, meaning *strong, victorious*. The message is that Kamose is not only a manly man, but a really tough son of a gun.

/Mos, Mes/ (F31), three *fox skins* tied together, *to be born, give birth*. This is an important one. Be sure to memorize it! Many of the big-name pharaohs, and some queens, too, use it in their names.

This sign has been called *three foxes' skins tied together* (GARDINER P 465), a *fox skin apron* (PETTY, HIEROGLYPHIC SIGN LIST P 44) and a *fly whisk* (BETRO P 128 and KAMIL, SAKKARA, P143). I would hate to see the fly large enough to require three fox pelts to whisk it away!

You usually cannot distinguish the foxy elements in this sign unless the inscription is extremely detailed. The little bumps on either side of the descending elements represent the ears and feet of the unlucky foxes.

I speculate that the fox skins have something to do with fertility. Did shamans or midwives in predynastic times use these skins as a talisman of some sort?

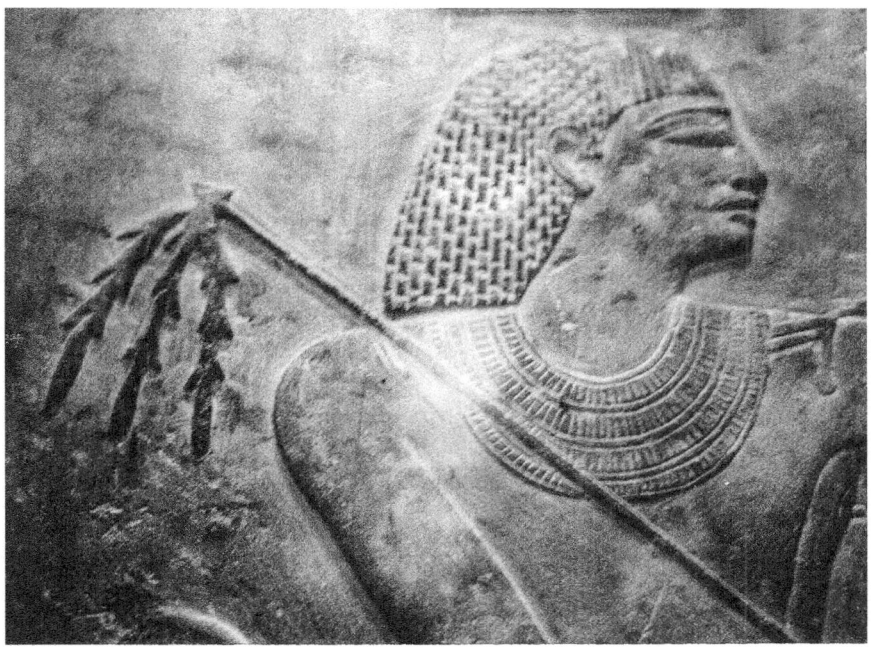

So-called *fly-whisk*

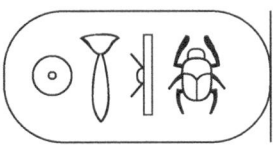

M13	L1	Y1	N5
𓇅	𓆣	𓏤	𓇳
Wadj	Kheper	-	Rᴀ

New Kingdom
Dynasties 18–20

D18:1B Ahmose I
D18:1T Nebpehtyra
Ahmosis

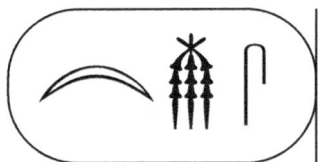

N11	F31	S29

Aн	**Mos**	**(S)**

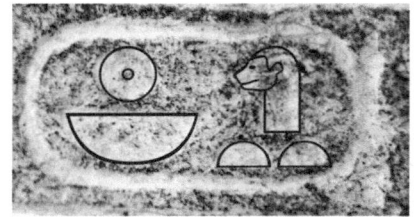

V30	F9	X1	N5
Neb	**Pehty**	**(Ty)**	**Rₐ**

 (N11, N12), /Ah/ the *moon god*. Ahmose means *the moon is born*. (Clayton p 100).

 /Pehty/, *leopard's head*, meaning *strength*. This sign is often written twice, to signify *double strength*. Perhaps the double /T/ bread loaves take the place of the double leopard's head.

D18: Queen Ahmose Nefertari

N12	F31	F35	X1	M17	D21	Z4
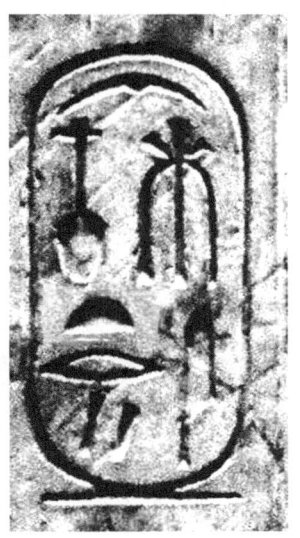						
AH	Mos	Nefer	T	A	R	Y

\\ /Y/, is a **DUAL MARKER**, meaning that a thing is doubled.

Ahmose Nefertari was wife of Ahmose I and mother of Amenhotep I.

Note that the /Mos/ in this inscription has been completely stripped of any foxiness, the hanging pelts showing up as smooth, curved lines.

D18:2B Amenhotep I
D18:2T Djeserkara
Amenophis

Cartouche, bottom

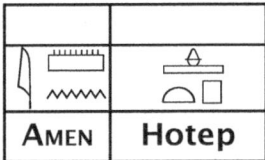

AMEN	Hotep

Cartouche, top

D45	D28	N5
		⊙
Djeser	Ka	RA

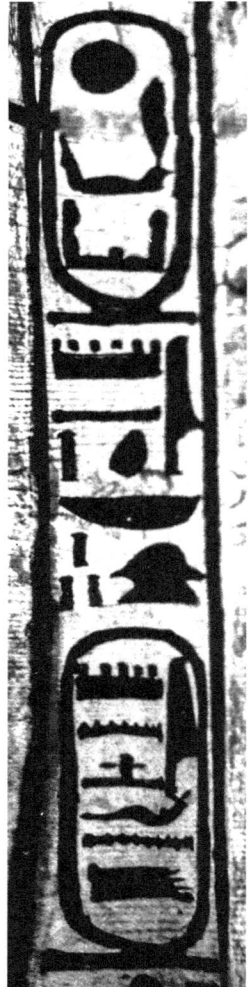

 /Djeser/ (D45), *hand holding a /nehbet/ wand*, meaning *holy, clear.*

I've included part of the inscription outside of the cartouches. Below /Djeserkara/ we find /Amen/. See how the /N/ in /Amen/ is reduced to a straight line.

/Si, Sa/ (H8) is a bird's *egg* and here means *son, (Son of Amen.)*

 /Kha/ (N28) follows, rendered in a curious fashion.

Next are three strokes denoting plural, shorthand for repeating the sign three times. As seen below, these three strokes can be written in various configurations, including the pyramid shape seen in the photo. /(Neb)Kha-u/, in the plural can be translated *(Lord of) Appearings.*

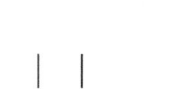

Inside the second cartouche, /Amenhotep/ is straightforward, but is followed by an unusual trio of signs:

〰〰〰 /N/ *water*, often meaning *pertaining to, of.*

〜 /F/ *horned viper*, meaning *he, him, his.*

/Kem/(I6), a *crocodile*'s spiky *tail*, meaning *black* or *gray*. In combination with other signs (below), you get /Kemet/, *Egypt*, presumably referring to the black fertile soil of the Nile valley.

These three extra signs are not "standard" for this cartouche, and are not documented in **Quirke, Clayton,** or even **von Beckerath**, although **Gauthier (vol 2 p 203)** cites this one instance. But since they are written on this pharaoh's coffin, they must be important. The meaning of this phrase has puzzled me for years. I can only assume it is a reference to *Egypt belonging to him.*

Just for fun, here is how to write /Kemet/, Egypt. It is not in any cartouches, but is often found associated with them. The example on the right is from a box belonging to King Tutankhamen:

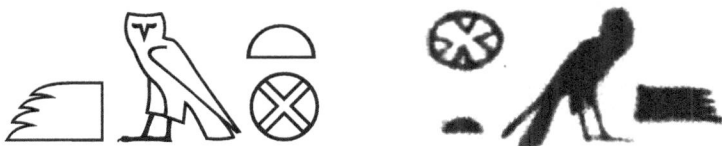

⊗ (O49) is a silent determinative denoting a *crossroads*, meaning a *town* or *inhabited area.*

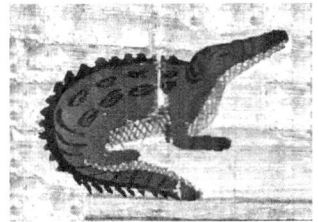

D18:3B Thutmose I
D18:3T Aakheperkara
Thutmosis, Djehutymes

G26	F31	O34	N28	W19	N5
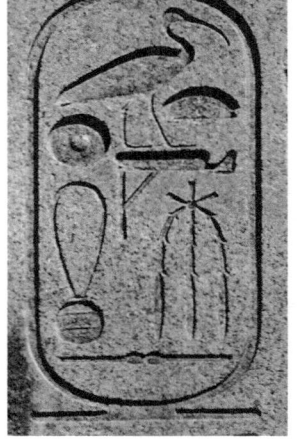					
THUT	Mos	(S)	Kha	Mi	RA

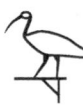 /Thut/, sacred ibis bird on a **STANDARD**. This bird represents the god *Thoth*, or more accurately, *Djehuty* in Egyptian. Thoth is the god of knowledge and writing.

 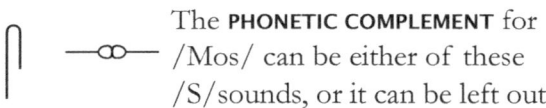 The **PHONETIC COMPLEMENT** for /Mos/ can be either of these /S/ sounds, or it can be left out

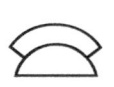 /Mi/, is a milk jug carried in a rope net, meaning *like*, or *as*.

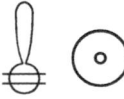 /Kha-mi-Ra/ (did you see the /Kha/ hiding under the ibis's throat?). This is translated as *Appearing in Glory Like Re* by **WILLOCKX (p 9)**. It is not an essential part of Thutmose I's **BIRTH NAME**. It is what is known as an **EPITHET**, a title or description which expands upon the name and often makes a name unique—there are four Thutmoses, for instance. Epithets can help distinguish them from one another.

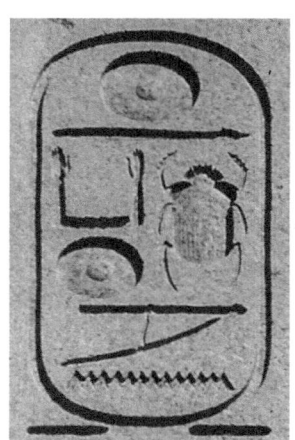

This epithet, /Kha-mi-Ra/ seems unique to Thutmose I.

O29	L1	D28	N5	U6	N35	N5
𓉻	𓆣	𓂓	☉	𓌻	𓈖	☉
Aa	**Kheper**	**Ka**	**Ra**	**Mer**	**(e)n**	**Ra**

Tutmose I's **THRONE NAME** also features an epithet, /Merenra/, containing
hieroglyphs we have seen earlier. This means *beloved of Ra*, and is a very popular
epithet from here until the end of pharaonic history.

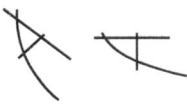 /Mer/ (U6 and U7) are variations of the sign for a *hoe*,
introduced with Teti and the Pepys of Dynasty Six. The
meaning is *love* or *beloved*. This tomb painting shows two
perfectly matched laborers, one beside the other, using hoes
like this.

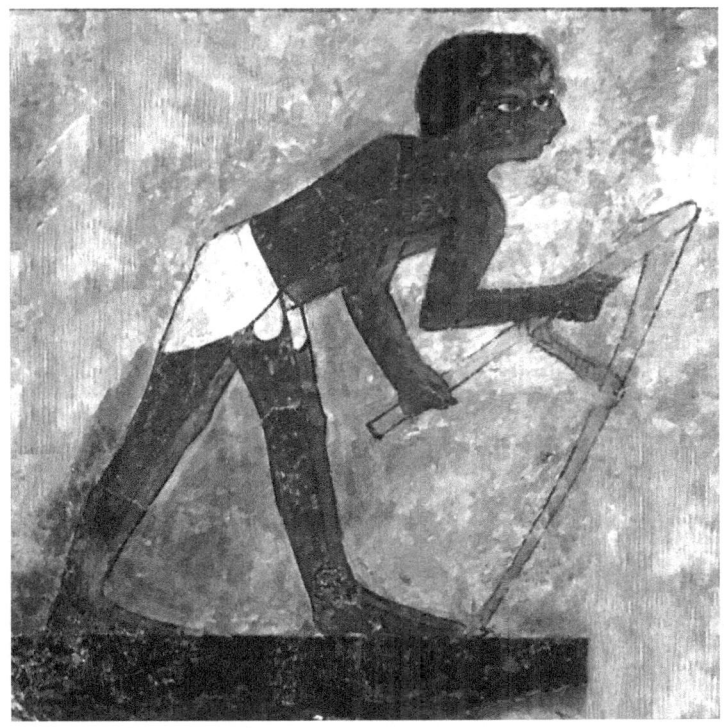

D18:4B Thutmose II
D18:4T Aakheperenra
Thutmosis, Djehutymes

Thutmose II used two epithets with his
BIRTH NAME. /Neferkha-u/ is the most
commonly seen. Once again, note that
placement of individual signs has
as much to do with symmetry as
with pronunciation.

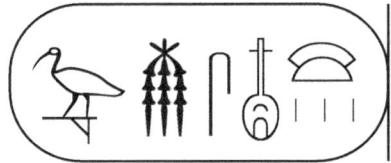

G26	F31	S29	F35	N28	Z2
🦤	🌾	∩	🎋	⌒	‖ ‖
THUT	**Mos**	**(S)**	**Nefer**	**Kha-**	**U**

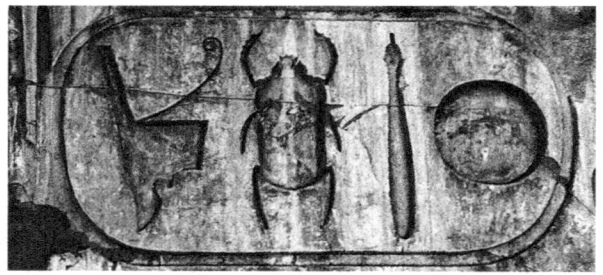

O29	L1	S3	N5
𓉻	🪲	🜪	⊙
Aa	**Kheper**	**(e)N**	**RA**

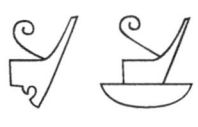

(S3. S4) are alternative writings for /N/. They represent the
red crown, traditionally identified as that of Lower (Northern)
Egypt. The second sign is the same *crown on a basket*, the
basket that can normally be read as *lord*, *master (of)* or *all*,
/Neb/ (V30).

D18:5B Hatshepsut Khenemet Amen
D18:5T Maatkara

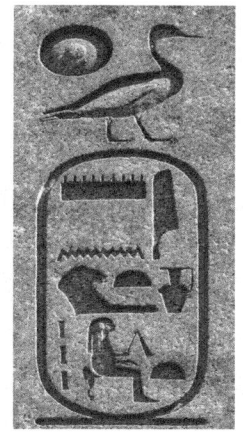 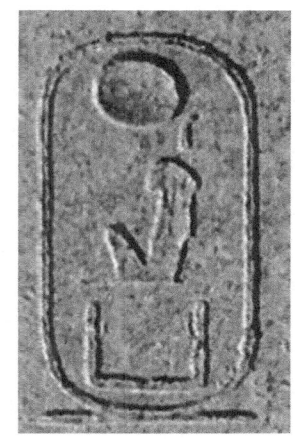

F4	A51	Z3	X1	W9	X1	
Hat	Sheps	U	T	(Khnem	(e)T	Amen)

C10	D28	N5
Maat	Ka	Rₐ

Hatshepsut, the most famous of the queens who reigned as kings, is conflicted. Here we see her identified as *Son of Ra*, like any other king, but she retains her feminine **BIRTH NAME**, which includes the **FEMININE GRAMMATICAL ENDING**.

 /Sheps/ *noble person*, seen in Shepseskaf, D4:6B. Here the figure is holding a flail, which does not change the meaning of the sign. In the carved sign, it even looks like the figure is wearing a woman's wig. Add a /T/ to the three strokes marking plural and you get feminine plural /-Ut/. So Hatshepsut is *First of the Noble Ladies.*

/Khnem/ is a ceramic *pitcher*, here with a /T/ **FEMININE ENDING**, /Khenemet/. The meaning is *unite, join*. Khenemet Amen means *united with Amen* (**WILLOCKX P 19**).

/Khenemet Amen/ is one of the **EPITHETS** mentioned earlier, so its inclusion in Hatshepsut's name is optional.

 /Maat/ is the personification of the concept of *Maat*; same as the second syllable of Nimaatra, D12:6B. Just as Superman on TV stood for *Truth, Justice and the American Way*, Maat represents *Truth, Justice and the Egyptian Way*, the right and order that keeps the cosmos together.

What distinguishes Maat from any other goddess is the *Maat feather*, a fluffy ostrich plume. When a deceased's soul reached the Underworld, his or her heart (we have seen *heart* /Ib/ earlier) was balanced against this feather of truth, or against Maat wearing the feather. If the person's sins were too heavy, the heart was devoured by a monster; if the heart was light, the person would enter a blessed afterlife.

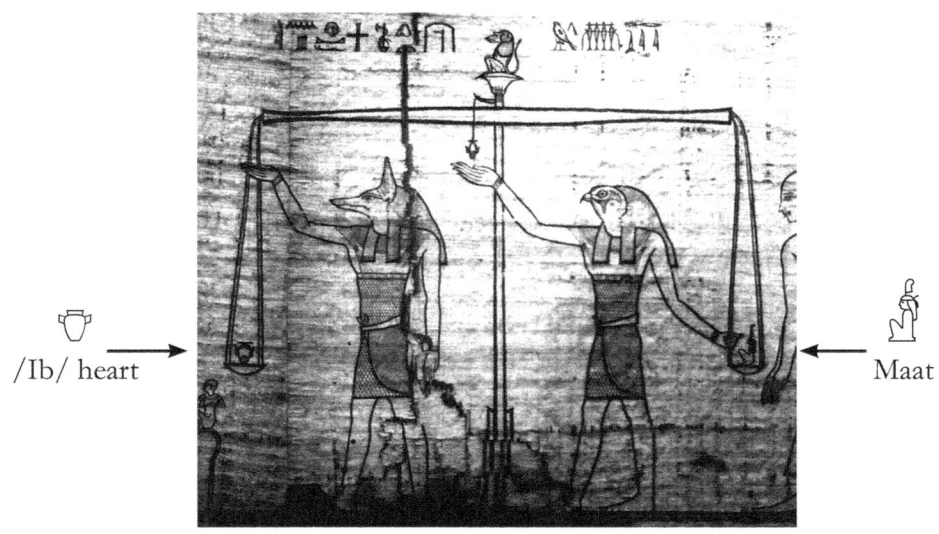

/Ib/ heart ⟶　　　　　　　　　⟵ Maat

The feather can be used alone, without the goddess figure. Remember to distinguish the feather from the reed.

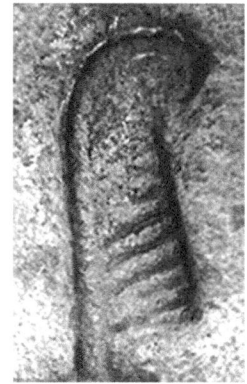 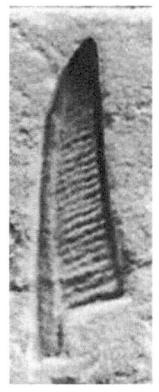

Maat feather (H6)   Reed (M17)

Here Maat is both wearing *and* holding a plume.

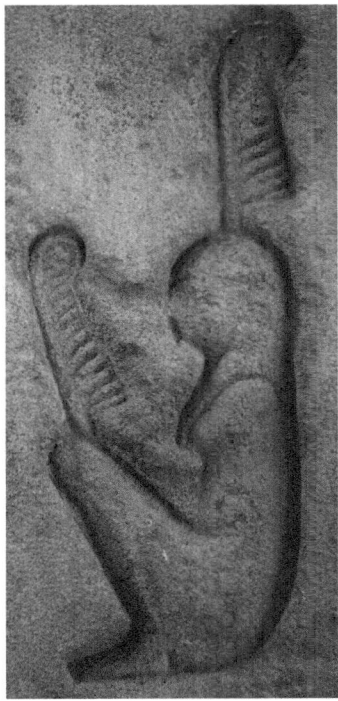

Review of *Maat*

Maat is the Egyptian concept of *Truth, Justice and Cosmic Order*, and one of the most common concepts used in cartouches

The main duty of the pharaoh was to maintain Maat in the kingdom. As ultimate high priest of every temple and cult in Egypt, he was responsible to see that proper rituals were observed.

As an all-pervasive concept, Maat is represented in many ways, including the following signs and combinations of signs:

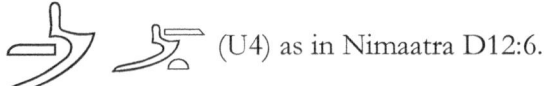 (U4) as in Nimaatra D12:6.

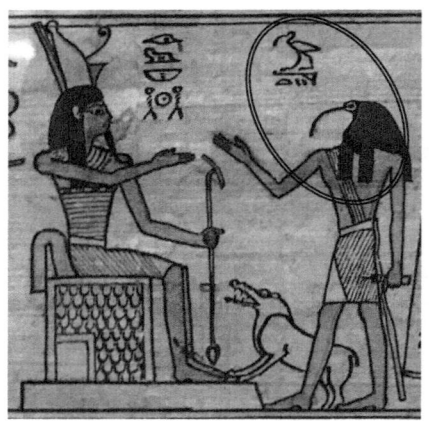 (Aa 11) This is often seen as the base of thrones or statues, as in the illustrated papyrus below:

While we're here, notice the ibis representing the god Thoth written both as an ibis on a standard (G26) and in human form with an ibis head.

At the foot of the seated figure is the crocodile-headed beast that devours your heart if you don't measure up at judgment.

 (H6) the fluffy *ostrich plume*. It can stand alone or be held or worn by almost any figure.

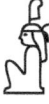 (C10) *Maat* personified. We see her seated on the ground, kneeling, seated on a throne, or standing. The key to identifying her is the feather headdress.

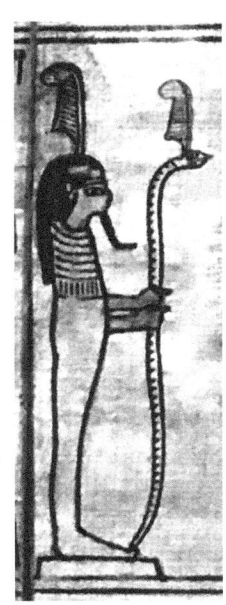

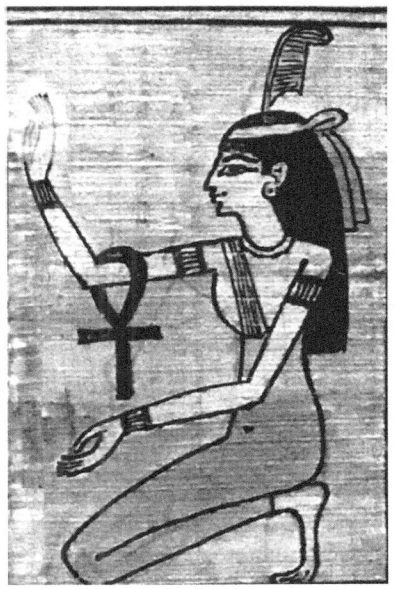

A divine figure standing on a Maat platform, wearing a Maat plume, and holding a protective serpent, also wearing a Maat feather. You can't have too much Maat!

Maat kneeling, with Ankh, *life*, draped over her arm.

D18:5 Princess Neferura

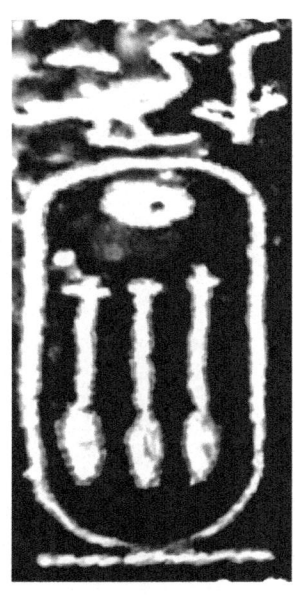

G39	X1	M23	F35	N5
🦆	⌒			⊙
Sa	**T**	**Su**	**Nefer-u**	**Rᴀ**

Neferura was Hatshepsut's daughter. She is introduced by the title *Daughter of the King (Queen!)*.

Remember, *daughter* is *son*, the duck sign, plus the feminine ending /T/.

The plural of /Nefer/ takes an /U/ sound at the end, /Nefer-u/.

D18:6B Thutmose III
D18:6T Menkheperra
Thutmosis, Djehutymes

G26	F31
🦅	🌿
Thut	Mos

Y5	L1	N5
▭	🪲	⊙
Men	Kheper	Ra

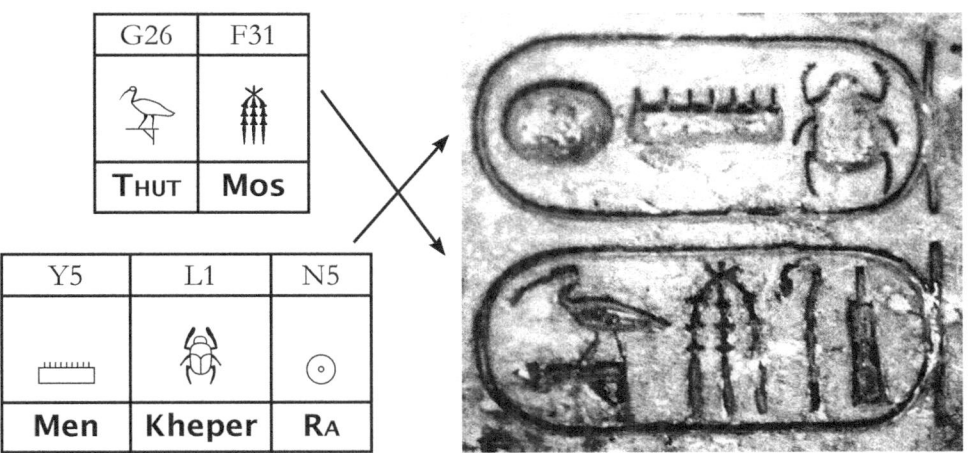

The order of the name breakouts are switched here, in relation to the carved cartouches, but I always like to list the **BIRTH NAME** first, since that is usually the most unique of a pharaoh's names, as well as the one he had first, and the one by which he is best known to us.

Thutmose III was not only king of Egypt, but king of **EPITHETS. WILLOCKX (P 32)** points out, "...in his cartouches, no one used more different epithets than he did (16), and no one added more new ones to the existing corpus (11)." Was it because he had an inferiority complex after being under the thumb of King/Queen Hatshepsut for so long?

Here are a *few* examples of his epithets:

S38	O28
⌒	▯
Heqa	Iunu

/heqa/ is a staff called a *crook*, and means *ruler*. The crook is part of the royal regalia.

/Iunu/is an architectural *column*. Iunu represents *Heliopolis*, one of the oldest and most important cities of ancient Egypt.

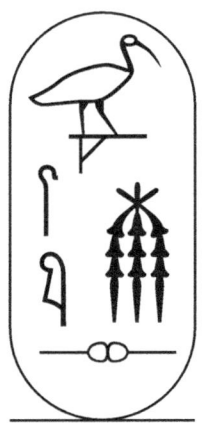

This cartouche is simple. We have the Thutmose name plus /Heqa Maat/.

S38	H6
Heqa	**Maat**

Another Heqa (ruler) name: Heqa Waset.

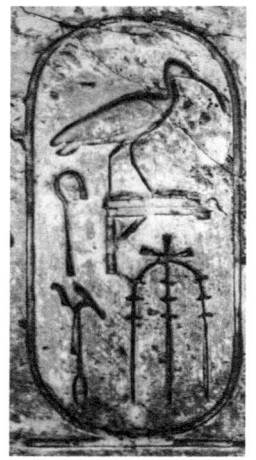

/Waset/ is a *Was* scepter with attached plume. It means the city of *Thebes*, or the modern Luxor area, site of Karnak temple, the Valley of the Kings, and other monuments.

S38	R19
Heqa	**Waset**

Here's another variation with Nefer Kheper, *Beautiful of Shape.*

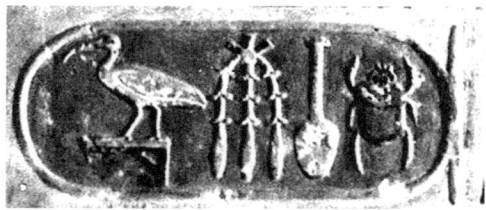

F35	L1
Nefer	**Kheper**

/Khepesh/ is the *foreleg of an ox*, meaning *power, strength, strong arm or thigh*, another example of using cattle parts to represent human attributes (see D12:1; D4:1) So, *Lord/Master/Owner of a Strong Arm*.

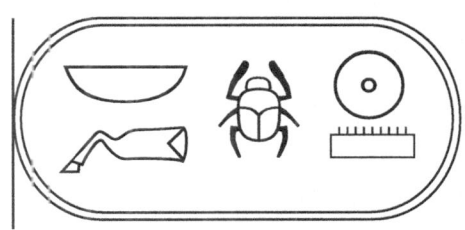

Y5	L1	N5	V30	F23
 	🪲	⊙	⌣	
Men	**Kheper**	**Rᴀ**	**Neb**	**Khepesh**

Below is another instance of including royal titles and other signs inside the cartouche that properly belong outside of it. Can you read it?

The only new thing in this cartouche is mention of Amen-Ra, a fusion between the gods Amen and Ra.

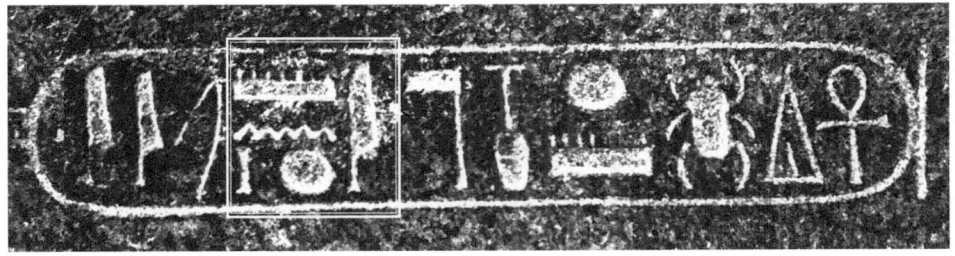

This is a good time to remind you that in many cases you need *both* the **BIRTH NAME** *and* the **THRONE NAME** to identify a king. For one thing, many names are repeated: there are 11 kings named Ramses, and 15 Ptolemies!

Also, no matter how many seemingly random signs are included within the oval frames, there is a minimum set that will "always" be there. For Thutmose III, they are:

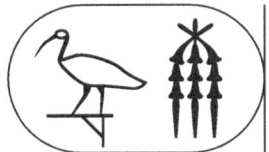   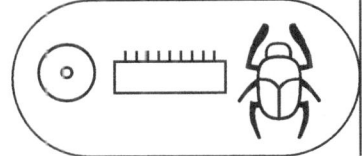

D18 Queen Sitiah
Ahsat

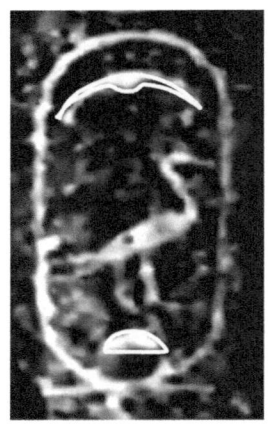

G39	X1	N12
🦆	⌒	👁
Si	**T**	**I**ᴀʜ

Sitiah is one of the wives of Thutmose III. The name means *Daughter of the Moon.* We saw Iah, or Ah, in Ahmose and Ahmose Nefertari in Dynasty 18.

D18:7B Amenhotep II
D18:7T Aakheperura
Amenophis

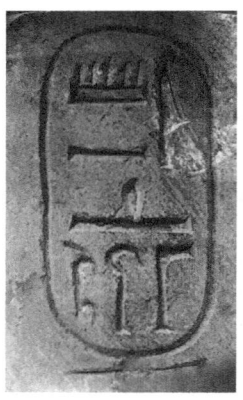

		S38	R8	R19
		👑	🚩	♀
Aᴍᴇɴ	**Hotep**	**Heqa**	**Netjer**	**Waset**

Optional Epithet: Divine Ruler of Thebes, /Heqa Netjer Waset/.

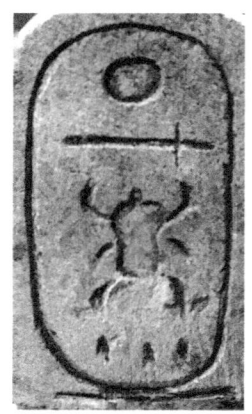

O29	L1	Z2	N5
🗡	🪲	| | |	☉
Aa	**Kheper**	**U**	**R**ᴀ

D18:8B Thutmose IV
D18:8T Menkheperura
Thutmosis

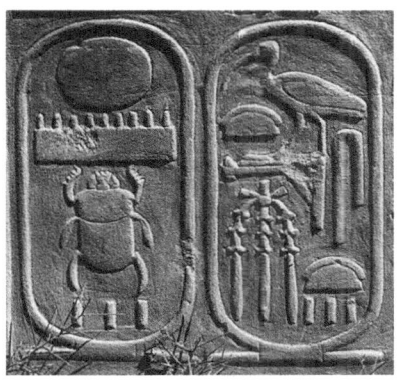

Cartouche, right

G26	F31	S29	N28	N28	Z2
🦤	𓇋	⫯	⌒	⌒	|||
Tнuт	Mos	(S)	Kha	Kha	u

Optional epithet: *Shining of Appearings* (**Willockx p 26)**, /Khakha-u/.

Cartouche, left

Y5	L1	Z2	N5
▭	🪲	|||	☉
Men	Kheper	U	Rᴀ

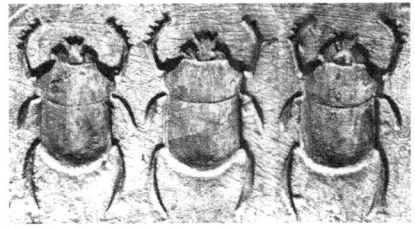

A full writing of 🪲 | | |. A chorus line of beetles!

D18:9B Amenhotep III
D18:9T Nebmaatra
Amenophis

		S38	R19
AMEN	**Hotep**	**Heqa**	**Waset**

Epithet: *Ruler of Thebes,* optional.

V30	C10	N5
Neb	**MAAT**	**RA**

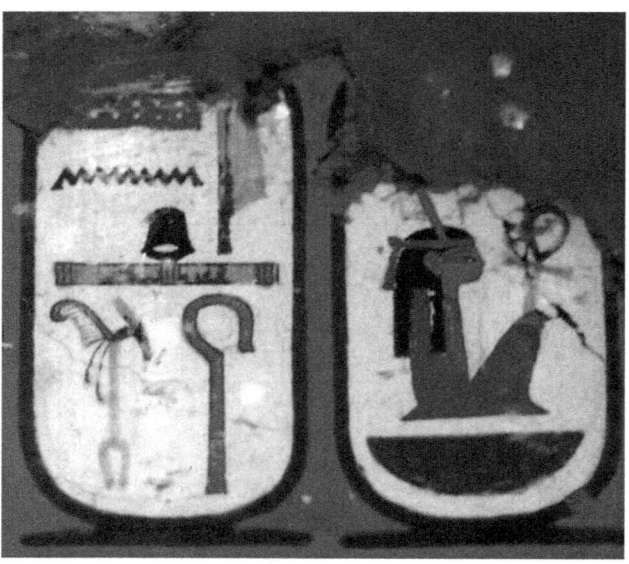

Although these cartouches are damaged, the detail is amazing. We can assume that the **THRONE NAME** includes Ra, since they virtually all do.

D18 Queen Tiye

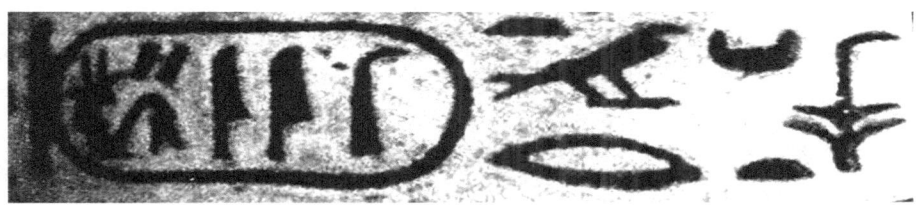

U33	M17a	Z4	B7
Ti	Y	Y	-

 /Ti/ is a pestle.

 is a silent **DETERMINATIVE** for *queen*. The typed sign shows a flat crown with a protective cobra (*uraeus*) on the brow, the figure holding a lotus blossom on a floppy stem. In this inscription, she wears a pair of plumes as well.

Queen Tiye was the wife of Amenhotep III. The signs preceding her cartouche make it clear that she was the *Great Wife of the King*.

N41	X1	M23	G36	D21	X1
Hem	(e)T	Nesut	Wer	(eR)	(e)T

/Hem/ *(water) well*, with the feminine /T/ ending, means *wife*.

We have seen /(Ne)sut/ plenty of times: the *sedge* plant meaning *king*.

/Wer/ *great*, is interesting. The sign (G36) depicts a *swallow* or *martin*. GARDINER points out the *swallow tail* on this bird.

What is interesting is that this sign (G36), *swallow*, meaning *great* is almost identical to (G37), *sparrow*, which refers to anything *bad, evil,* or *false*.

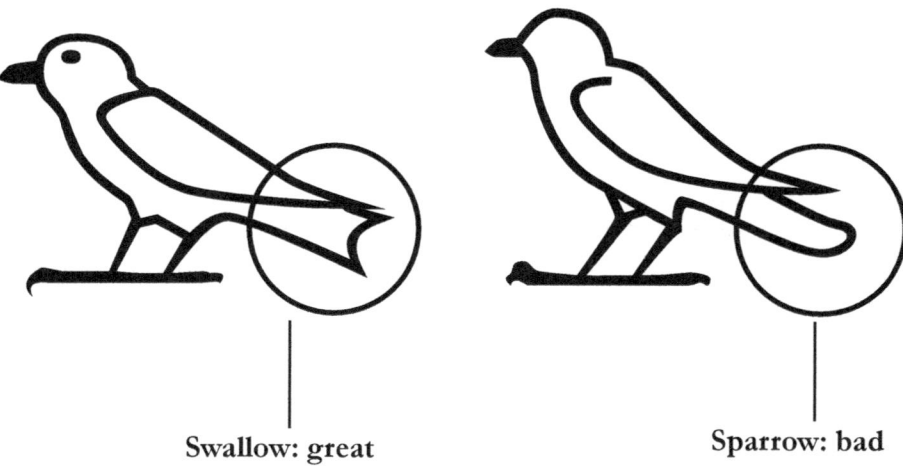

Swallow: great   **Sparrow: bad**

Why the distinction between the birds? What makes one nice and the other naughty? Speculation: house sparrows are extremely common (thus "vulgar") and can be terrible agricultural pests. Swallows, on the other hand, eat agricultural pests (flying insects), and are associated with goddesses Isis and Nephthys.

D18:10B Akhenaten
D18:10T Nefer kheperura waenra
Amenhotep IV, Ikhnaten

With Amenhotep IV we are in for a wild ride! The plethora of names for him, his god and the members of his family is staggering. Amenhotep changed his **BIRTH NAME** to Akhenaten and adopted the sun disk, the Aten, as the sole god of Egypt, at the expense of the other gods and their very powerful priesthoods.

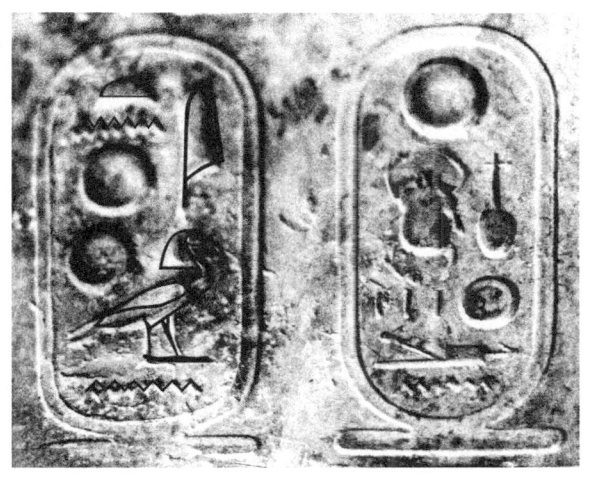

G25	Aa1	N35	M17	X1	N35	N5
Akh	(Kh)	(e)N	A	T	(E)N	-

F35	L1	Z2	N5	T21	N35	N5
Nefer	Kheper	U	Rᴀ	Wa	(e)N	Rᴀ

/Akh/ *crested ibis*. Here it means *beneficial* or *effective*. So the meaning of Akhenaten could be *Beneficial to the Aten*.

 /Aten/ is the *disk of the sun*. The *sun* here is a **DETERMINATIVE** for *Aten*.

/Wa/ *harpoon, unique one*. Waenra is *the unique one of Ra*.

At Akhenaten's behest, the name of Amen, heretofore the most influential Egyptian god, was hacked out of monuments throughout Egypt, as in this example where Akhenaten's own father's **BIRTH NAME** (Amenhotep) was entirely effaced. We know it's his cartouche, of course, by the **THRONE NAME**, Nebmaatra, and by the giveaway defaced name, with *Amen*, faintly visible.

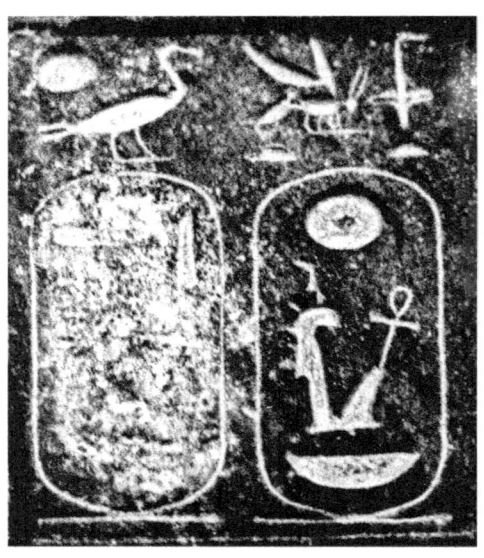

The god **ATEN'S** names were also written inside two cartouches, just like a king, translated together by **QUIRKE (P 32)** as *Ra-Horakhty jubilant in the horizon, in his name as Shu (daylight) who is in the Aton (sun disc)*.

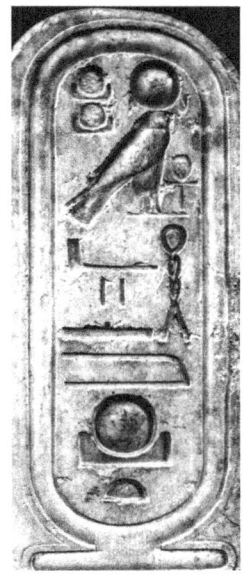 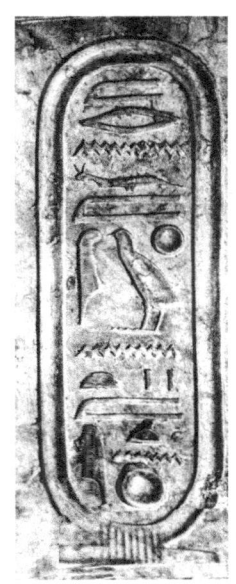

Cartouche, left

G9	N27	V28	D36	Z4	Y1	Aa13	N27	X1
RA-HOR	Akhti	H	A	-	-	(e)M	Akh	(e)T

 /Ra-Horakhti/ *Horus of the Two Horizons*. This sign alone, usually without the Ankh, is Ra-Horakhti, a combination of the sun god Ra and Horus /Hor/, a falcon god, introduced in D5:7T, Menkauhor. **WILKNSON (GODS AND CODDESSES P 239)** also adds a translation of the little *Ankh* tucked under the bird's breast, *Live, Re-Horakhti...*

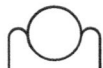 /Akhet/ *sun on the horizon*. In the first instance, there are two, so they take the unwritten /I/ ending.

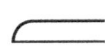 /M/ an alternative to 𓅓, meaning *in or on*. An unknown object.

/Ha/ is *joy*; means this is an abstract concept.

Cartouche, right, previous page

Aa13	D21	N35	I9	Aa13	H6	G43	N5
		wwww			𝑃	🐦	☉
M(e)	R(e)	N(e)	F	(e)M	Shu	(U)	-

				N35	X1	Z4	Aa13	
				wwww		| |		
				(e)N	T	Y	(e)M	Aten

 wwww /Ren/ is *name*, so wwww /Merenef/ is *In his name*.

𝑃 /Shu/ is the same fluffy *ostrich feather* that usually means *Maat*. Here, especially with the **PHONETIC COMPLEMENT** *quail chick* /U/, it means *Shu*, the primeval god of the air. In the Aten's case, QUIRKE (P 32) identifies Shu with *daylight*. That leaves /Enti em Aten/ meaning *(he) who is in the Aten* (IBID).

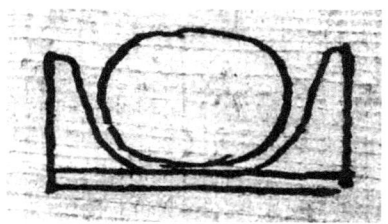

Sun on the Horizon

Only to confuse things more, the **ATEN** was later given a different pair of names. They still include the tell-tale Aten signs but manage to get those pesky gods Shu and Ra-Horakhti out of the picture. QUIRKE (P 32) translates these combined revised names as *"the sun, ruler of the horizon, jubilant in the horizon, in his name as the light which comes from the Aton."* Again, WILKINSON (GODS AND GODDESSES P 239) prefaces this with *Live*.

The Aten

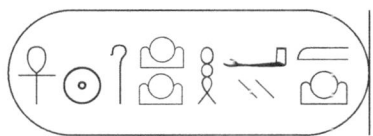

S34	N5	S38	N27	V28	D36	Z4	Aa13	N27
♀	⊙	?	▱	8	⟶	||	⊂	▱
Ankh	**Rᴀ**	**Heqa**	**Akhti**	**H**	**A**	**-**	**(e)M**	**Akh(et)**

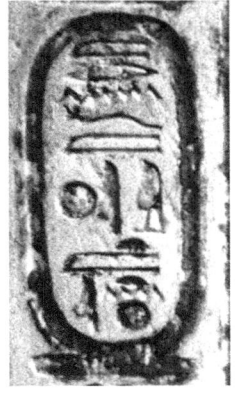

Aa13	D21	N35	I9	Aa13	N5	M17
⊂	⌒	〜〜	⤳	⊂	⊙	∫
M(e)	**R(e)**	**N(e)**	**F**	**M(e)**	**Rᴀ**	**A**

M18	X1	Aa13	
∫	⌒	⊂	(Aten glyph)
I	**T(e)**	**M**	**Aᴛᴇɴ**

/I/ *to come.* How would you illustrate this concept? The Egyptians took the reed sign (M17) which, as we know, sounds like /I/, which also sounds like their word *to come.* They added the cute little legs to show the concept of motion.

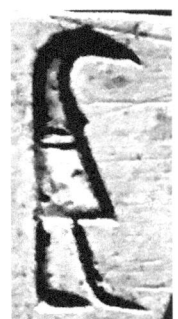
In this example of M18, the sign looks more like a Christmas elf than a *reed with legs*. I get the idea that the artisan who carved this had forgotten exactly what the sign was supposed to represent.

There is much discussion about the meaning and **TRANSLITERATION** of the Aten's names. The transliterations shown in the **BREAKOUTS** for Aten are not authoritative.

D18 Queen Nefer Neferuaten-Nefertiti

This is the cartouche of Akhenaten's wife Nefertiti, the queen whose bust inspired a world of Egyptian souvenirs. Very tasteful (sarcasm alert!) light-up "alabaster" Nefertiti heads were sold on all the street corners when I lived in Egypt.

Can you see the *King's Great Wife* title above the cartouche? The queen figure inside the cartouche (where is her sagging lotus blossom?) also tells us that we are looking at a queen's name.

She has the only cartouche with *five* Nefer signs.

TYLDSLEY (p 125) translates *Nefertiti* as *a beautiful woman has come.*

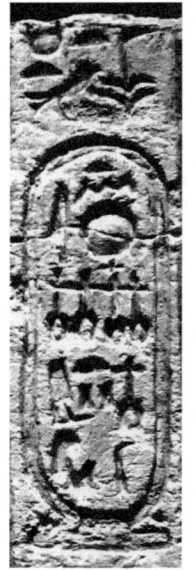

F35	F35		F35	X1	M18	U33	B7
Nefer	**Neferu**	**ATEN**	**Nefer**	**T**	**I**	**Ti**	**-**

/Ti/ *pestle*, seen in D18:1 Queen Tiye. Again, they found an object that sounded like the syllable they wanted to portray and used it for the phonetic value alone.

D18:12B Tutankhamen
D18:12T Nebkheperura
Tutankhaten

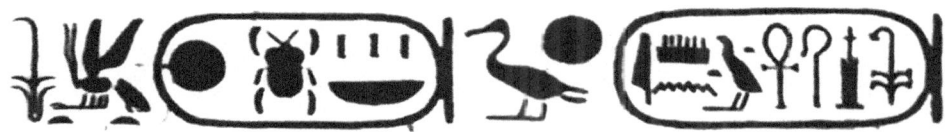

I love the script here. The signs are so crisp and economical, yet elegant. The beetle looks like a Chinese character done with a brush.

This is the legendary "King Tut." He started life as Tutankh*aten*, being raised in the Aten court. With the death of Akhenaten, the old priesthoods and bureaucracy retook power, and "Tut" became Tutankh*amen*.

Once again, don't be confused by my writing the **BIRTH NAME** first, contrary to Egyptian custom. It makes more sense to me to cite the more unique and well-known name first.

Cartouche, right

X1	G43	X1	S34		S38	O28	M26
▱	🐦	▱	♀	▯〰	?	▮	🌱
T	U	T	Ankh	A<small>MEN</small>	Heqa	Iunu	Shema

/Tut/ means *image*, so Tutankhamen is *Living image of Amun* (C<small>LAYTON</small> P 128). Note again how the *T*s of Tut are fitted into the empty spaces before and behind the chick, to maintain symmetry and equilibrium.

/Iunu/ is Heliopolis, as we saw with Tutmose II D18:6B.

(M26) /Shema/ is a *flowering sedge plant,* not to be confused with (M23), the *non-flowering sedge plant,* /Su/, meaning *King.*

O28 + M26 /Iunu Shema/ means *Heliopolis of the South,* the Thebes area.

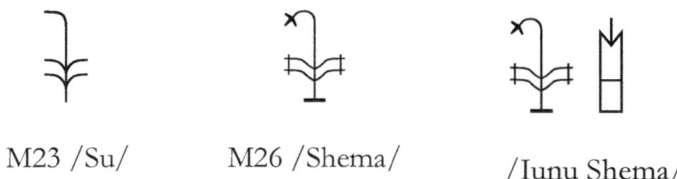

M23 /Su/   M26 /Shema/   /Iunu Shema/

Cartouche, left (previous page)

V30	L1	Z2	N5
⌣	🪲	| | |	☉
Neb	**Kheper**	**U**	**Ra**

D18 Queen Ankhesenamen
Ankhesenamun

N41	M23	X1	S34	S29	N35	-	B7
(☐)	⸶	◠)	♀	∩	∿∿∿	⎍ ∿∿	𓀀
Hem(et)	**Nesu**	**T**	**Ankh**	**(e)S**	**(e)N**	**Amen**	-

Tutankhamen's *Royal Wife* /Hemet Nesut/.

The only "tricky" thing here is the single stroke used both times for/N/, probably because of the difficulty of scratching neat zigzags into the alabaster jar.

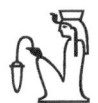 is extremely rudimentary, also. Without the title above the cartouche, we may not recognize it.

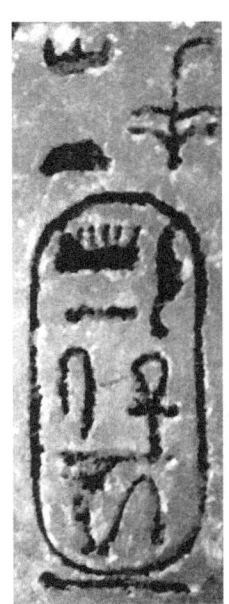

D18:13B Ay
D18:13T Kheperkheperura
Acherres

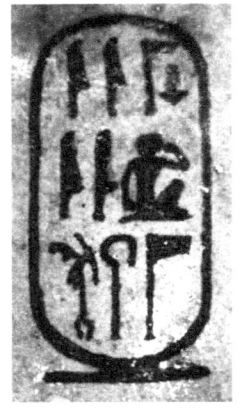 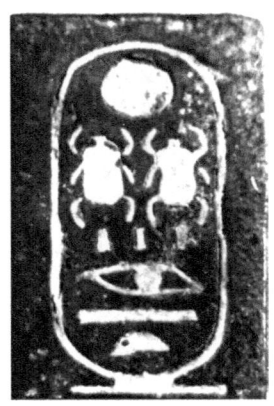

X2	R8	M17a	A2	M17a	R8	S38	R19
(I)t	Netjer	Ay	-	(Y)	Netjer	Heqa	Waset

Ay's "default" cartouche given by **CLAYTON (P 136)** and **QUIRKE (P 62)** is shown below. It starts with the title, **GOD'S FATHER** /It(f)-Netjer/, a priestly title **(GARDINER P 53)**. Unusually, the /f/ is silent.

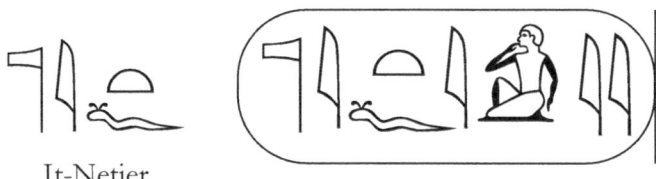

It-Netjer

 /A1/ represents a man with his hand to his mouth, as in eating, speaking, etc. I assume it is **DETERMINATIVE** for *father.* in this instance.

 /T/(X2) is a loaf of bread. $\ominus\urcorner$, seen in the photograph, is a variant of /It-Netjer. **(GARDINER P 531)**.

L1	L1	Z2	N5	D4	Aa11	S1
🪲	🪲	| | |	⊙	👁	▱	⌒
Kheper	**Kheper**	**U**	**Rᴀ**	**Ir**	**Mᴀᴀᴛ**	**(T)**

👁 /Ir/ *human eye*, means *to do, make*. Irmaat is *doing right*.

D18:14B Horemheb
D18:14T Djeserkheperura
Haremheb, Armesis

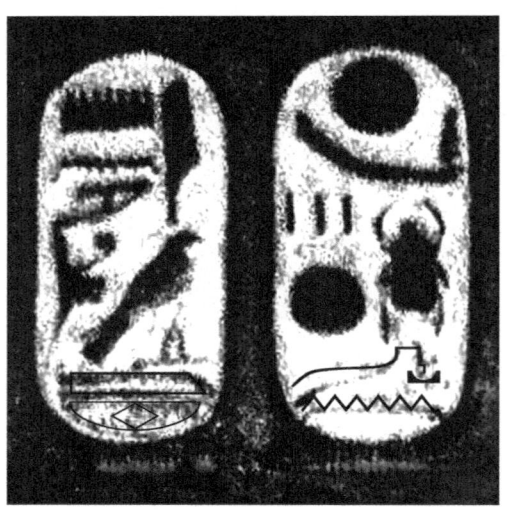

Cartouche, left

G5	S3	Aa13	W3	U7	-
🦅	🛆	⬭	⬭	⤙	𓏺
Hor	**(N)**	**(e)M**	**Heb**	**Mery**	**Amen**

 /Heb/ is an *alabaster bowl* or *basin* used in feasts and purifications. It means *feast or festival.* The diamond shape inside the bowl represents the banding present in the translucent stone.

 /S3/ the *red crown*, usually pronounced /N/, is not pronounced in Horemheb's name, nor is it usually written. I'm assuming it is an optional grammatical particle.

Cartouche, right, previous page

D45	L1	Z2	N5	U21	N35	N5
〰	🪲	| | |	⊙	⌐	〰〰	⊙
Djeser	**Kheper**	**U**	**Rᴀ**	**Setep**	**(e)N**	**Rᴀ**

/Setep/ is an *adze*, a carpenter's tool for forming large pieces of wood. The sign shows the adze cutting into a block of wood. A stone or metal blade is attached to a wooden handle, curved to give better leverage. The meaning is to *choose, select*.

It is shown here with the grammatical particle /N/. /Setepen/ means *chosen by/of* and is always followed by the name of a god.

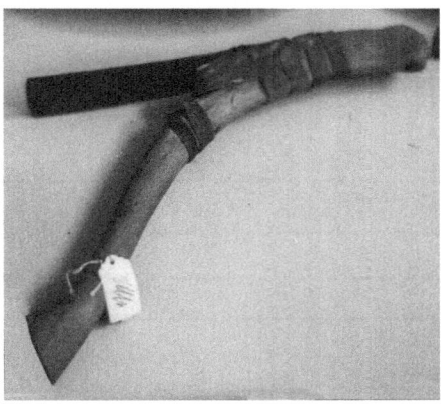

An adze

D19:1B Ramses I
D19:1T Menpehtyra
Ramesses, Ramessu

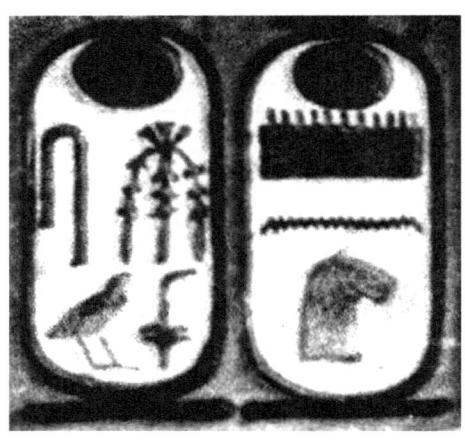

N5	F31	S29	M23	G43
⊙	🌿	∏	⤓	🐦
RA	Mes	(S)	Su	(U)

Y5	N35	F9	N5
▭	∿∿∿	🐆	⊙
Men	(N)	Pehty	RA

Ramses I, or Ramessu, is the first king of the 19th Dynasty, and the first of eleven kings of that name! As usual, the first, or early kings of a dynasty or period have short, simple names. Later kings of the same basic name tended to lengthen their names out with epithets and adjectives.

D19:2B Sety I
D19:2T Menmaatra
Seti, Sethos

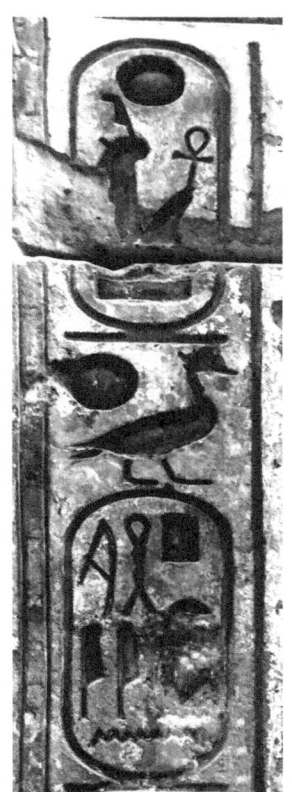

Poor Sety! The indignities his name has suffered!

The *Set* in Sety is the *god Set*, the god of the desert, chaos and storms, and the odd-looking brother and killer of Osiris.

Although there were at least three kings whose name included *Set* in the nineteenth and twentieth dynasties, during most of Egyptian history Set was considered unfit for polite society.

The usual remedy for later pharaohs was just to have Set's image chiseled out of his, Sety's, cartouches, as in the bottom cartouche to the left.

Even during Sety's lifetime (or shortly thereafter), when his name was meant to be carved into a wall or monument dedicated to Osiris, Set's sign was suppressed and changed to something more acceptable, such as the *Tyet* knot amulet (V39).

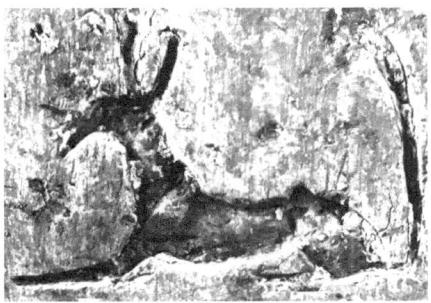

This is the so-called Set animal, which, unusually, cannot be identified with any living creature. Key features are the droopy snout, erect tail, and erect, straight-cropped ears.

Here is Sety's name carved into a wooden object, where instead of Set's figure, that of Osiris, wearing the white crown, was inserted. After the figure of Osiris, a sacred knot, the *Tit* or *Tyet* was added to approximate the sound of *Sety*.

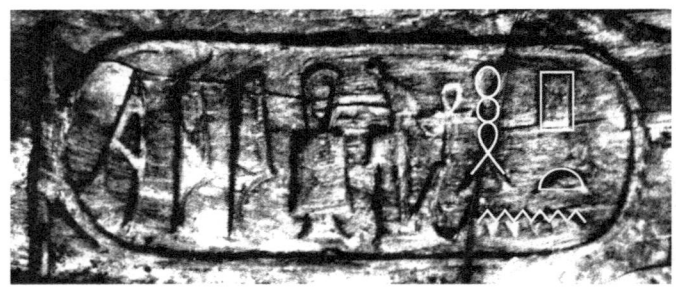

Bottom cartouche, previous page

C7	M17a	U6	N35	
SET	Y	Mer	(e)N	PTAH

Cartouche above

*	V39	M17a	U6	N35	
OSIRIS (USIR)	Ti	Y	Mer	(e)N	PTAH

Luckily, Sety's **THRONE NAME** is completely straightforward:

Top cartouche, previous page

Y5	C10	N5
Men	Maat	RA

Up to now, the only deity we have seen depicted as a human figure in a car-touche is Maat, the personification of Truth, Right and Justice. From here on out, more of the gods will be shown in human form, sometimes with animal heads. These gods can be shown in the usual position on the floor, sitting cross legged with knees up, crouching or, more imaginatively, walking or sitting, sometimes holding another sign as a staff.

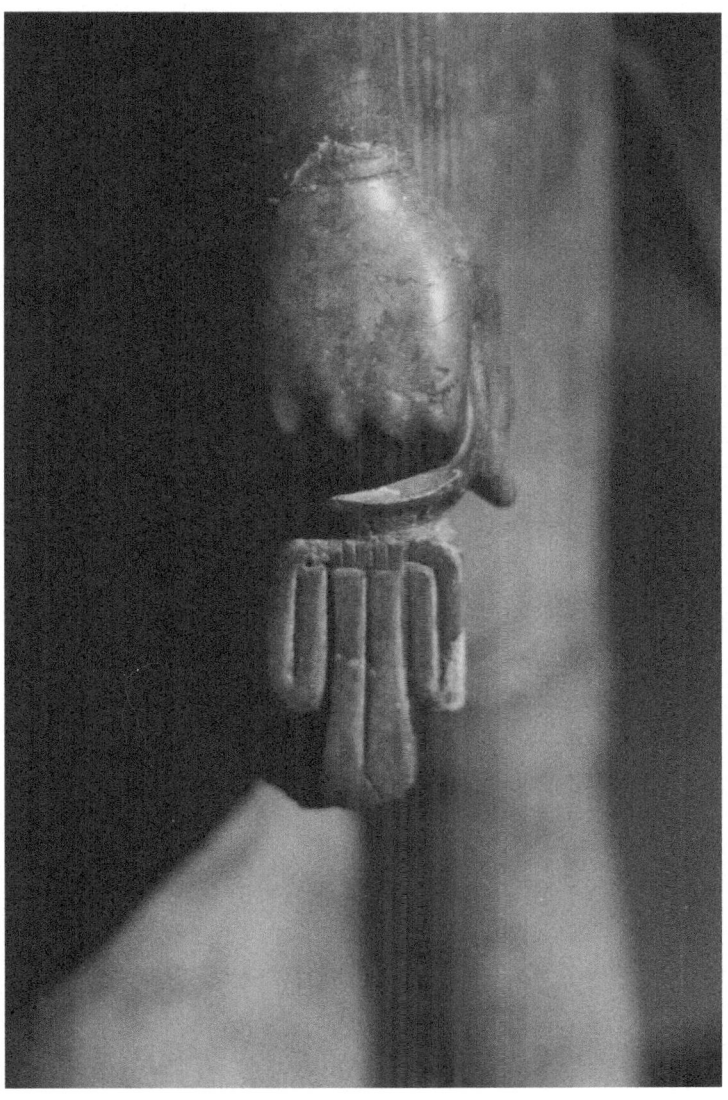

Tyet amulet in the hand of a king or deity

D19:3B Ramses II
D19:3T Usermaatra setepenra
Ramesses, Ramessu

We are in for a treat with Ramses II, Ramses the Great. He reigned for 67 years! I can only imagine the consternation his priests and advisors felt trying to keep the king amused for such a long time. Having worked in government myself, I'm sure those advisors were under pressure to come up with new achievements to document on their performance appraisals, including new, imaginative ways to write the king's name. He used many different epithets.

Here are his "default" cartouches:

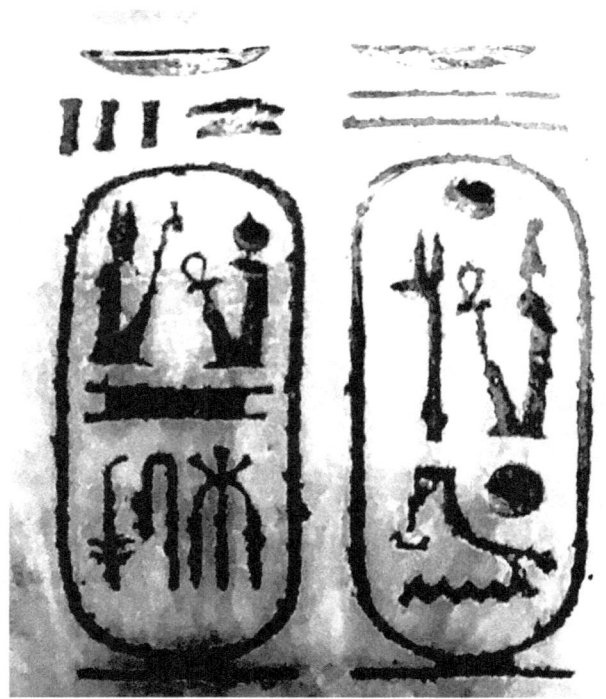

Left hand cartouche, previous page

C2	F31	S29	M23	N36	C12
🝙	𓇑	𓂋	𓇓	𓏋	𓁩
RA	Mes	(S)	Su	Mer(y)	AMEN

 Ra is now an anthropomorphic *falcon-headed god* with the sun disk on his head.

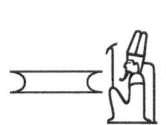 /mer/ represents a *water channel*, a homophone of 〵 (U6), *beloved*.

Amen is now a human with a beard and two impossibly tall plumes like rabbit ears on his head. He often holds the *was* scepter, (S40), which looks a little like a hot dog on a stick, and means *dominion*.

/Mery Amen/ is *beloved of Amen*. Under the principle of **HONORIFIC TRANSPOSITION**, Amen, even though pronounced last, moves to the head of the queue and faces Ra. I always think of this construction as the *tea party (wienie roast?)* position..

Right hand cartouche, previous page

F12	C10	N5	U21	N35	N5
𓄤	𓁦	⊙	𓋴	〜〜〜	⊙
User	Maat	RA	Setep	(e)N	RA

You may as well go ahead and memorize this name now: Ramses Meryamen Usermaatra-setepenra. Due to Ramses II's long reign, it is one of the most widely seen names. **JACQ (P 207)** translates this name *The Harmony of Divine Light is Powerful*.

Fun with names!

Here are some variations of Ramses II's names.

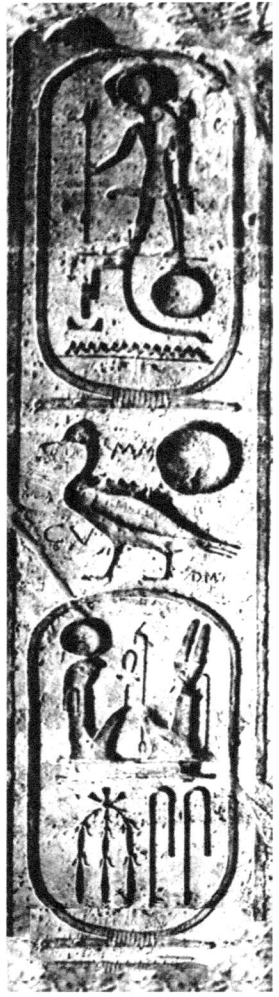

To the left, *Ra* is a *falcon-headed man with sun disk* striding forward, carrying an *User* staff in one hand and a *Maat* feather in the other. The sculptor messed up the carving of the sun disk on *Ra*'s head. It was repaired with plaster, which has since fallen out.

In the photo below, *Maat* sits on a throne and holds the *User* scepter An alternate /S/, the *door bolt* (O34), is used in some versions of *Ramses* (see cartouche, right).

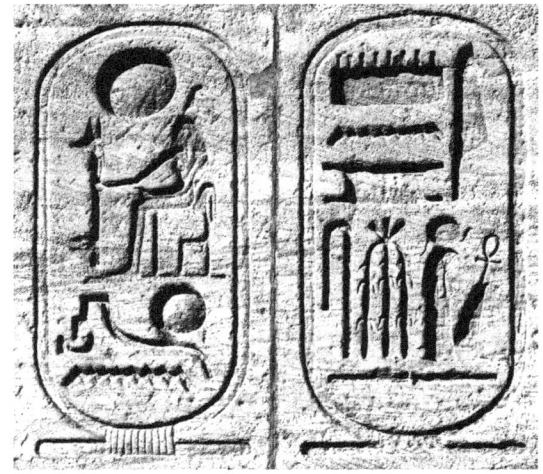

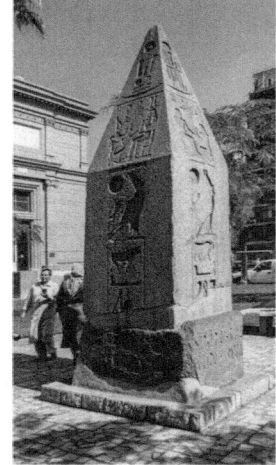

To the right is an obelisk in the courtyard of the Egyptian Museum, Cairo, bearing some of the names of Ramses II, including his Horus name. In the close-ups, opposite, you can see that the hieroglyphs have slipped out of their cartouche frames and are "messing about in boats."

Can you identify each hieroglyph in these illustrations?

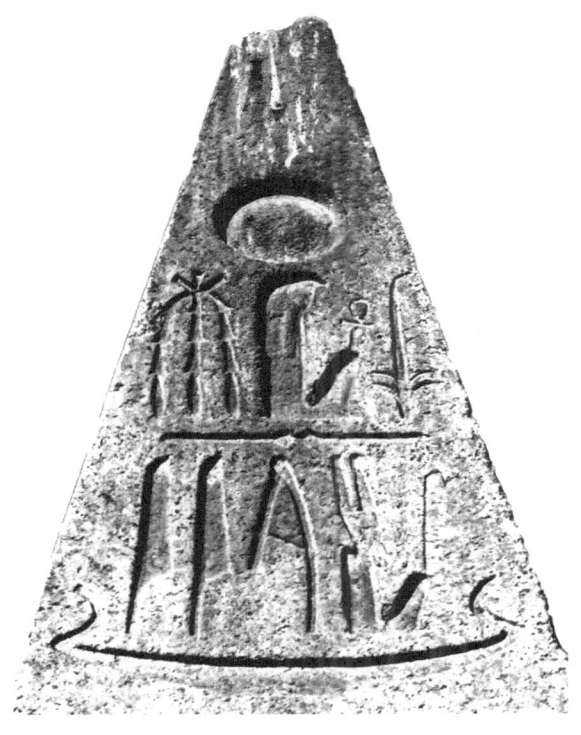

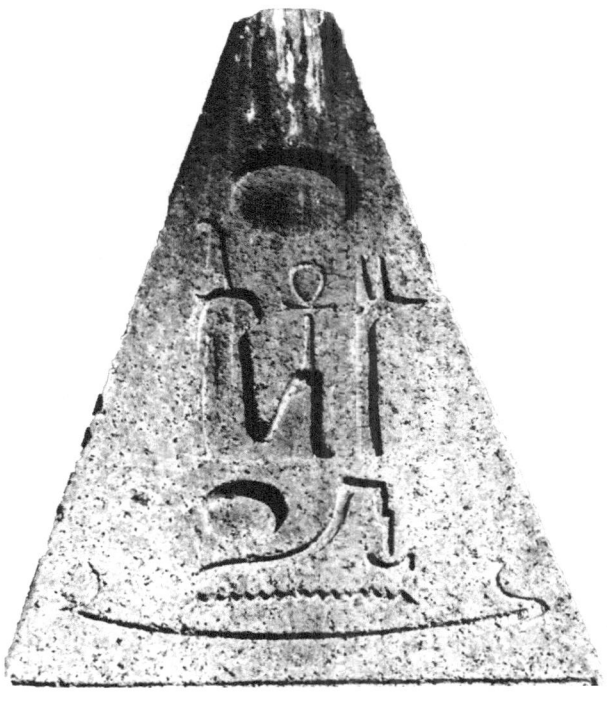

CLAYTON (p 148), lists eight wives of Ramses II. Here are a few:

D19 Queen Nefertari

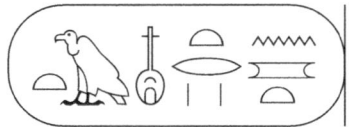

F35			G14
(Nefer symbol)	(Tari symbol)	(Meret(en) symbol)	(Mut symbol)
Nefer	**Tari**	**Meret(en)**	**Mut**

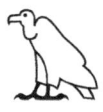
This is the *vulture goddess, Mut,* spouse of *Amen.* Oddly, to our way of thinking, the vulture stands for *mother* in ancient Egyptian. Nefertari-Meretmut then, is, *Nefertari Beloved of Mut* (the /N/ is silent here).

D19 Queen Bintanath

			D36	N35	V13
(B symbol)	(i)N symbol	(T symbol)	(A symbol)	(N(a) symbol)	(Th symbol)
B	**(i)N**	**T**	**A**	**N(a)**	**Th**

This is a very interesting cartouche. The lady's name is Canaanite (TYLDESLEY P 155). The *Bint* part is straight up Arabic, meaning *daughter (of),* **COGNATE** to *Bat (Mitzvah).* Here the reference is to Canaanite goddess Anath. There are special rules for writing non-Egyptian names. (See **GROUP WRITING, GARDINER P 52**) The *ram* (E10) and *incense bowl* (R7) with the plural marker give a /B/ sound. The *loaves* (X1 and X2 plus the *land sign* N18 *plus* the plural marker combine to make a /T/. We'll see this phenomenon later in some other non-Egyptian names.

D19 Queen Meritamen

Nothing peculiar about this name, thank goodness!

U6	M17a	X1	U21	X1
Mer	**Y**	**T**	**Amen**	**(T)**

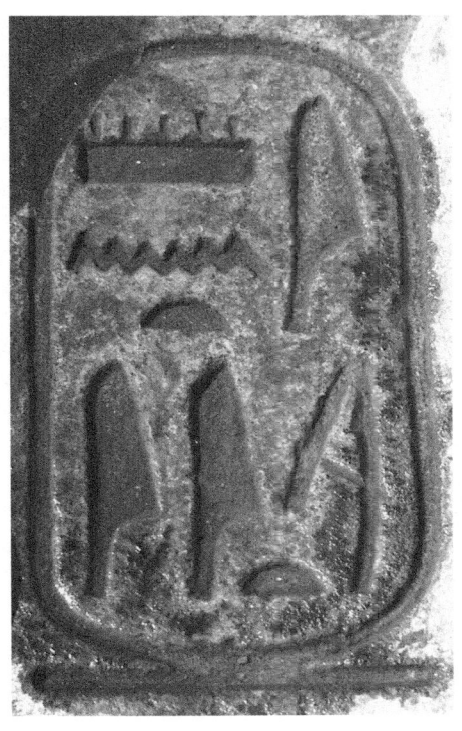

D19:4B Merenptah
D19:4T Baenra meryamen/merynetjeru
Ammenephthes, Merneptah

Cartouche, right

N36	N35	C19a	R4	D2	C10
⟞⟞	∿∿	🧍	⌂	😐	🧍
Mer	**(e)N**	**Ptah**	**Hetep**	**Her**	**Maat**

Ptah is a god we have seen before, spelled out, but here he is portrayed in the form of a bearded, mummified man, with feet together and wrapped in a form-fitting shroud or robe.

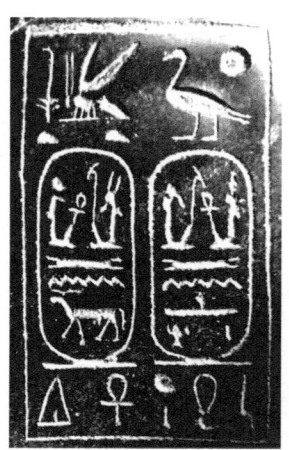

😐 /Her/ *face* is used as a preposition: *on, in, at.* It is the nature of prepositions that they can mean almost anything, depending on context. Clayton (p 156) translates /Hetep-hermaat/ as *Joyous is Truth.*

Cartouche, left

E10	N35	C2	N36	N35	C12
🐏	∿∿	🧍	⟞⟞	∿∿	🧍
Ba	**(e)N**	**Ra**	**Mer**	**(e)N**	**Amen**

A common variation:

E10	N35	N5	N36	R8
🐏	∿∿	⊙	⟞⟞	𓂉𓂉𓂉
Ba	**(e)N**	**Ra**	**Mery**	**Netjeru**

🐏 /Ba/ *ram*, which we saw with Bintanath, here stands for the *Ba*, one of the aspects of the Egyptian soul. Baenra is *Soul of Ra.*

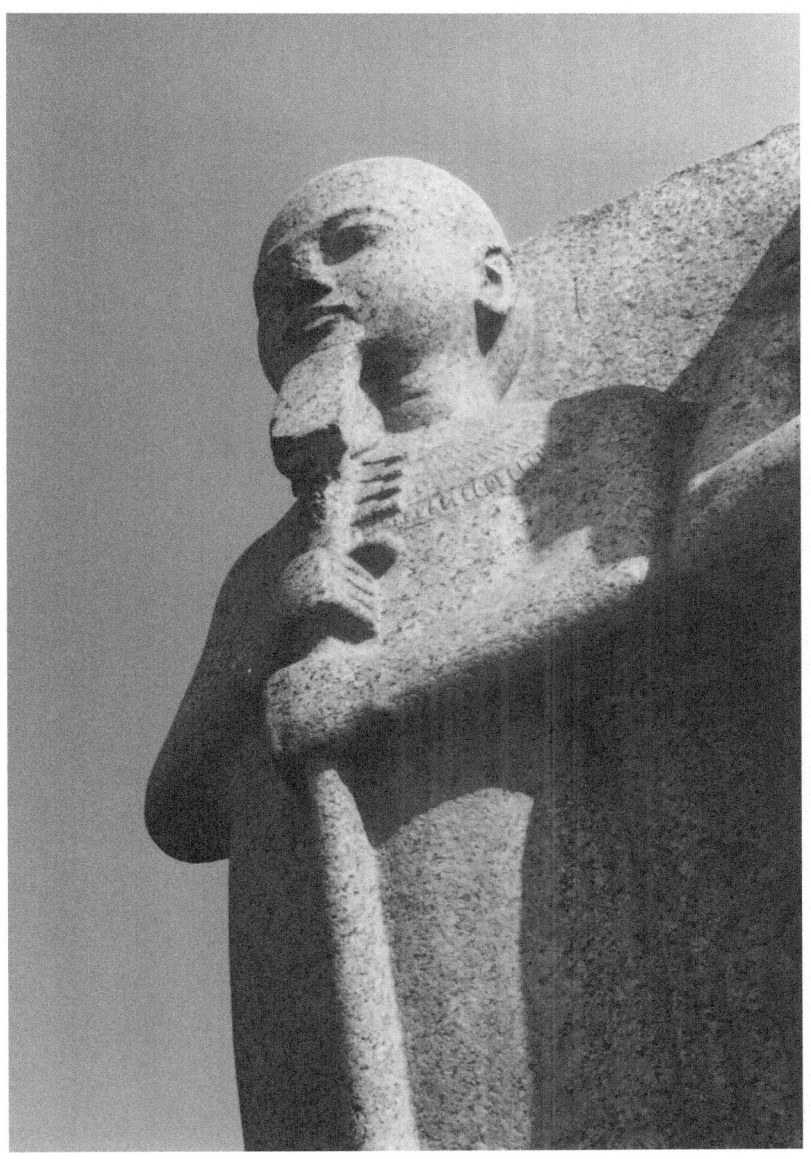

God Ptah, with shaved head or skull cap, djed scepter,
tight fitting robe or shroud and squared off beard.

D19:6B Sety II
D19:6T Userkheperura
Seti, Sethos

C7	U33	M17a	N36	N35		C19
𓆐	(𓊪)	𓇌	⊐⊏	〜〜	𓊪𓎛	𓁧
S<small>ET</small>	(T)	Y	Mer	(e)N	P<small>TAH</small>	(Ptah)

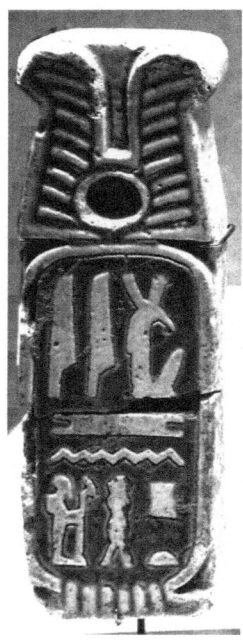

𓁧 this goofy-looking Set figure escaped the mutilation that most of its larger counterparts suffered.

𓁧 Here we see Ptah standing in his skull cap, shroud, and holding his *was* scepter. He usually looks like he's wearing a backpack.

Cartouche left, opposite

F12	L1	Z2	N5	N36	N35	
𓄃	𓆣	|||	⊙	⊐⊏	〜〜	𓇋𓏤
User	**Kheper**	**U**	**R**<small>A</small>	**Mer**	**(e)N**	**A**<small>MEN</small>

In the tile to the right, the Set figure didn't fare so well. But the piece features both **BIRTH** and **THRONE NAMES** of this king combined in one cartouche.

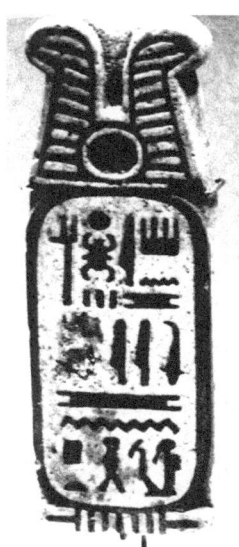

Sety is spelled differently: the pestle figure (U33), used earlier in queens' names, serves as the /T/.

Here we see Ptah both spelled out and engraved seated on the ground.

This is a good place to remind you that pharaohs could mix and match epithets. The important thing in identifying cartouches is to isolate the basic name in each cartouche if possible, disregarding the **EPITHETS**, then see if the corresponding **THRONE** or **BIRTH NAME** matches your identification.

Here is another example of Sety II's cartouches.

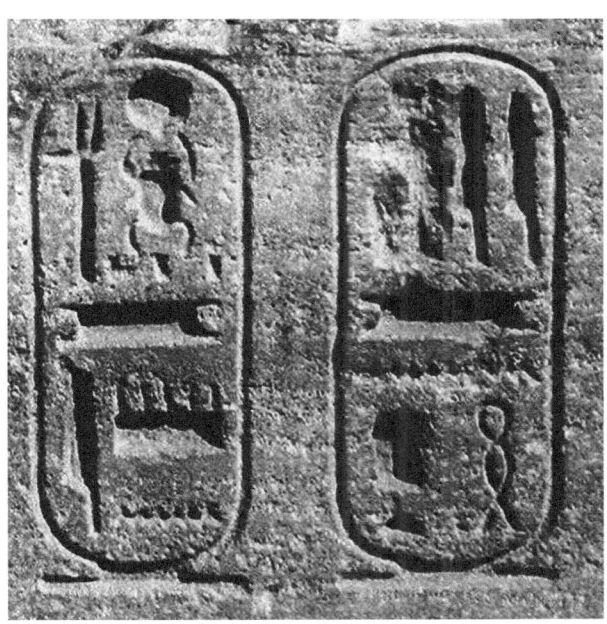

D19:7B Siptah
D19:7T Akhenra
Menephtes Siptahs

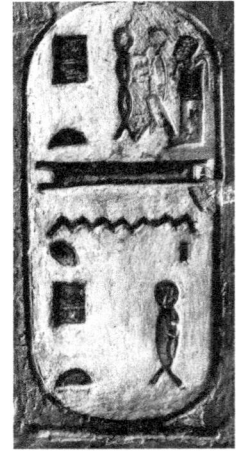

H8		N36	N35		C19a
○	🜂	⊏⊐	〰	🜂	👤
Si	PTAH	Mer	(e)N	PTAH	(PTAH)

○ Remember, the *egg* is /Si or Sa/ and means *son (of)*.

There are three *Ptahs* in this cartouche, two spelled and one illustrated.

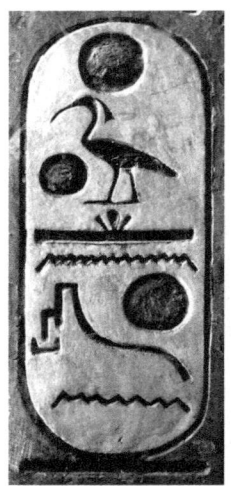

G25	Aa1	N35	Y1	N5		N5
🦅	⊜	〰	⌣	⊙	〰	⊙
Akh	(Kh)	(e)N	-	RA	Setep-en	RA

 This *crested ibis* is the /Akh/ from Akhenaten, meaning *beneficial, beautiful*.

Look at the detailed, flowing style in these hieroglyphs.

D19:8B Queen Tausret
D19:8T Sitra Meryamen
Tausert, Twosre, Tawosret

Another reigning queen, she was the wife of Sety II and regent for Siptah before taking the crown herself.

GARDINER does not list a hieroglyph for Mut.

X1	F12	X1		
⌒	𓏤	⌒	𓐙	𓁟
T(a)	Usr	(e)T	Setep-en	MUT

H8	X1	C2	N36	M17a	C12
◯	⌒	𓀀	▭	𓇋𓇋	𓀭
Si	T	RA	Mer	Y	AMEN

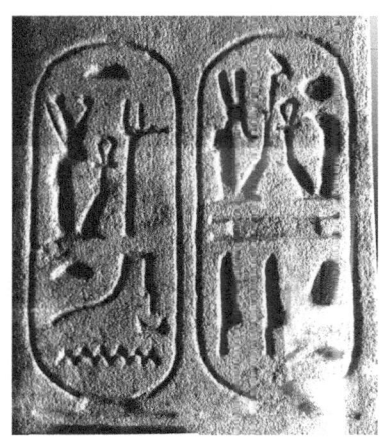

D20:1B Setnakht
D20:1T Userkhaura Setepenra
Setnekhtes

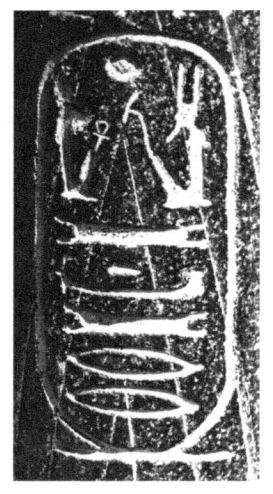 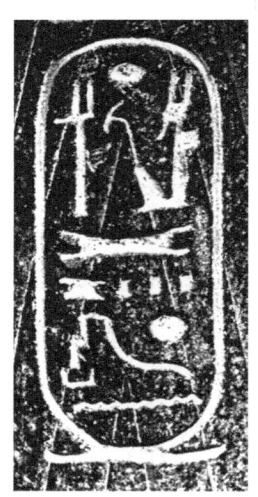

C7	D40	X1	N36	D21	C12	N36	N5
𓋴	𓂡	𓏏	𓏇	𓂋	𓀭	𓏇	𓇳
SET	Nakht	(T)	Mer	(R)eR	AMEN	MER(EN)	RA

F12	N28	Z2	N5		N5	N36	C12
𓄊	𓈍	|||	𓇳	𓊃𓈗	𓇳	𓏇	𓀭
User	Kha	U	RA	Setep-en	RA	MER(EN)	AMEN

 /Nakht/ is a *forearm and hand holding a stick*, and means *victorious, strong*.

Notice the epithet *Mereramen*, in the left hand cartouche, instead of the usual *Meryamen* or *Merenamen*. **WILLOCKX (P 17)** interprets *Mereramun* as *Continuously Loved by Amen* "The implication seems to be, that for the king, Re's love only mattered once (when Re decided that he should be king), while Amun's affection was required on a more permanent basis.. "

D20:2B Ramses III
D20:2T Usermaatra Meryamen
Ramesses, Ramessu

Cartouche, right

C2	F31	O34	S38	O28
🛡	⚘	⚌	↾	⬚
RA	Mes	(S)es	Heqa	Iunu

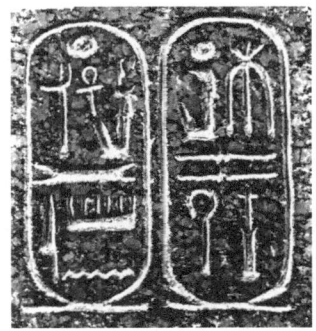

Cartouche, left

F12	C10	N5	N36	
⚑	⚶	⊙	⚊	⚏
User	Maat	RA	Mer(y)	AMEN

   In the cartouche below left the *sedge* /Su/ (M23) makes the name *Ramessu*.

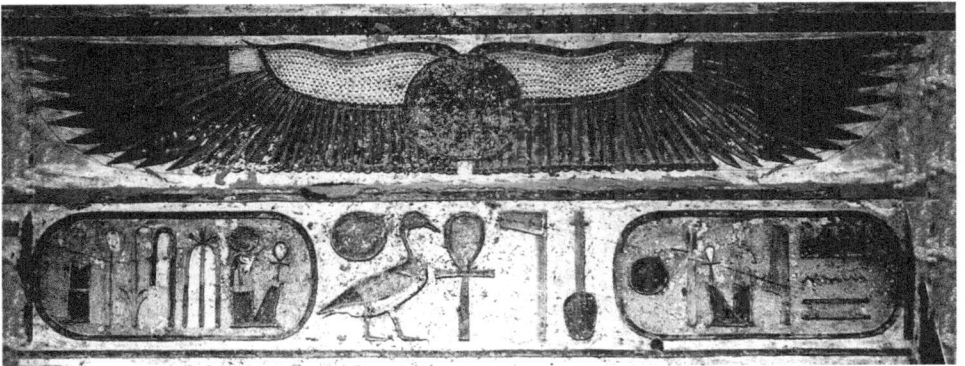

D20:3B Ramses IV
D20:3T Heqamaatra
Ramesses, Ramessu

N5	F31	S29	M23
⊙			
Rᴀ	Mes	(S)	Su

S38	C10	N5	N36	C12
		⊙		
Heqa	Maat	Rᴀ	Mer(y)	Aᴍᴇɴ

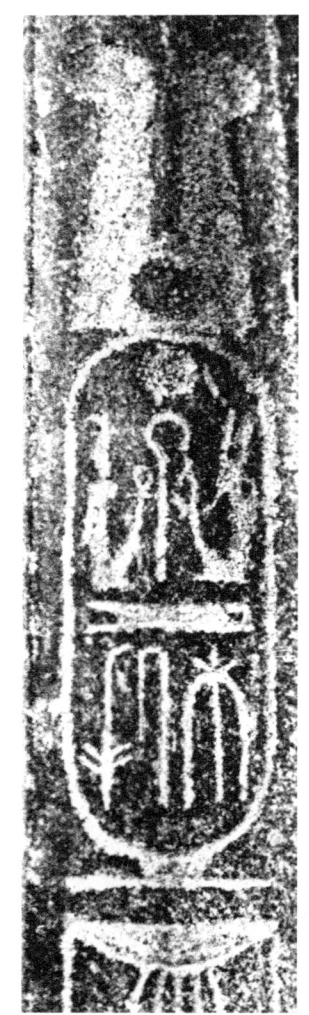

 Here's an interesting example (left) of a combined cartouche, topped with sun disk and double plumes, and seated on the sign for *gold* /Nub/ (S12)

It looks as if the sun disk at the top, inside the cartouche, is doing double duty for *Ra*mses and Heqamaat*ra*, unless the disk at the base of the plumes, on top, is taking one of those roles.

Here (below) is a more conventional treatment of the **THRONE NAME**, with *setepen-amen* (Amen holds the Maat feather).

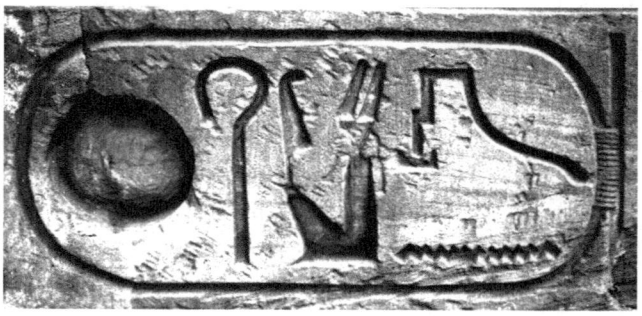

D20:5B Ramses VI (Amenherkhepshef Netjerheqaiunu)
D20:5T Nebmaatra Meryamen
Ramesses, Ramessu

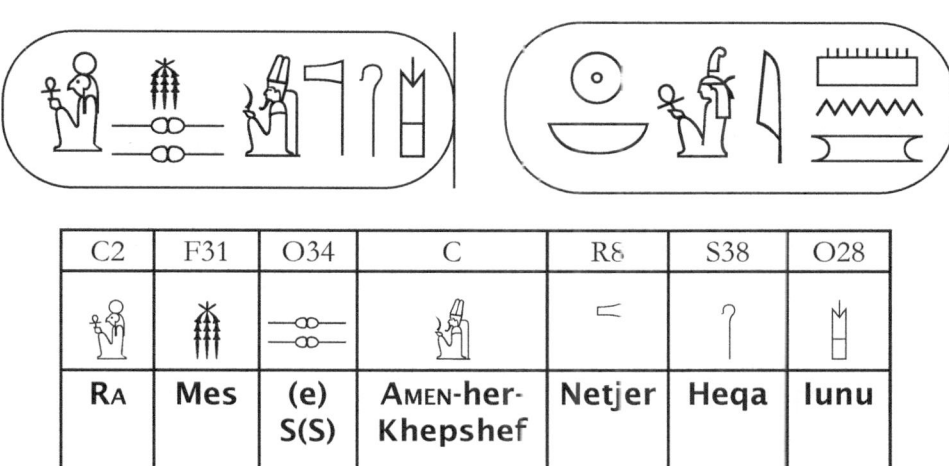

C2	F31	O34	C	R8	S38	O28
Rᴀ	Mes	(e) S(S)	Aᴍᴇɴ-her- Khepshef	Netjer	Heqa	Iunu

 Amenherkhepshef, *Amen with his khepesh or khopesh scimitar* representing *strength* (T16).

The epithet /Netjer Heqa Iunu/ is *Divine Ruler of Heliopolis.* .

V30	C10	N5	N36	
Neb	Mᴀᴀᴛ	Rᴀ	Mery	Aᴍᴇɴ

Notice how, in the spirit of oneupmanship, the Ramses' names are getting longer and longer as we progress through the nineteenth and twentieth dynasties. We find this trend throughout Egyptian history. It seems that the biggest, most powerful rulers were content with their **BIRTH NAMES** plus a short and simple **THRONE NAME**. Ramses I, who founded the dynasty, and Ramses II, the Great, were satisfied with very modest names in terms of number of signs. Their namesakes of the twentieth dynasty seemed to compete to see how long their names could be.

The **PTOLEMIES**, the dynasty that Cleopatra belonged to, are notorious for this. General Ptolemy I had *Ptolemy* only. The fourteen (!) succeeding Ptolemies went crazy with their names, as we shall see in Dynasty 33.

D20:8B Ramses IX (Khaemwaset Mereramen)
D20:8T Neferkara setepenra
Ramesses

N5	F31	S29	M23	N28	S40	-	C12
⊙							
RA	Mes	(S)	Su	Kha	(em) Was (et)	Me(rer)	AMEN

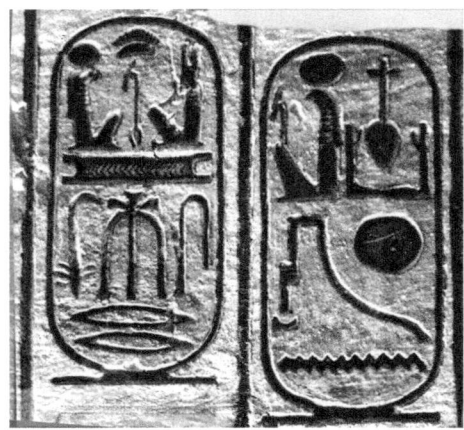

Here the **BIRTH NAME** uses the ordinary *Was* scepter (*dominion*) instead of the full *Waset* sign (R19, *Thebes*), consisting of the *was* scepter and a plume:

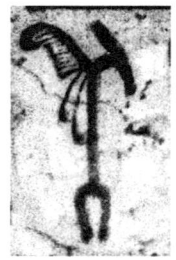

F35	D28	C2	
Nefer	Ka	RA	SetepenRA

D20:9B Ramses X (Amenherkhepshef)
D20:9T Khepermaatra
Ramesses, Ramessu

C2	F31	S29	M23	Cx8
RA	Mes	(S)	Su	AMEN-her-Khepshef

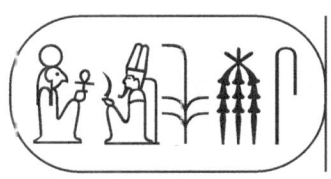

L1	C10	N5	S29
Kheper	MAAT	RA	SetepenRA

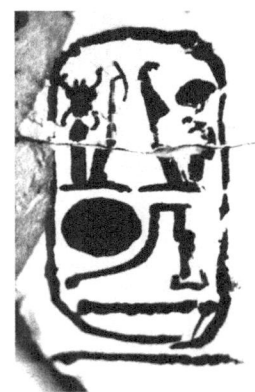

This is a fun cartouche (right). You have *falcon-headed Ra* holding the *Maat feather*, facing the *solar god Khepri, the beetle*, in the *tea party position*. Placing the beetle on top of the human body raises it up physically to the level of Ra so they can chat face to face as equals.

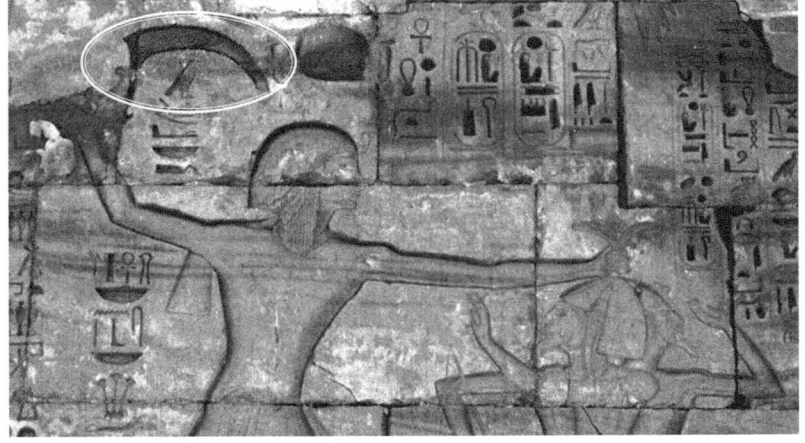

Ramses III wields his khepesh scimitar (See D20:5)

D20:10B Ramses XI (Khaemwaset merreramen netjerheqaiunu)
D20:10T Menmaatra setepenptah
Ramesses

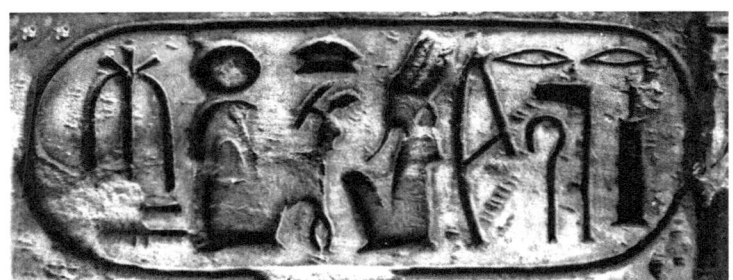

C2	F31	S29	N28	R19	U6	D21	C12
R_A	Mes	(e)S(S)	Kha	(em-) Waset	Mer	(re)R	A_{MEN}

R8	S38	O28
Netjer	Heqa	Iunu

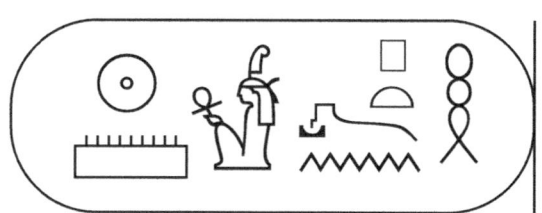

Y5	C10	N5		
Men	M_{AAT}	R_A	Setepen	P_{TAH}

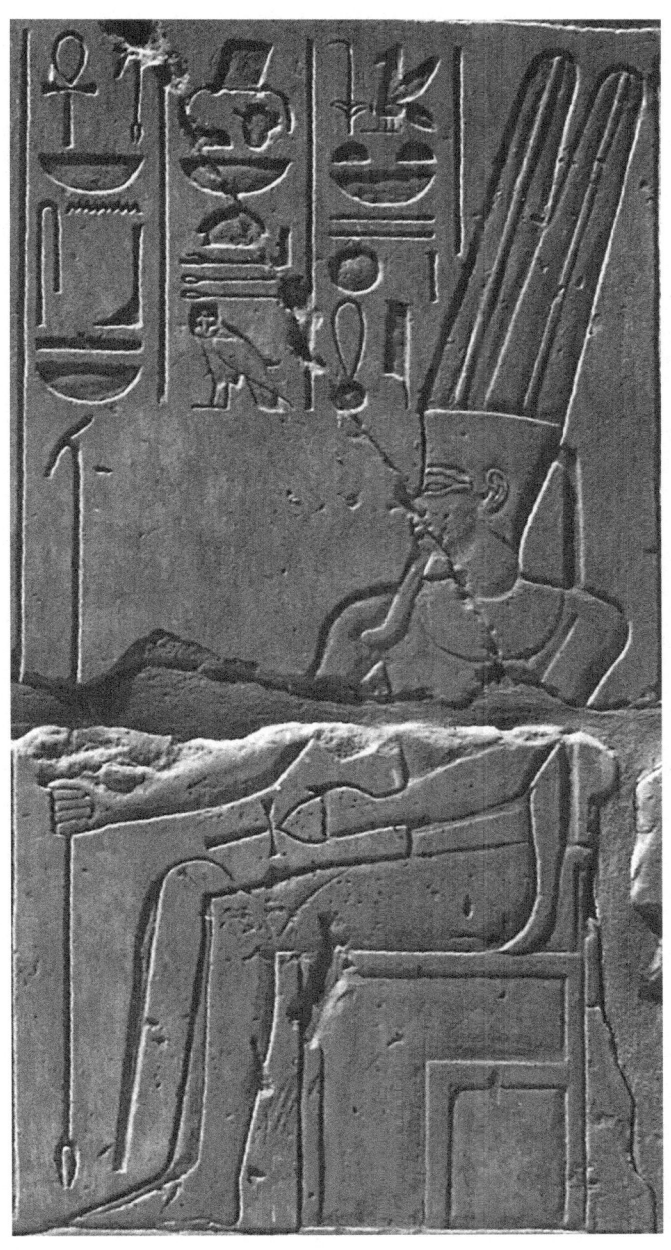

Amen, with his impossibly
tall plumes, ankh, and "was" scepter

Third Intermediate Period
High Priests, Dynasties 21–26

D20:11B Herihor siamen
D20:11T Hemnetjer tepyenamen

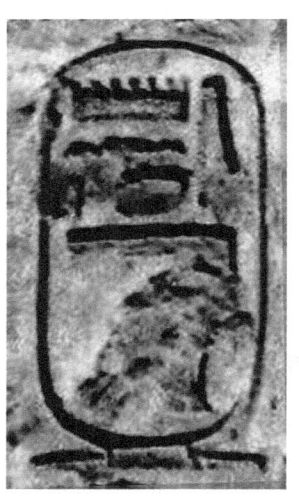
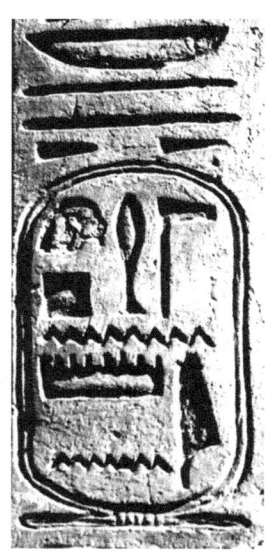

N1	G5	H8	Z1	
Her(i)	Hor	Si	-	Amen

U36	R8	D1	Q3	
Hem	Netjer	Tep	(Py-en)	Amen

Numbering for High Priests at Thebes, Herihor, above, D20:11, and Pinedjem D21:7, is not taken directly from **VON BECKERATH**. Rather than use his slightly complicated system for this period, I have just added the next available number in the series in the interest of simplicity.

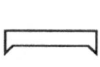 /Her/ means *heaven* or *sky* (often pronounced /Pet/), denoting someone or something that is *above*. **CLAYTON (P 175)** translates Herihor as *Horus protects me.*

We've seen *Siamen* as *Son of Amen* (D18:2, see photograph).

 /Hem/ is a *washerman's club* for beating clothes. Here /Hem-Netjer/ means *slave*, or *servant* (of god), a *prophet or high priest.*

 /Tep/ is a *human head.* /Tep/, with the phonetic complement /P/, modifies /Hem-netjer/ to reiterate that he is the Number One, First High Priest of Amen.

D21:3B Pasebakhaenniut I
D21:3T Aakheperra setepenamen
Psusennes I

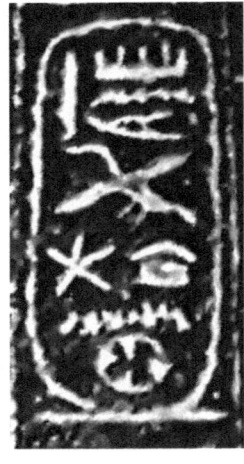

G40	N14	N28	N35	O49	U7	
Pa	Seba	Kha	(e)N	Niut	Mer(y)	Amen

 /Seba/ is clearly a *star*. This pharaoh styles himself *the Star that appears in the City* (Thebes) (**Clayton p 178**).

 /Pa/ the *flying duck* means *the*.

⊗ /Niut/ means *city*.

O29	L1	N5		C12
Aa	Kheper	Ra	Setepen	Amen

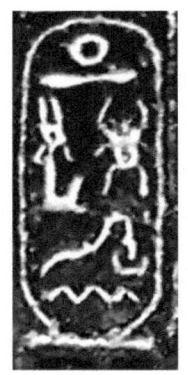

D21:6B Siamen
D21:6T Netjerkheperra
Psinaches

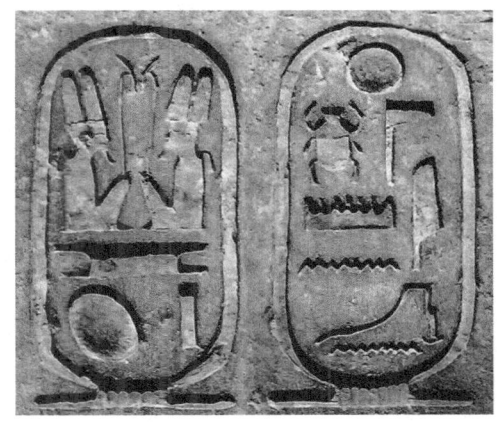

In the **BIRTH NAME**, we are treated to the sight of *two* Amen figures facing each other having a tea party. Or maybe roasting hot dogs.

Cartouche, left

H8	Z2	C12	N36	C12
○	|	🪶	⚬	🪶
Si	-	**A**MEN	**Mer(y)**	**A**MEN

Cartouche, right

R8	L1	N5		
⚑	🪲	⊙	〰	〰
Netjer	**Kheper**	**R**A	**Setepen**	**A**MEN

D21:7B Pinedjem
D21:7T Khakheperra

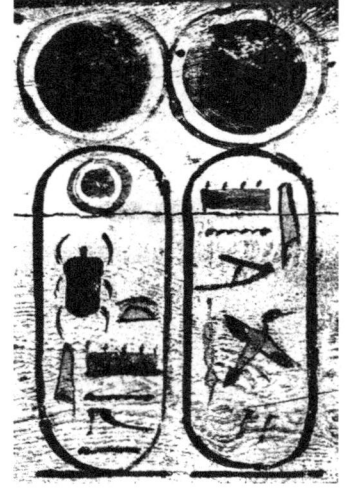

Cartouche, right

G40	M29	U6	
Pi	Nedjem	Mer(y)	Amen

Cartouche, left

N28	L1	N5		
Kha	Kheper	Ra	Setepen	Amen

Pinedjem is another of the High Priests at Thebes.

 This (carob?) *pod*, means *sweet* or *pleasant*. **Clayton (p 175):** *He who belongs to the Pleasant One* [Horus or Ptah].

D22:1B Sheshonq I
D22:1T Hedjkheperra
Sesonchis, Shoshenq

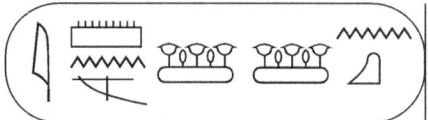

Sheshonq began a dynasty of
Libyan origin, hence the unusual names.

M8	M8	N35	N29	U7	
𓈗	𓈗	〰	𓈎	𓌸	𓋴 〰
Sh(e)	Sh	(o)N	Q	Mer(y)	Amen

𓈗 /Shesh/ a *marsh*, phonetic.

𓈎 /Q/, a *hill*, phonetic.

S1	L1	N5		
𓋴	𓆣	⊙	𓊃〰	𓋴 〰
Hedj	Kheper	Ra	Setepen	Amen

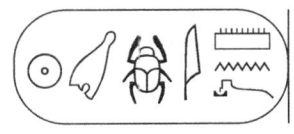

 /Hedj/, the *white crown of Upper (Southern) Egypt*. Here, according to
Clayton (p 185) it means *bright. Bright is the Manifestation of Re.*

D22:2B Osorkon I
D22:2T Sekhemkheperra
Osorthon

 /O/ lasso.

 /S/ an unidentified object

Cartouche, right

V4	Aa18	M17	D21	V31	N35	N36	
O	S	O	R	K	N	Mer(y)	AMEN

Cartouche, left

S42	L1	N5		N5
Sekhem	Kheper	RA	Setepen	RA

D22:3B Sheshonq II
D22:3T Heqakheperra
Sesonchis, Shoshenq

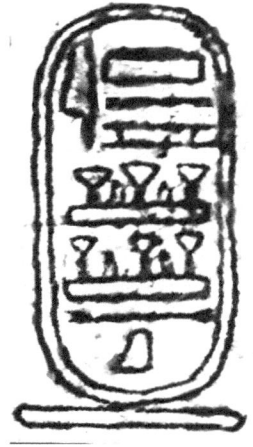

M8	M8	N35	N29	N36	
🐚	🐚	〰	◁	⊐⊏	𓂋〰
Sh(e)	Sh	(o)N	Q	Mer(y)	Aᴍᴇɴ

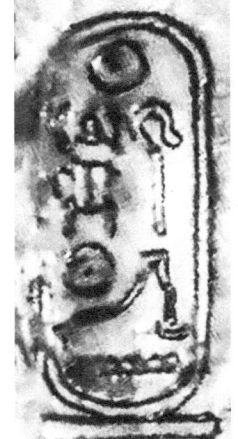

S38	L1	N5		N5
𓋾	🪲	⊙	〰	⊙
Heqa	Kheper	Rᴀ	Setepen	Rᴀ

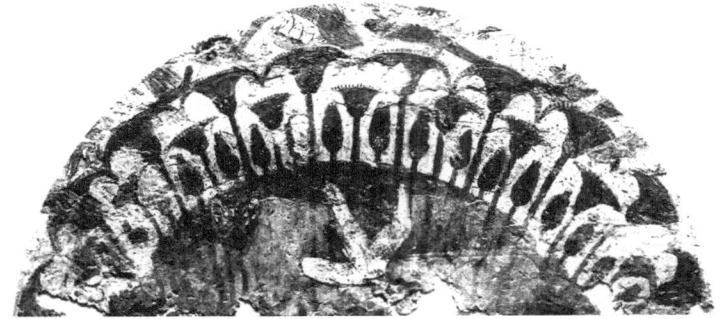

Depiction of a marsh, with alternating lotus buds and papyrus umbels, as in the hieroglyph.

D22:5B Osorkon II
D22:5T Usermaatra setepenamen
Osorthon

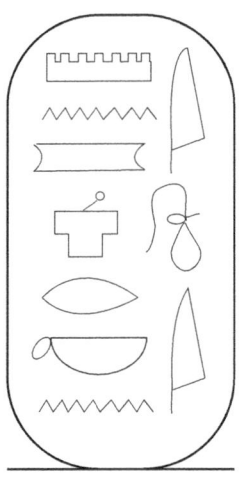 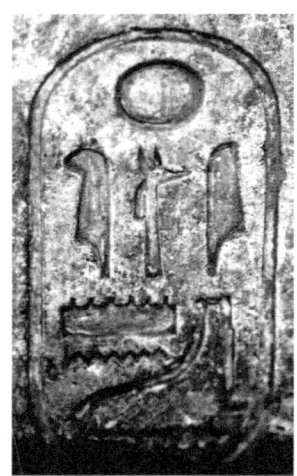

Cartouche, left

V4	Aa18	M17	D21	V31	N35	N36	
O	S	O	R	K	N	Mer(y)	Amen

Cartouche, right

F12	H6	N5		
User	Maat	Ra	Setepen	Amen

D25:3B Piankhi I
D25:3T Menkheperra
Piyi, Piye

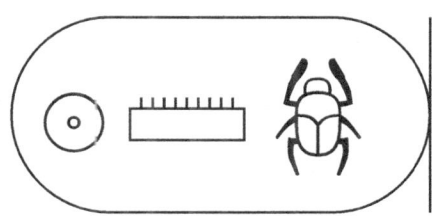

Cartouche, left

Q3	S34	M17a
□	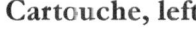	
P(i)	Ankh	i

Cartouche, above

Y5	L1	N5
Men	Kheper	Rᴀ

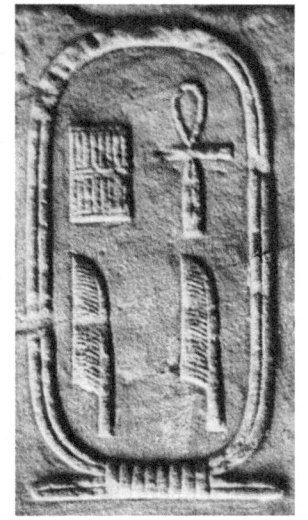

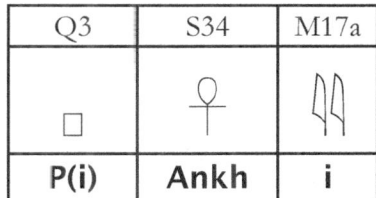

D25:4B Shabaka
D25:4T Neferkara
Saba Sabacon, Shabako

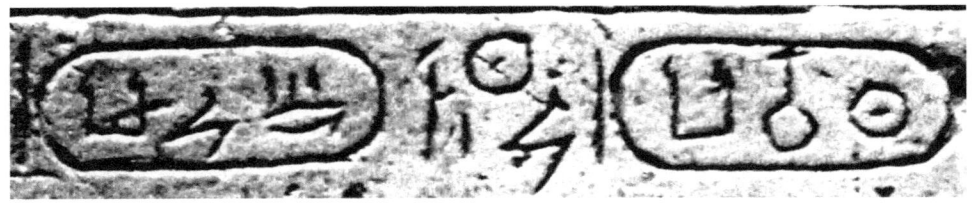

M8	E10	D28
ꜣ	𓃒	𐤫
Sh(a)	**Ba**	**Ka**

F35	D28	N5
𓄤	𐤫	☉
Nefer	**Ka**	**RA**

The photograph shows an unusually cursive inscription in a style closer to **HIERATIC** handwriting.

D25:5B Shabitko
D25:5T Djedkara
Sebichos, Shabitka, Djedkaura

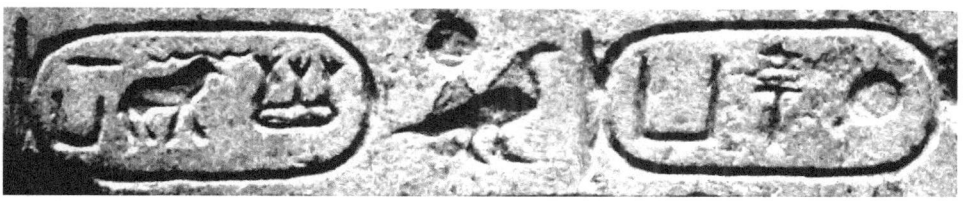

M8	E10	N17	D28
𓊖	𓃒	—	𓂓
Sh(a)	Bi	T	Ko

R1̲	D28	N5
𓊽	𓂓	☉
Djed	Ka	RA

D25:6B Taharqa
D25:6T Nefertemkhura
Tarcus

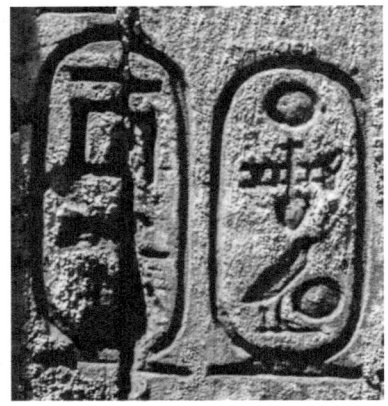

N17	O4	E23	N29
—	▢	🦁	◿
Ta	**Ha**	**R**	**Q(a)**

F35	U15	Aa1	G43	N5
🜊	🛷	⊜	🐦	☉
NEFER	TEM	**Kh**	**U**	RA

 Nefertem is a god, the son of Ptah. His name is written with the well-known /Nefer/ plus a *sledge*, combined into one glyph.

 /L or R/ *Lion*, used in foreign names.

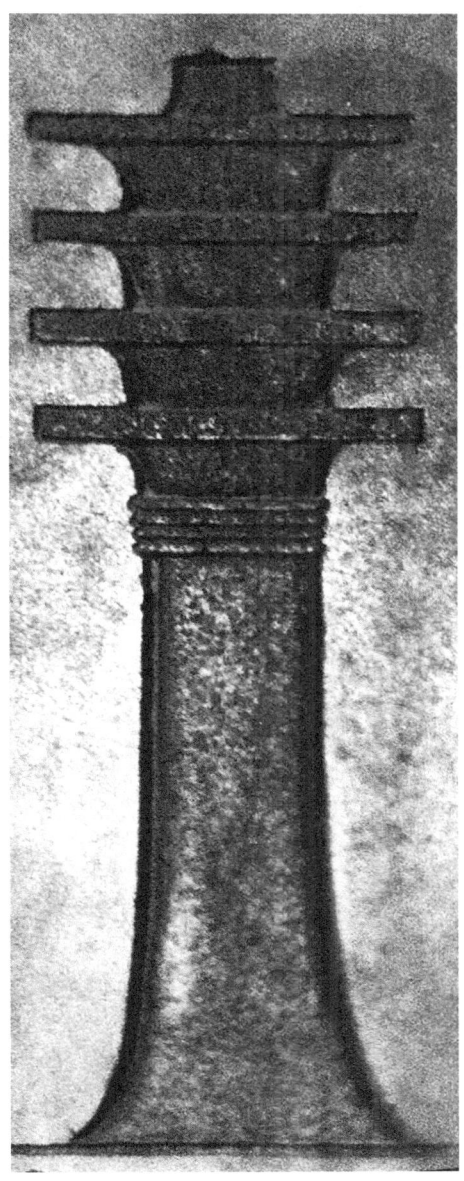

Djed Pillar
See D5:8T and D25:5T,
Djedkara

D25 Divine Adoratrice Shepenwepet I, II
Shepenupet
D25 Divine Adoratrice Amenirdis I, II

During the 25th Dynasty there were some High Priestesses of Amen who bore the title **DIVINE ADORATRICE (OR GOD'S ADORER) OF AMEN** and/or **GOD'S WIFE OF AMEN**. There were two called Shepenwepet and two called Amenirdis.

They were not pharaohs, but they held real power and had cartouches. **CLAYTON (P 192)** and **TILDESLEY (P 184)** explain the concept and history of the *God's Wife* and *Divine Adoratrice* titles and roles.

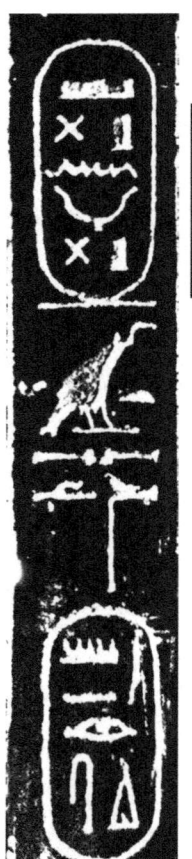

Cartouche of Shepenwepet, top

N37	Q3	Z9	N35	F13	Q3	Z9
▭	□	✕	〜〜〜	⩗	□	✕
Sh(e)	P	-	(e)N	Wep	(P)	et?

▭ /Sh/ a *pool*.

✕ This is a silent determinative of some sort, often meaning *to divide*. It is not clear to me what function it has in Shepenwepet's name.

⩗ /Wep/ A *bull's horns*. This sign is commonly seen in the name of *Wepwawet*, the jackal-headed god, *Opener of the Ways*, vivid symbolism of a bull crashing through whatever passed for a china shop in ancient Egypt, *opening the way*.

Cartouche of Amenirdis, bottom, opposite

	D4	X8	S29
Amen	Ir	Di	(S)

/Ir/ *eye; do or make.* Mentioned with D5:3T, Neferirkara

Amenirdis I also had a **THRONE NAME** cartouche, Khaneferumut:

N28	F35	G14	X1
Kha	Nefer-u	Mut	(T)

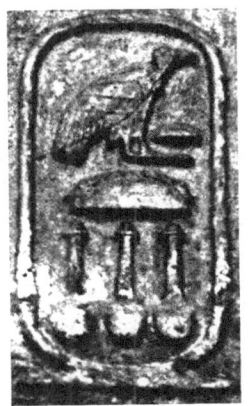

D26:1B Psamtik I
D26:1T Wahibra
Psammetichus, Psammuthis

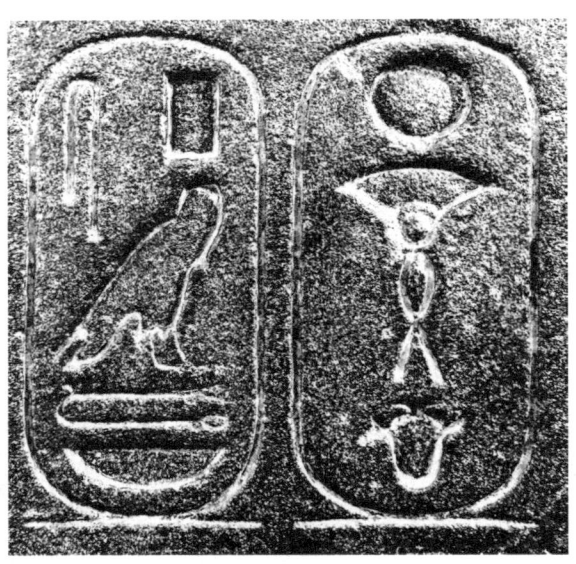

Q3	S29	G17	V13	V31
(P)	S(a)	M	T(e)	K

V29	F34	N5
Wah	Ib	Rᴀ

 /Wah/ (V29) is a *swab*. The sign is based on V28, *twisted flax*.

D26 Divine Adoratrice Nitocrit
Nitocris, Nitiqret

Another **GOD'S WIFE**, daughter of Psamtik I. You can see the signs for *God's Wife* above the cartouche.

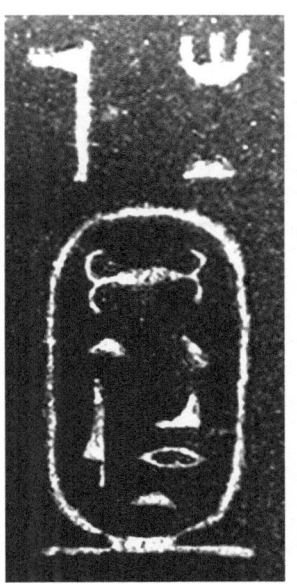

R24	X1	H8	N29	D21	M17	X1
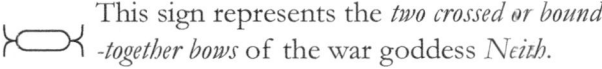						
Nit	(T)	-	(o)Q	R	I	T

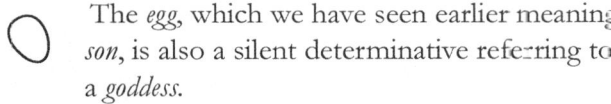 This sign represents the *two crossed or bound -together bows* of the war goddess *Neith*.

The *egg*, which we have seen earlier meaning *son*, is also a silent determinative referring to a *goddess*.

D26:2B Nekau II
D26:2T Wehemibra
Necho

Cartouche, left

N35	E1	G43
∿∿∿	𓃒	𓅱
N(e)	Ka	U

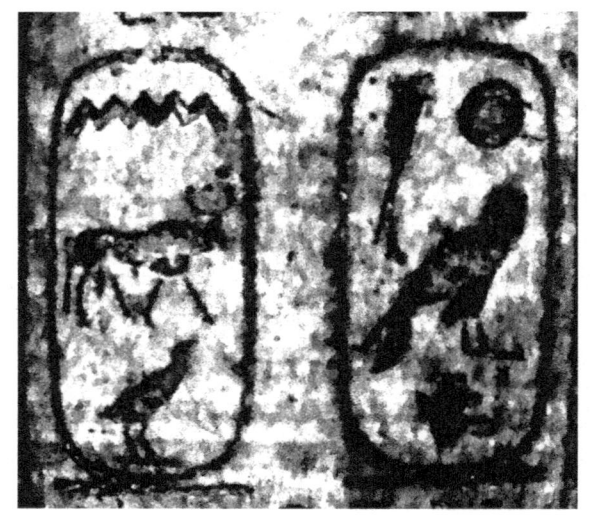

Cartouche, right

F25	G17	F34	N5
𓂾	(𓅓)	𓄣	☉
Wehem	(M)	Ib	Rᴀ

 /Ka/ (E1) the *bull*, is here a graphic variant of the raised arms, *Ka* (D28), with which Nekau's name is also written.

 /Wehem/ (F25) is the *hoof and leg of an ox* (remind me of the difference between a bull and an ox, again?) and signifies *repeating*.

D26:3B Psamtik II
D26:3T Neferibra
Psammetichus, Psammuthis

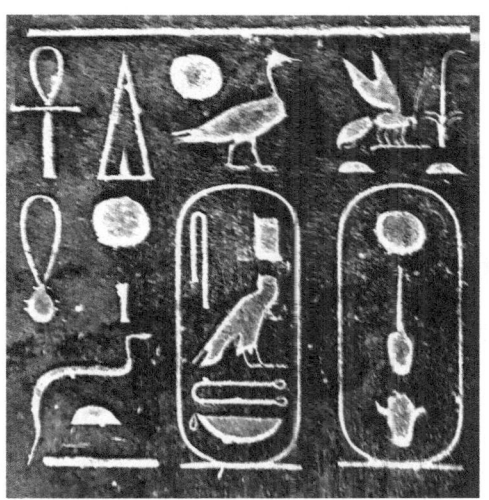

Q3	S29	G17	V13	V31
□	⌠	🦉	⟿	⟝
(P)	S(a)	M	T(e)	K

F35	F34	N5
⚱	♡	☉
Nefer	Ib	RA

Are you detecting a trend in these **THRONE NAMES**? There are at least half a dozen /Ib Ra/ names in this dynasty.

In this illustration I have included some of the external signs, in other words those outside of the cartouches. We have seen them all before. *He of the Sedge and the Bee, Son of Ra, Given Life Like Ra Eternally.* See D12:2 for review of these titles.

D26: Divine Adoratrice Ankhnes Neferibra

Another **DIVINE ADORATRICE**, daughter of Psamtik II, D26:3B. She includes her father's **THRONE NAME**, Neferibra, in her cartouche. This is a type of name we saw given to Old Kingdom queens, here meaning *She Lives for (King) Neferibra.* **(See TILDLESLY P 186)**.

This cartouche is a mystery to me, actually. That this is the cartouche of Ankhnes Neferibra is well attested, but it also contains the hieroglyph for the god Amen, without the usual *beloved of* sign, as well as what possibly looks to be the name of Piankhi (Piye), D25:3B. I can speculate, but won't. If you know, please tell me.

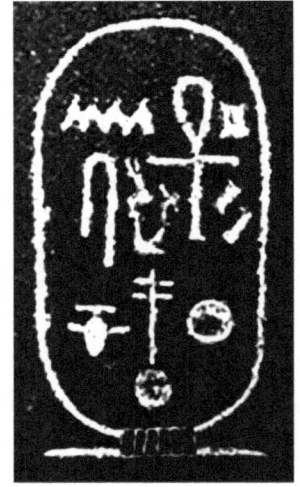

S34	N35	S29	F35	F34	N5	C12		Z4	S34
☥	〜〜〜	┃	⚲	⛿	☉	🜨	□	＼＼	(☥)
Ankh	**N**	**(e)S**	**Nefer**	**Ib**	**Rᴀ**	**Aᴍᴇɴ**	**P**	**Ye**	**(Ankh?)**

Father's throne name

D26:4B Wahibra
D26:4T Haaibra
Apries, Uaphres

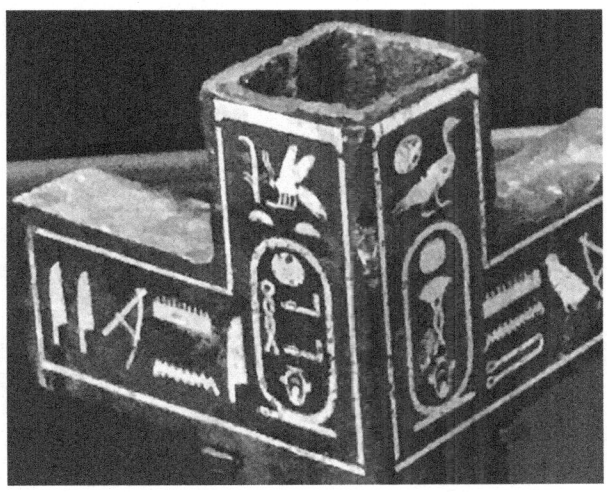

Cartouche, right

V29	F34	N5
𓏶	𓄤	☉
Wah	**Ib**	**RA**

Cartouche, left

V28	D36	D36	F34	N5
𓏴	𓂝	𓂝	𓄤	☉
H	**A**	**A**	**Ib**	**RA**

Did I mention the /Ib Ra/ phenomenon in Dynasty 26? This pharaoh uses it in both his names.

In another twist, Wahibra's **BIRTH NAME** is the same as a predecessor's **THRONE NAME** (D26:1).

On this piece of furniture, you can see not only the royal titles, but *Beloved of Amen* and *Beloved of Montu* (see D11:5B for *Montu*)

D26:5B Ahmose Sineit
D26:5T Knemibra
Amosis

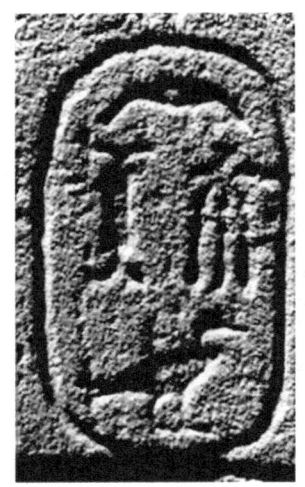

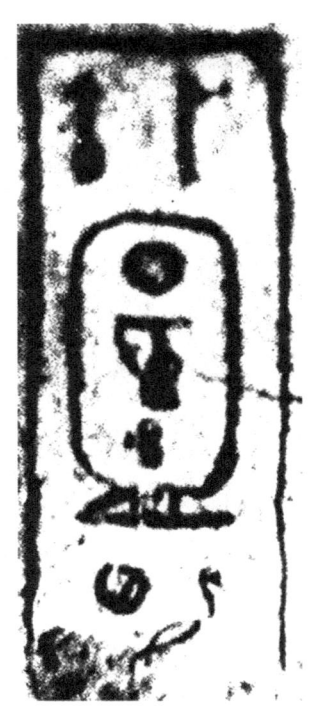

N12	F31	G39	R24
⌒	🌾	🦆	⊂⊃
Aн	Mos	Si	Nɪт

W9	F34	N5
🏺	🏺	⊙
Khnem	Ib	Rᴀ

Late Period
Dynasties 27-31

D30:1B Nakhtnebef
D30:1T Kheperkara
Nectanebes, Nectanebo I

We've skipped a number of Persian conquerors and other pharaohs with short reigns.

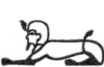

Nakhtnebef often uses a *sphinx* in lieu of the regular *basket* for /Neb/, *Lord*. GARDINER did not include the sphinx in his list.

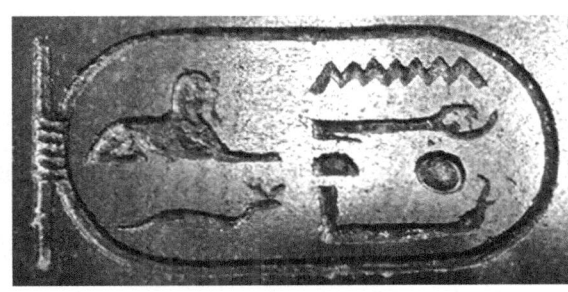

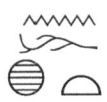

/Nakht/ *strength*, is what I call a LIGATURE, namely several signs that occur together almost as one hieroglyph, like *Amen* and *Hotep*

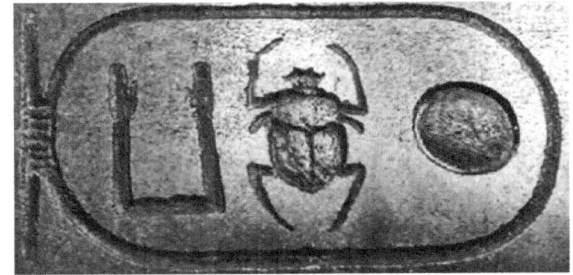

/Khet/ (M3) is a *branch*, representing *wood*, or a *tree*. By extension it means *strong*. Combined with the /N/, /Kh/, and /T/ it is /Nakht/, *strong* or *victorious*. The *hand brandishing a stick* (D40) is a determinative. Sometimes a *man*, not just a hand, holds the stick.

	D40		I9		L1	D28	N5
Nakht	**(Nakht)**	**Neb**	**(e)F**		**Kheper**	**Ka**	**RA**

D30:3B Nakht horheb
D30:3T Senedjem ibra
Nectanbus

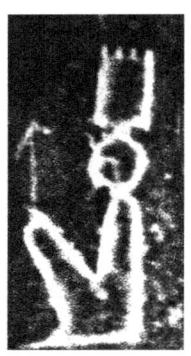

Anhur

Cartouche, right

D40	G5	W4	U6	Cx2	O49	X1
Nakht	HOR	Heb	Mery	ANHUR	Niut?	(T)

Cartouche, left

S29	M29	F34	C2		Cx2
S	Nedjem	Ib	RA	Setepen	ANHUR

/Heb/ is a combination of two signs: (W3) the *alabaster basin* meaning *feast, topped by a booth supported by a column* (O22). The combined sign means *festival*.

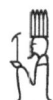 /Anhur/ *Onuris*, is a warrior god from Abydos. He wears four tall plumes which, when the stone will not take detail, can be abbreviated as a rectangle, sometimes with crenelations (three examples, opposite). Not in GARDINER.

I can't explain the presence of /Niut+T/, the *city* hieroglyph. Both VON BECKERATH and CLAYTON include these two signs in their cartouches, but uncharacteristically, neither includes the transliteration of O49 or offers any explanation of this group of signs in this cartouche.

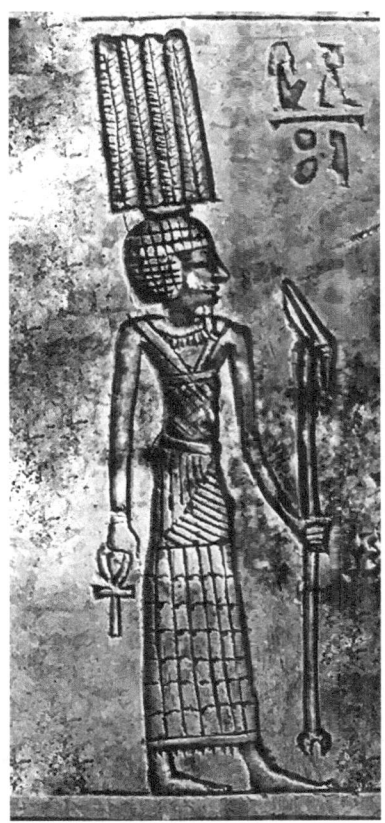

**Anhur (Onouris), with
headdress of four plumes**

Greco-Roman Period
Macedonian Kings
"Dynasty 32"

D32:1B Alexander I the Great
D32:1T Meryamen setepenra
Alexander III of Macedon, Alexandros

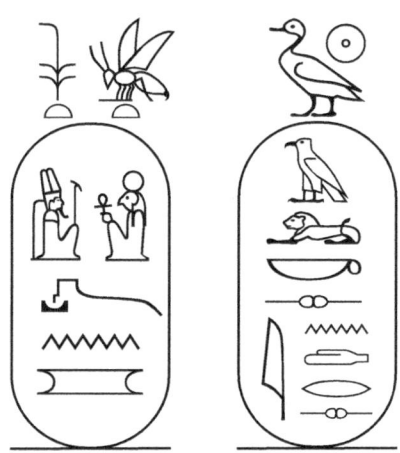

Cartouche, right

G1	E23	V31	O34	M17	N35	D46	D21	O34
🦅	🦁	🥄	—∞—	𓏭	∿∿∿	▱	◯	—∞—
A	L(e)	K	S	A	N	D	R	(o)S

Cartouche, left

	N36	C12		N5
	▭	🧍	🔨∿∿∿	⊙
	Mer(y)	Amen	Setep-en	Ra

Although Alexander the Great's name is pretty straightforward, from here on we are in for some adventures in spelling. While the **PTOLEMIES** went in for incredibly long names, they stay pretty much within the Egyptian framework. The names of the Macedonian kings and Romans, however, are (obviously) not in the Egyptian language. I suspect that certain of the sounds in their names sounded just a little bit unusual to the Egyptians, so they experimented with different ways to represent those sounds. "Experimented" is the key word, because any kind of standard spelling goes out the window in the **GRECO-ROMAN** period.

We've seen three alternate/S/ sounds. They are all quite common.

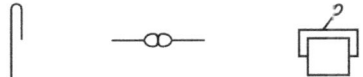

Similarly, (WII), a *jar stand*, which normally has a hard /G/ sound, stands in for /K/.

That pesky /L or R/ sound, here represented by the *lion*, can also be written with the *mouth* /R/ sign (D21).

The *Egyptian vulture* /A/ can be swapped out for the *reed* (M17)

Thus Alexander I's /Alexandros/ name can be written with these alternate signs, as below:

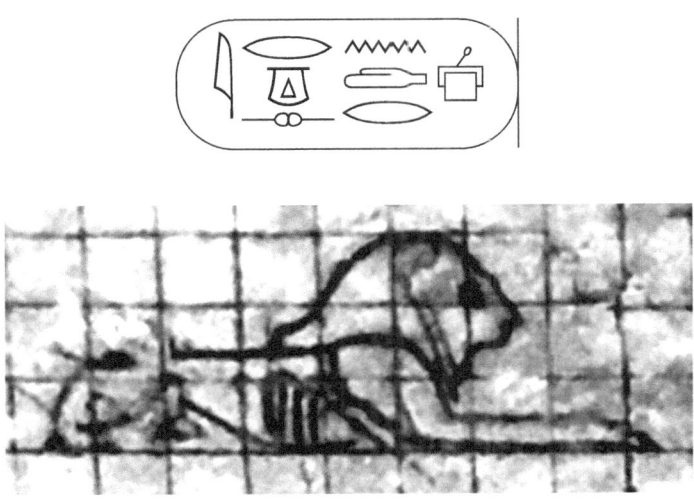

D32:3B Alexander II
D32:3T Haaibra setepenamen
Alexander IV

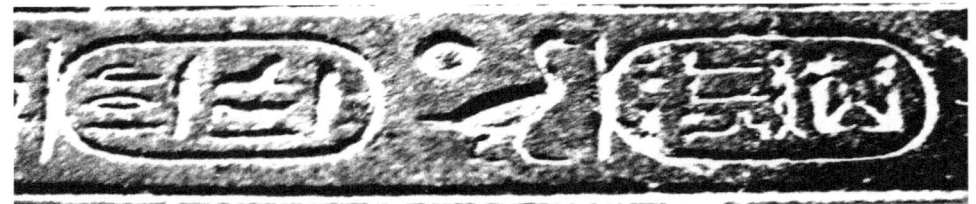

Cartouche, left

M17	E23	V31	O34	M17	D46	D21	O34
A	L(e)	K	S	A	D	R	(o)S

Cartouche, right

V28	D36	D36	F34	C2		C12
H	A	A	Ib	Rᴀ	Setepen	Aᴍᴇɴ

The Ptolemies
"Dynasty 33"

As I mentioned earlier, there were 15 **PTOLEMIES**, not counting their queens. While "manly-man" Ptolemy, one of Alexander the Great's generals, was satisfied with using just his given name, most of his successors went out of control with their names. And for some perverse reason, it seems that most of their monumental texts were carved in soft sandstone, so they look like they were molded from cookie dough and are very hard to read.

Even when they are clearly rendered, it can be very hard to make sense of some of these names. As **RITNER (P 1)** points out, "the student of Ptolemaic titularies is poorly served by available studies... The full phraseology of the hieroglyphic cartouches...has received little attention, probably on the assumption that these formal titles in then-arcane script were of little historical importance. When reproduced, the cartouches are only rarely transliterated or translated."

I have a fanciful picture in my mind of these gullible foreign pharaohs, or at least their prime ministers, who except for Cleopatra VII didn't even understand the Egyptian language, "shopping" for their cartouches at the bazaar. Just like at a Damascus rug emporium, shop assistants bring out and unfurl, one after another, ever longer and more glorious cartouches, the proprietor (High Priest?) offering advice about which gods need to be propitiated, which ancestors honored, or which combination of hieroglyphs is in fashion at the moment

D33:1B Ptolemy I
D33:1T Meryamen Setepenra
Ptolemaios Soter I

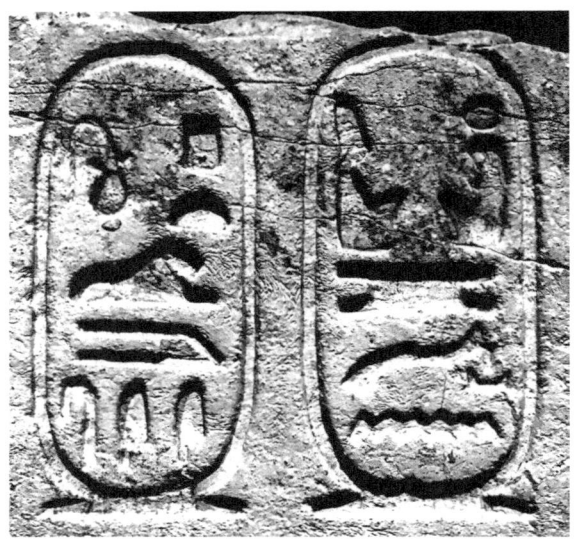

Q3	X1	V4	E23	Aa13	M17a	S29
□	⌒					
P	T	O	L(e)	M	(a)y	(o)S

N36	C12		C2
Mer(y)	AMEN	Setep-en	Ra

Ptolemy I chose to use just his name, unadorned, for his **BIRTH NAME** cartouche. His **THRONE NAME** borrows that of Alexander the Great.

D33:2B Ptolemy II
D33:2T Userkaenra Meryamen
Ptolemaios Philadelphos

Cartouche, right

Q3	X1	Z7	E23	Aa13	M17a	S29
□	◠	℘	🦁	◁	𓏭	⌐
P	**T**	**O**	**L(e)**	**M**	**(a)y**	**(o)S**

Cartouche, left

F12	D28		C2	N36	C12
𓄹	𓂩		𓁪	⟷	𓁩
User	**Ka**	**(eN)**	**Rᴀ**	**Mer(y)**	**Aᴍᴇɴ**

 The spiral (Z7) is said to be an abbreviation for (G43), the quail chick. Both have an /U/ or /O/ sound.

D33:3B Ptolemy III
D33:3T Iwaennetjerwysenwy sekhemankhra setepamen
Ptolemaios Euergetes I

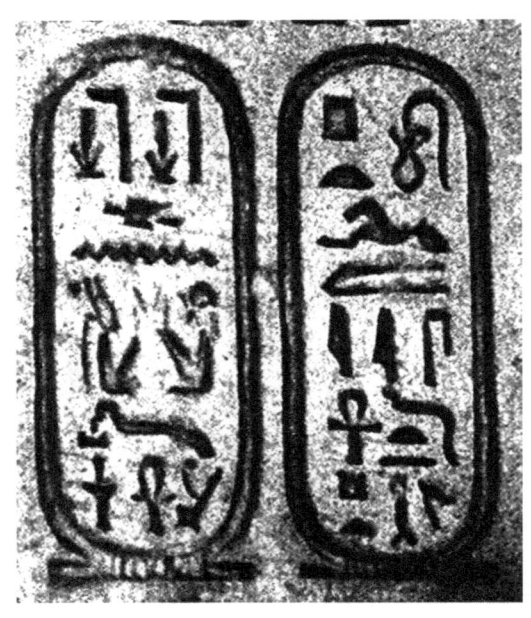

Cartouche, right

Q3	X1	V4	E23	Aa13	M17a	S29	S34		U6	
P	T	O	L(e)	M	(a)y	(o)S	Ankh	Djet	Mery	PTAH

Cartouche, left

F44	N35	R8	T23	S42	S34	C2	U21	C12
Iwa	(e)n	Netjerwy	Senwy	Sekhem	Ankh	RA	Setepen	AMEN

/Iwa/ is a *joint of beef*, meaning *heir*. Think of *bone of my bones, flesh of my flesh*. Unfortunately, in a carved inscription this sign often looks more like either a flying saucer or a hamburger than a bone-in Sunday ham.

 /Sen/ is a *barbed arrowhead* and means *brother*.

The /wy/ endings on Netjerwy and Senwy make the nouns **DUAL**, in other words, it doubles them. These syllables are not written in the cartouche but the doubled signs make the meaning clear.

CLAYTON (P 209) translates the phrase Iwaennetjerwy Senwy as *Heir of the Twin Gods*,. **RITNER (P 2)** gives a clue as to who these twin gods were: "The **PRENOMEN** itself, after Ptolemy III, invariably begins with the declaration that the king is the heir of a predecessor's epithet." So, the *Twin (or other) Gods* refer to a Ptolemy's parents or recent ancestors. **RITNER'S** 27-page study dissects this name thoroughly.

Note that **CLAYTON (P 208)** and **VON BECKERATH (P 118)** differ as to the order of phrases in the **THRONE NAME**. **VON BECKERATH** says Setep-(en)ra Sekhemankhamen, reversing position of the two gods. As Clayton's book is the more recent, I will defer to it, although I believe that the fact that at least seven Ptolemies end their names with Sekhemankh*amen* tends to support that reading.

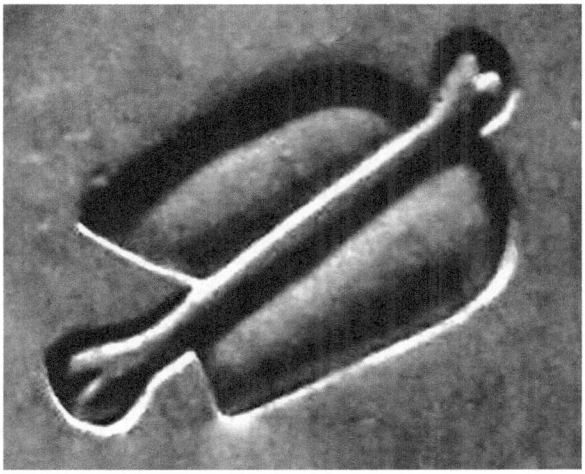

D33:4B Ptolemy IV
D33:4T Iwaennetjerwymenkhwy setepptah userkara-sekhemankhamen
Ptolemaios Philopator

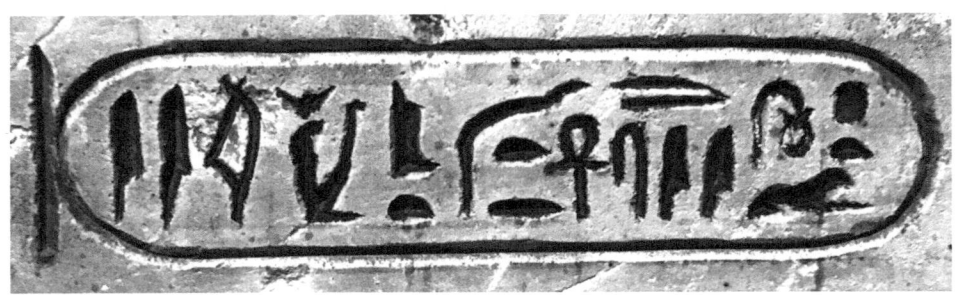

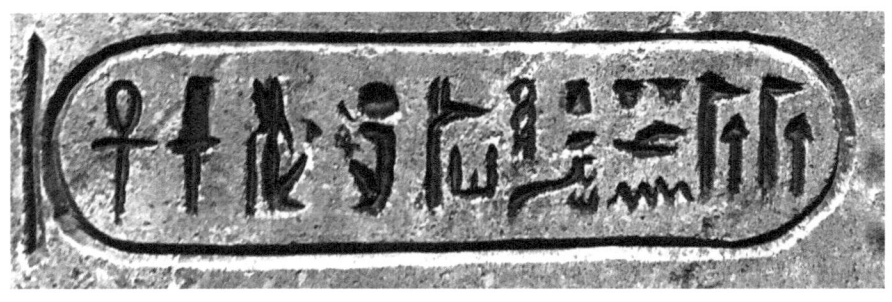

Q3	X1	V4	E23	Aa15	M17a	S29	S34	
□	◠							
P	T	O	L(e)	M	(a)y	(o)S	Ankh	Djet

U6	M17a	Q1	X1	C9
			◠	
Mery	(y)	Ese	(T)	(Isis)

F44	N35	R8	U22	W10	U21	
Iwa	(e)n	Netjerwy	Menkhwy	?	Setep	PTAH

F12	D28	C2	S42	S34	C12
User	Ka	RA	Sekhem	Ankh	AMEN

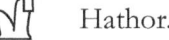

/Eset/ a *throne*, with the following /T/ and optional *egg*, is the name of the *goddess Isis*. This is followed by the figure of Isis, wearing the *cow's horns and sun disk* that had in earlier dynasties been the signature of Hathor.

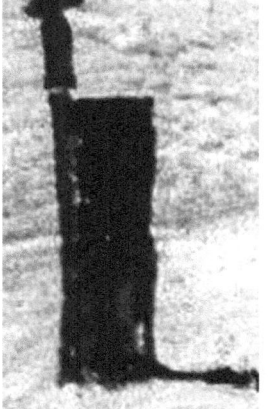

/Menkh/ is a chisel. CLAYTON (P 209) translates Netjerwy Menkhwy as "*the [Two] Beneficent Gods.*" This tall version of the chisel reminds me of a mushroom.

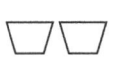

This sign, *a cup*, has several different pronunciations. Neither CLAYTON (P 209) nor VON BACKERATH (P 119) transliterates these signs.

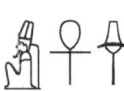

CLAYTON (P 209) translates /Sekhem Ankh Amen/ as *Living Image of Amun*. As mentioned under Ptolemy III, this EPITHET is used by seven of the Ptolemies.

D33:5B Ptolemy V
D33:5T Iwaennetjerwy merwytu setepptah userkara sekhemankhamen
Ptolemaios Epiphanes

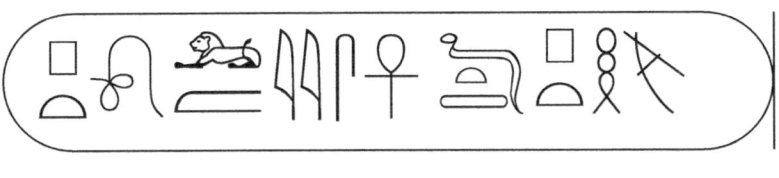

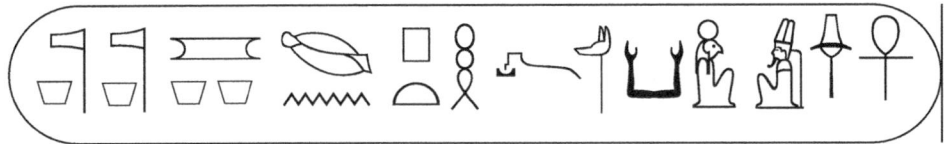

Q3	X1	V4	E23	Aa15	M17a	S29	S34	
P	T	O	L(e)	M	(a)y	(o)S	Ankh	Djet

U6	
Mery	P<small>TAH</small>

F44	N35	R8	W10		U21	
Iwa	(e)n	Netjerwy	-	merwyitu	Setep	P<small>TAH</small>

F12	D28	C2	S42	S34	C12
User	Ka	R<small>A</small>	Sekhem	Ankh	A<small>MEN</small>

The only difference between Ptolemy V's **THRONE NAME** and that of Ptolemy IV is that V has cups instead of chisels. In their **BIRTH NAMES**, IV honors Isis and V honors Ptah. You might think that which god or goddess a given Ptolemy was "chosen by" would vary, but in the case of these two, at least among the examples cited by **GAUTHIER (P 275)** and **VON BECKERATH (P 119)**, they are consistent.

GAUTHIER (VOL 4 P 275) tells us that /Netjerwymerwyitu/ means *The Father-loving Gods, "les dieux Philopators."*

(W10) alone is a determinative for a cup or basket.

D33:6B Ptolemy VI
D33:6T Iwaennetjerwyper-setepenptah Khepri Irmaaten Amenra
Ptolemaios Philometor

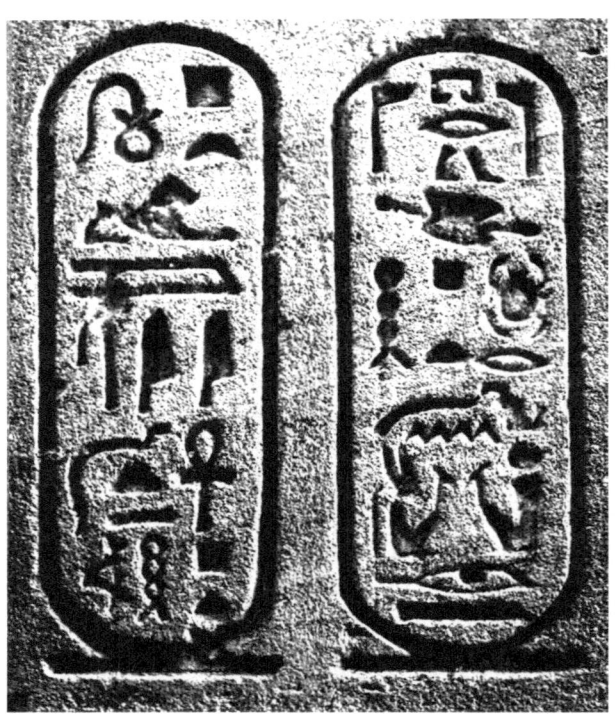

Q3	X1	V4	E23	Aa13	M17a	S29	S34	
□	◠	🐍	🐆	▭	𓏭	𓂑	☥	🐍
P	T	O	L(e)	M	(a)y	(o)S	Ankh	Djet

U6	
⟋	□⚭ ◠⚭
Mery	PTAH

F44	N35	R8	O1			
〰	〰〰	🚩🚩	⬜	🔱	🐾〰〰	🏺
Iwa	**(en)**	**Netjerwy**	**Per**	**(R)(wy)**	**Setepen**	**P**TAH

	L1	D21	D4	aa11	C12	C2
	🪲	⬭	👁	▱	𓀀	𓁩
	Khepr	**(Ri)**	**Ir**	**Maat(en)**	**A**MEN	**R**A

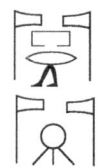

/Per/ (O1) is *house*. The following /R/ *mouth with legs* may be an elaborate phonetic complement for /Per/. CLAYTON (P **209**) translates this phrase as *Heir of the [two] houses of the Gods.*

/Pri/ means *to go forth*. I don't know if there is a play on words at work here or not.

Alternatively, GAUTHIER (VOL **4** P **286**) notes that variations of both these groups of signs mean *the Two Illustrious Gods*, les *deux dieux Épiphanes*, a title of Ptolemy V (remember, we're working on Ptolemy VI now) reflecting his Greek epithet, although neither of these groups appear in his (V's) cartouche. Von Beckerath transliterates both groups the same, /Perwy/.

The sun with rays can replace the *house + walking mouth* in Ptolemy VI's cartouche.

Whether intentional on the part of the original sculptor or not, I have to draw attention to the rays on this sun (taken from Ptolemy VIII's cartouche, next). The rays appear to be garlands of flowers. What a lovely image.

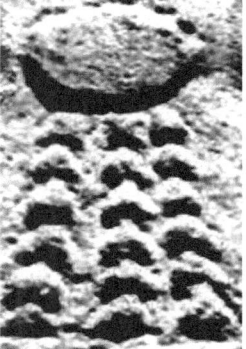

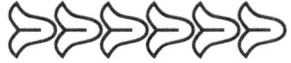

D33:8B Ptolemy VIII
D33:8T Iwaennetjerwyperwy setepenptah Irmaatenra sekhemankhamen
Ptolemaios Euergetes II Tryphon

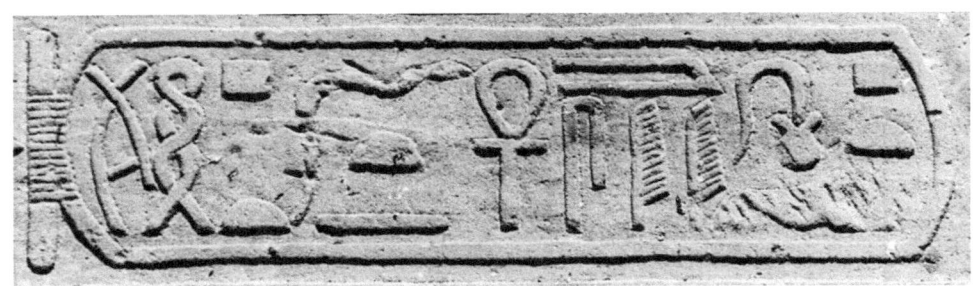

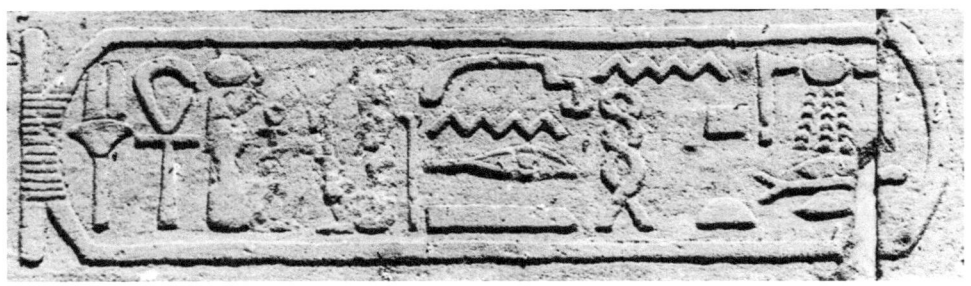

Q3	X1	V4	E23	Aa15	M17a	S29	S34	
□	⌒			⌒				
P	T	O	L(e)	M	(a)y	(o)S	Ankh	Djet

U6	
Mery	Pᴛᴀʜ

F44	N35	R8	N6		
	〰				
Iwa	(en)	Netjerwy	Perwy	Setepen	PTAH

D4	aa11	C2	S42	S34	C12
Ir	Maat(en)	RA	Sekhem	Ankh	AMEN

CLAYTON wavers, or maybe "wearies" is a better word, on Ptolemies VIII, IX and X. He gives their THRONE NAME cartouches but does not offer a TRANSLITERATION, that is, writing them out in Latin letters. QUIRKE leaves VIII, IX and X out altogether (Ptolemies VII and XI did not have cartouches). I will base my transliterations for VIII, IX and X on VON BECKERATH (PP 119-121).

 /Ra/ *Sun with rays*, treated in the entry for Ptolemy VI, D33:6T

 This cartouche looks just like that of Ptolemy VI, but VI often features the *beetle* /Khepri/ (L8).

Let me note that there seems to be disagreement on the order of the last two gods in some of these cartouches. Is it /Irmaaten *Ra*, sekhem ankh *Amen*/ or /Irmaaten *Amen*, sekhem ankh *Ra*?/

D33:9B Ptolemy IX
D33:9T Iwaennetjermenkh netjeretmeretmutes
nedjetsetepenptah Irmaatenra sekhemankhamen
Ptolemaios Philometor Soter II

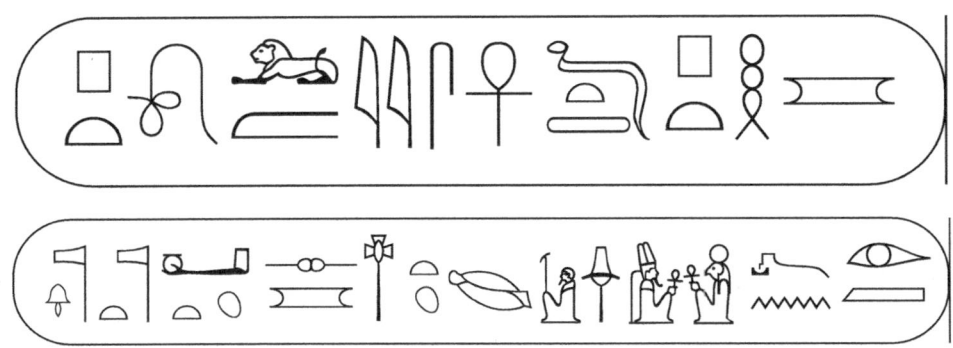

Q3	X1	V4	E23	Aa13	M17a	S29	S34		U6	
P	T	O	L(e)	M	(a)y	(o)S	Ankh	Djet	Mery	P**TAH**

F44	R8	U22		N36	D39	O34
Iwa(en)	Netjer	Menkh	Netjeret	Mer(et)	Mut	S

Continued on next page

Continued from previous page

Aa27		Cx6	D4	aa11	C2
⚑	～	👤	👁	▱	👤
Nedjet	Setep-en	Pᴛᴀʜ	Ir	Maat(en)	Rᴀ

S42	S34	C12
⚚	☥	👤
Sekhem	Ankh	Aᴍᴇɴ

(D39) *Arm holding a /Nu/ pot* (W24), probably of wine or milk. This is a silent determinative meaning *offering*. Pharaohs are seen in statues and reliefs offering one in each hand to various gods. Vᴏɴ Bᴇᴄᴋᴇʀᴀᴛʜ (ᴘ 120) transliterates this /Mut(es)/.

/Nedj/ (Aa27) This unidentified object is part of a number of words, including to *ask, protect, greet* and *counsel.*

Gᴀᴜᴛʜɪᴇʀ (ᴠᴏʟ 4 ᴘ 346) states that the THRONE NAME of Ptolemy IX, whom he calls Ptolemy X, by the way, includes the phrases *héritier au dieu Euergète, aimé de sa mère la déesse Éuergète, vengeur, Heir of the God Euergetes (Benefactor), Beloved of his Mother the Goddess Euergetes, the Avenger.*

The group on the left, below, means, for some reason, *Beloved of his Mother.* In other versions of the cartouche it is replaced with the *vulture* /Mut/(G14), right, which is a more commonly seen sign for *mother* (Gᴀᴜᴛʜɪᴇʀ ᴠᴏʟ 4 ᴘ 360; ᴠᴏɴ Bᴇᴄᴋᴇʀᴀᴛʜ ᴘ 292).

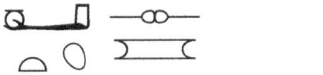
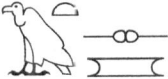

D33:10B Ptolemy X
D33:10T Iwaennetjermenkh netjeretmenkhetsatra
setepenptah Irmaatenra senenankhenamen
Alexander I

Q3	X1	V4	E23	Aa15	M17a	S29	I10	U33	W24	Z7
□	⌒	⋔	⚊	𓏺𓏺	⌐	⟋	⌑	○	⌒
P	T	O	L(e)	M	(a)y	(o)S	J	T	Nu	U

M17	D21	V31	S29	S3	D46	D21	O34
⎩	⬯	⌣	⌐	𓈖	⬯	⬯	—⊙—
A	R(e)	K	S(a)	N	D	R(o)	S

S34		U6	
⚲	🐍	⚒	⚖
Ankh	Djet	Mery	PTAH

The **BIRTH NAME** contains the delightful surprise *Alexander* embedded in it, all spelled out in simple hieroglyphs! Only the /N/, the red crown, is a bit unusual.

 Other versions of this cartouche use this *blossom* instead of the mouth sign for the /R/ *and* the /L/ in *Alexander*. Not listed in **GARDINER**, **PETTY** calls it (M85).

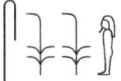 /Senen/ means *image*. The *mummy*, or here, *statue*, serves as a silent **DETERMINATIVE** for that word.

F44	N35	R8	U22		U22	
⬭	〰	⚑	⚒	⚑	⚒	⚙⊙
Iwa	(en)	Netjer	Menkh	Netjeret	Menkhet	Sat-RA

		D4	aa11	C2	S29	M23
𓃀〰	⚖	⬮	⚊	🧍	⌐	𓇓
Setepen	PTAH	Ir	Maat(en)	RA	S	(S)enen?

A53	S33	S3	C12
🧍	⚲	𓈖	✋
-	Ankh	(e)N	AMEN

D33:12B Ptolemy XII
D33:12T Iwaenpanetjer entynehem setepenptah Irmaatenra sekhemankhamen

Ptolemaios Neos Dionysos

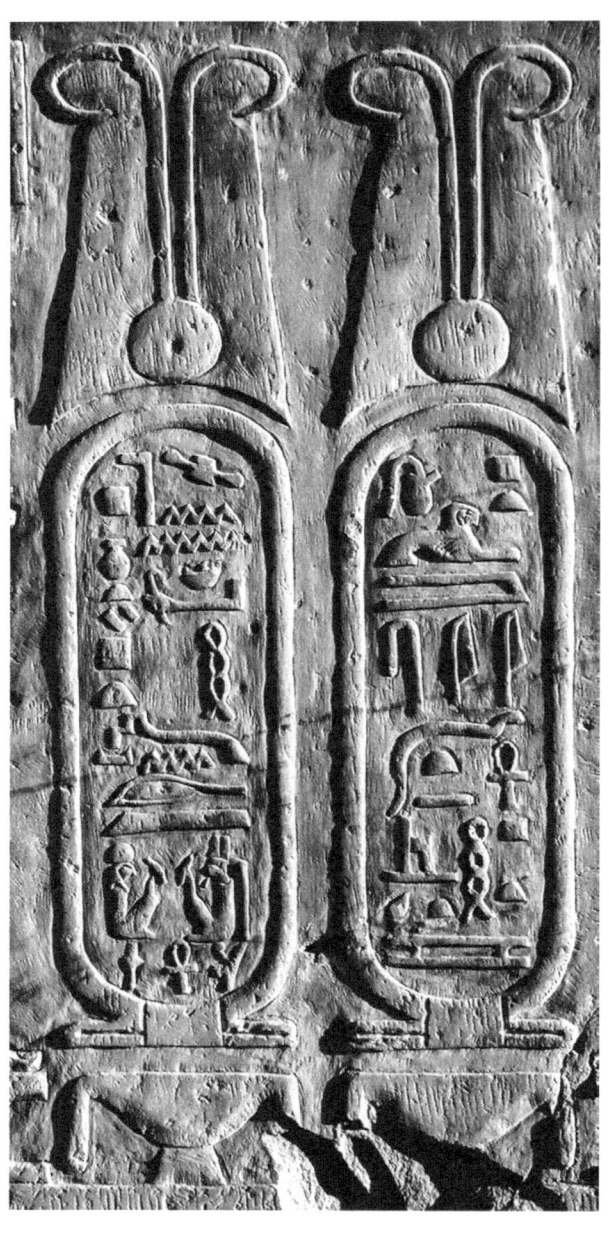

Cartouche, right

Q3	X1	V4	E23	Aa13	M17a	S29
P	T	O	L(e)	M	(a)y	(o)S

	S34			N36			
	Ankh	Djet		Mery	Ptah	Eset	

Cartouche, left

F44	N35	Q3	R8	W24	X1	Z4	N41	D40
Iwa	en	P(a)	Netjer	(e)N	T	Y	Nehem	-

		D4	Aa11	S3	N5
Setepen	Ptah	Ir	Maat	(e)N	Ra

	S42	S34	C12
	Sekhem	Ankh	Amen

This is a variation on /Eset/, the *goddess Isis*, represented by the *throne* (Q1), *loaf* (X1), and *egg* (H8). The *egg* sign, (H8), as seen with Nitocrit, D26, can be a **DETERMINATIVE** for *goddess*.

Ptolemaic Queens

The fifteen Ptolemies had their queens, of course, many of whom had their names written in cartouches. With these women, the Ptolemaic monotony is broken by each assuming one of *three different* names: Berenice, Arsinoë, and Cleopatra. There are several of each, and their spellings can vary a bit. What is confusing about these queens is the habit the Ptolemies had of marrying their sisters, stepmothers, nieces, cousins and half-sisters—"their sisters and their cousins, whom they reckon up by dozens, and their aunts!"—to paraphrase Gilbert and Sullivan. Married them and often killed them, as well. They invented Byzantine intrigue 600 years before the Byzantines were invented.

Here are two versions of each of these queens' names. They are easy and short, but with no corresponding **THRONE NAMES**, except for Cleopatra VII, it is hard to tell them apart by the names alone. More on these later:

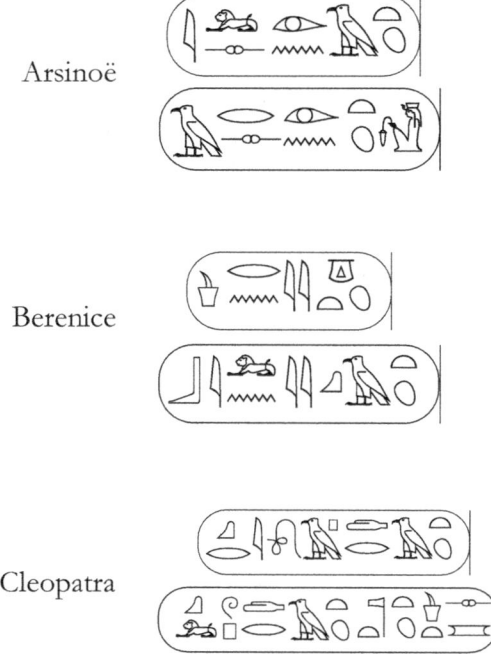

Arsinoë

Berenice

Cleopatra

Ptolemaic Writing

As I mentioned before, the Ptolemaic kings used more or less standard phonetic letters and phrases in their cartouches, even though they did multiply epithets and titles.

Outside the cartouches, however, the carved Ptolemaic temple inscriptions displayed an explosion of unusual phonetic signs, all derived from earlier forms. According to FAIRMAN (PP 56-57), PTOLEMAIC WRITING was characterized by an "increase in the signs in common use and in the values they could bear…, a big increase in the number of ideograms and in the number of determinatives that are used as ideograms and phonograms…(and) the deliberate employment of a variety of alternatives for known signs, values and spellings."

GAUDARD (P 173) describes PTOLEMAIC WRITING as "…the script employed by the scribes of Egyptian temples after the conquest of Egypt by Alexander the Great until the end of the second century AD." In other words, temple writing under the auspices of the Roman emperors is included in PTOLEMAIC WRITING, even though the actual Ptolemaic rulers were all dead by then.

I bring this up here because these hieroglyph variants begin to show up in the Ptolemaic queens' names, opposite.

Rather than give BREAKOUTS for these names, I will treat this phenomenon and explain some of the signs in the section dealing with Roman names.

To tell the truth, I just stumbled upon FAIRMAN's paper as I undertook the final proofreading of the *Field Guide*. He explained what was going on with the crazy Roman spellings. I was happy to see that my deductions on the readings of the unusual signs were mostly correct.

D33:13B Cleopatra VII
Philopator

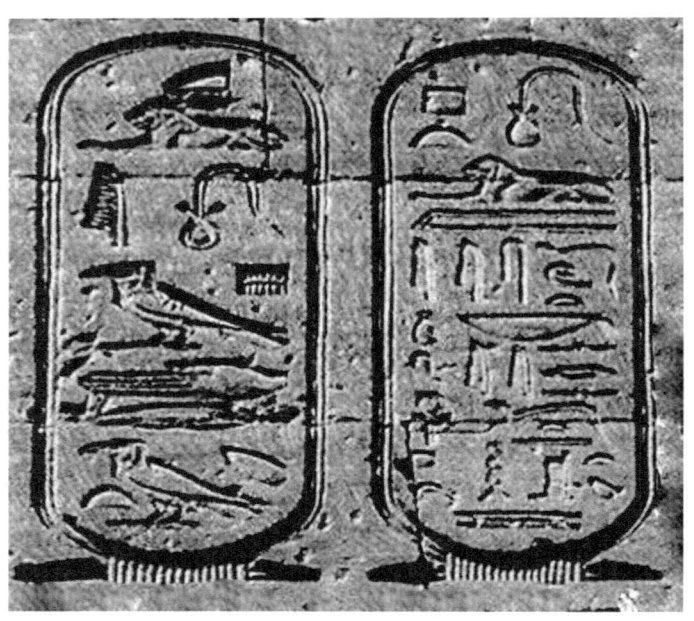

Cleopatra VII is *the* Cleopatra. I once took my four-year-old granddaughter to an exhibit on Cleopatra, but it consisted of nothing but paintings of the queen pressing the asp to her bare bosom. Needless to say, neither of us cared much for the exhibit. Her cartouche is pictured above (left) with that of her son, Ptolemy XV Caesarion (right, see next entry).

Cartouche, left

N29	E23	M17	V4	Q3	G1	D46	D21	G1	X1	H8
Q	L	I	O	P	A	T	R	A	T	-

⊂▭ *hand*, normally /D/, is used here to write /T/.

D33:13cB Ptolemy XV
D33:13cT Iwapanetjer entynehem Sepetenptah Irmaatenra Sekhemankhamen
Kaisar(os), Caesarion

Ptolemy XV was the son of Cleopatra VII and Julius Caesar, and was named after him. As such, for our purposes he serves as sort of a bridge between the Ptolemies and the Romans.

His **BIRTH NAME** cartouche may contain the title *Caesar (Kaisaros)*, or else the title can be placed in a separate cartouche, as below left, on this page.

The title *Caesar* began as a name specific to Julius Caesar's family, but evolved to mean *emperor*. The word survives into modern times as Kaiser and Czar. It was pronounced in Latin something like Kaisar.

BREAKOUT on next page

Here is the breakout for the two-part Ptolemy XV COMBINED CARTOUCHE, shown to the right of Cleopatra VII's entry (D11:13) on page 182. It combines the names and EPITHETS of *Ptolemy* and *Caesar, living forever, beloved of Ptah and Isis.*

Q3	X1	V4	E23	G17	M17a	S29
□	⌓	🐍	🦁	🦅	⸗⸗	⌐
P	T	O	L(e)	M	(a)Y	(o)S

V31	M17a	S29	E23	O34	S34		N36		
⌣	⸗⸗	⌐	🦁	⚊	☥	🐍	⚌	📿	🔱
K(a)	(a)y	S(a)	R(o)	S	Ankh	Djet	Mer(y)	Pᴛᴀʜ	Eꜱᴇᴛ

Below are the same names of *Ptolemy* and *Caesar, living forever, beloved of Ptah and Isis*, divided into two separate cartouches and shown under the entry for Ptolemy XV (D11:13cB), page 183. Both Ptolemy and Caesar show minor variations in spelling.

Q3	X1	V4	E23	Aa13	M17a	S29	I10		
□	⌓	🐍	🦁	▭	⸗⸗	⌐	🐍	⌓℮	⊙℮
P	T	O	L(e)	M	(a)Y	(o)S	Dj(et)	Tu?	Nu?

V31	M17a	S29	S34		N36		
⌣	⸗⸗	⊜	☥	🐍	⚌	📿	🔱
K(a)	(a)y	S(a)R(o)S	Ankh	Djet	Mer(y)	Pᴛᴀʜ	Eꜱᴇᴛ

Complete **THRONE NAME** of Ptolemy XV (no photo)

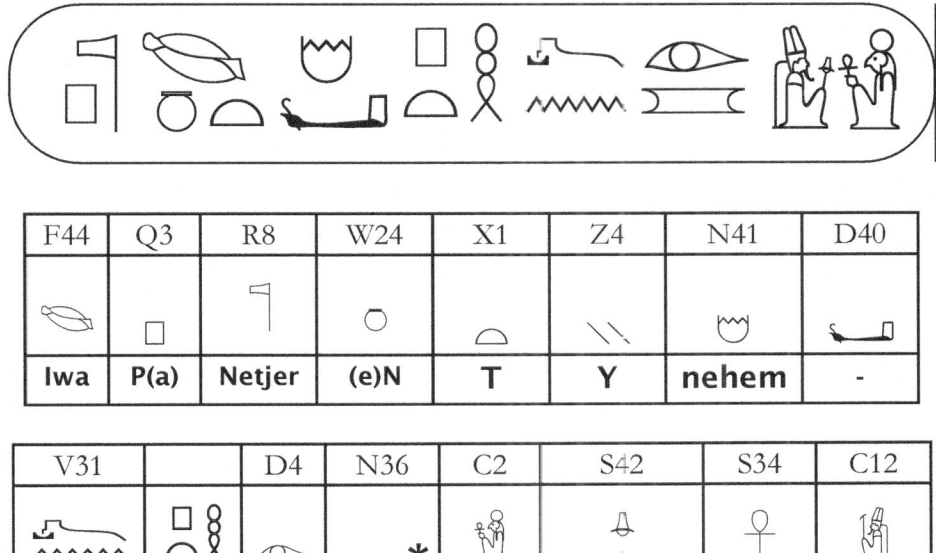

F44	Q3	R8	W24	X1	Z4	N41	D40
Iwa	P(a)	Netjer	(e)N	T	Y	nehem	-

V31		D4	N36	C2	S42	S34	C12
Setepen	PTAH	Ir	(Maat)	RA	Sekhem	Ankh	AMEN

* /Mer/, in the **THRONE NAME** above, seems to be an ancient "typographical error" for the /Maat/ *platform.*

should be

Ptolemy XV's **THRONE NAME** does not seem to have been used very much—I've never seen it in person. The **THRONE NAME** cartouche is interesting in that the last phrase, Sekhemankhamen, *Living image of Amun,* **(CLAYTON P 213)** rather than each sign being written separately, has the *sekhem* scepter (left) and the *ankh* signs held in *Amen's* and *Ra's* hands respectively instead of standing alone

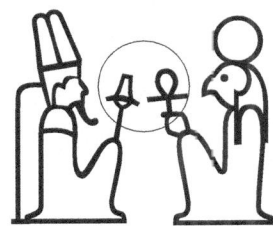

Alternate Phonetic Symbols

Here is an exercise where you can decipher *some* of the phonetic signs favored by the **GRECO-ROMANS**. I'm going to leave out the supplied *e* in this exercise, so each letter will be represented by one sign. The Greek endings will be included. Not all spelling variations are shown.

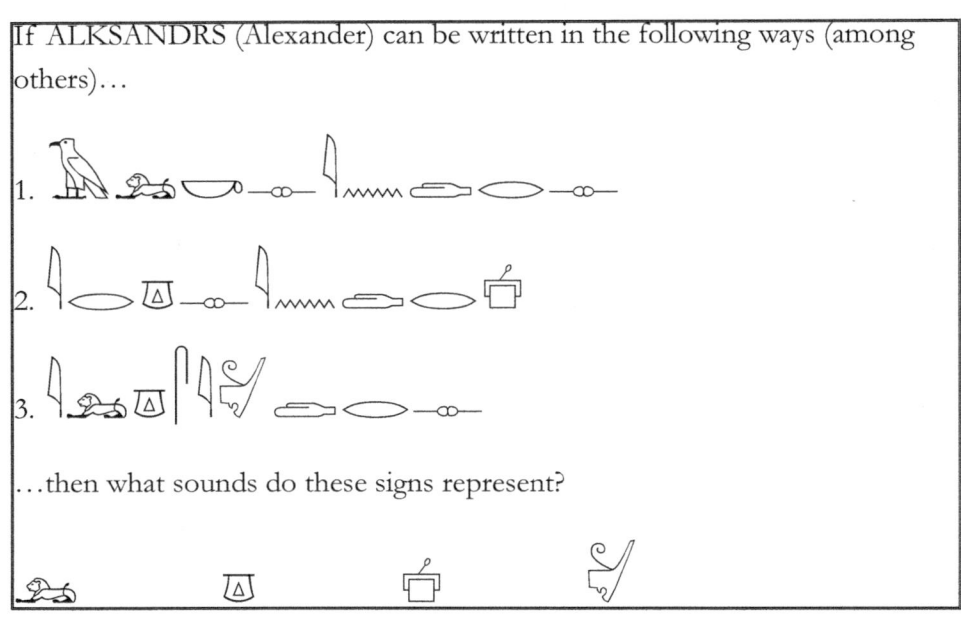

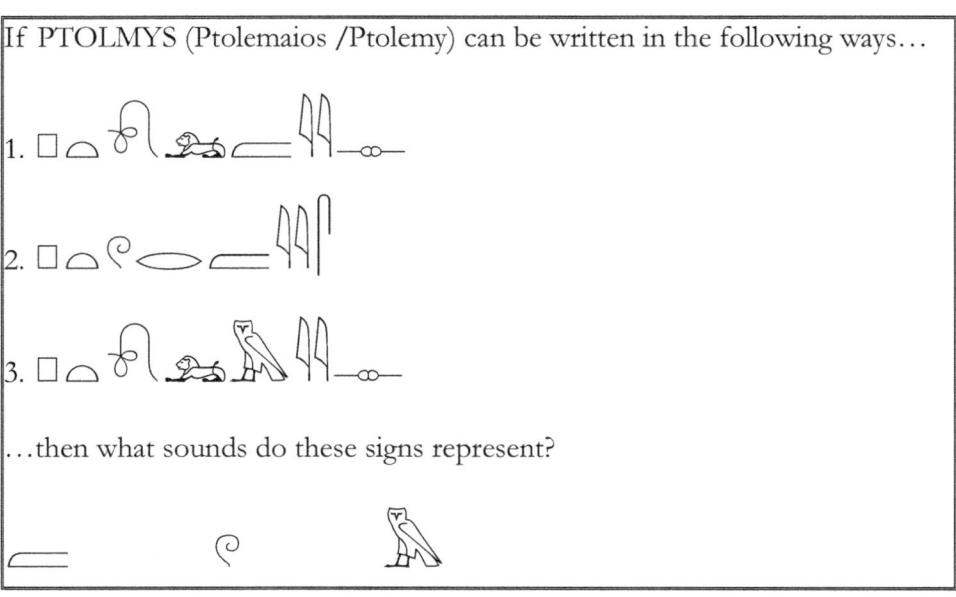

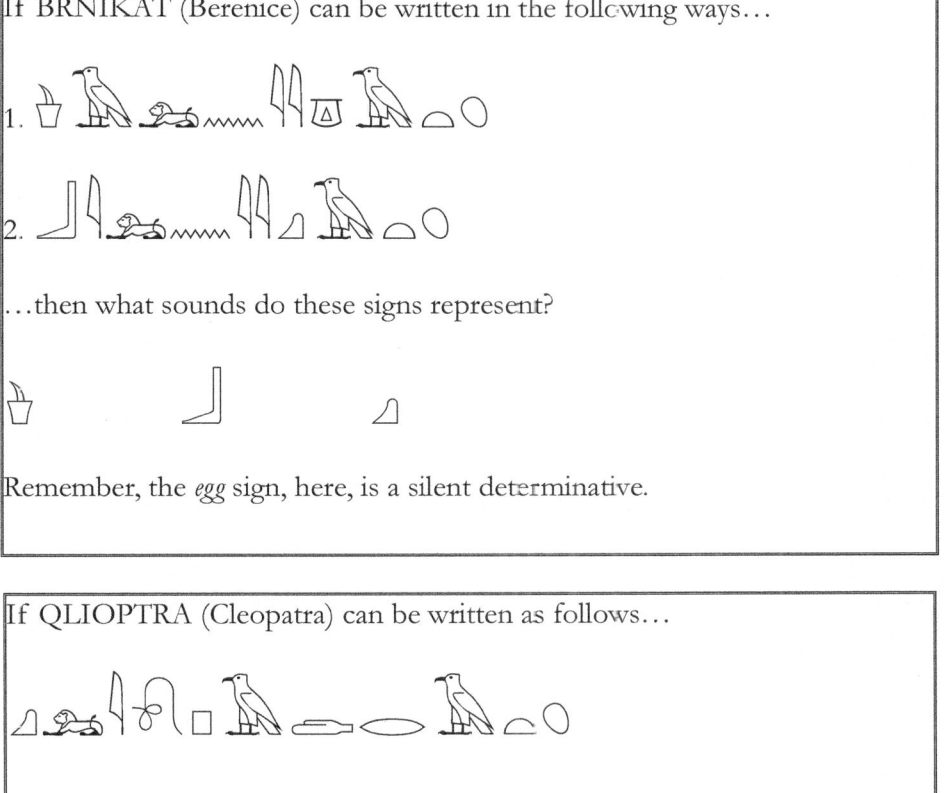

If BRNIKAT (Berenice) can be written in the following ways...

1. [hieroglyphs]

2. [hieroglyphs]

...then what sounds do these signs represent?

[hieroglyph]   [hieroglyph]   [hieroglyph]

Remember, the *egg* sign, here, is a silent determinative.

If QLIOPTRA (Cleopatra) can be written as follows...

[hieroglyphs]

...then what sound does [hieroglyph] represent? (Note: it's normally *d*)

If ARSINAT (Arsinoë) can be written as follows...

[hieroglyphs]

...then what sound does [hieroglyph] represent? (Hint: oddly enough, it's a vowel).

Remember these signs. We will see them used extensively by the Roman emperors.

Roman Emperors
"Dynasty 34"

Roman names being so obnoxious, it has been suggested that I end the *Field Guide* with Ptolemy XV. Some of my best sources assert that the scope of their work ends with "the last native pharaoh, Nectanebo II in 343 BC…" (**Clayton p 217**), but to me that would be cheating. Some of the books that skip over the Romans *do* address the Ptolemaic dynasty (as well as non-native Libyan and Persian rulers); **Rose (pp 140-142)** gives just a smattering of Greco-Roman Rulers' names. The *Field Guide's* purpose is to allow novices to read and identify commonly-seen cartouches. If that includes Roman cartouches, then I will present Roman cartouches.

Von Beckerath lists the names of over 40 Roman emperors who ruled Egypt. The Greek barbarians who were the Ptolemies (I imagine that is how they were regarded by the native priests and scholars), wrote their names in a way that conformed, more or less, to standards that went back to the pyramid builders. Yes, they favored a few different phonetic symbols and were gluttons for epithets and titles, but the names are mostly readable, translatable and standardized.

The Romans are another kettle of fish. First of all, even at home in Rome, their names and titles shape-shifted through time and space. Nicknames turned into permanent family names; titles and names were reused. Adding further confusion, an emperor's conquests were sometimes added to his name.

Augustus adopted the titles "…*Imperator Caesar*," which "…became standard nomenclature for all subsequent Roman emperors up to the fourth century AD." (**Scarre p 17**). *Autokrator* became the standard Greek translation of *Imperator (***Kazhdan p 235)**.

Appropriately enough, there is a species of butterfly found in Afghanistan and Tajikistan called Parnassius *autocrator*. The Wikipedia article illustrates ten varieties of this butterfly, all with slightly varying colors, patterns, and sizes. In the same way, the Roman rulers of Egypt spelled *Autocrator*, as well as *Caesar*, in at least that many ways. The variations in "spelling" would cross a third-grade teacher's eyes.

I was at a loss as to why this is. I thought it went back to my supposition that most of these emperors knew or cared next to nothing about Egypt and its culture, religion and history beyond their economic and strategic value. It seemed to me that those who fashioned the names of these Roman pharaohs were either semi-literate in ancient Egyptian or were gripped by a need for innovation. My last-minute discovery of two papers on **PTOLEMAIC WRITING**, mentioned just prior to Cleopatra VII's entry (D33:13), showed me that the originators of **PTOLEMAIC WRITING** were extremely well-versed in every aspect of hieroglyphic writing from the Old Kingdom on. Why they went crazy with variations is anybody's guess.

My compliments to those scholars who initially figured out how Ptolemaic writing worked and deciphered the Roman cartouches!

I'm going to repeat my Ptolemies exercise, using the titles *Caesar* and *Autocrator*, starting with Ptolemy XV, Caesarion, already treated above. I'm leaving off epithets. It's fun to pick out the signs not seen previously and figure out what sounds they represent:

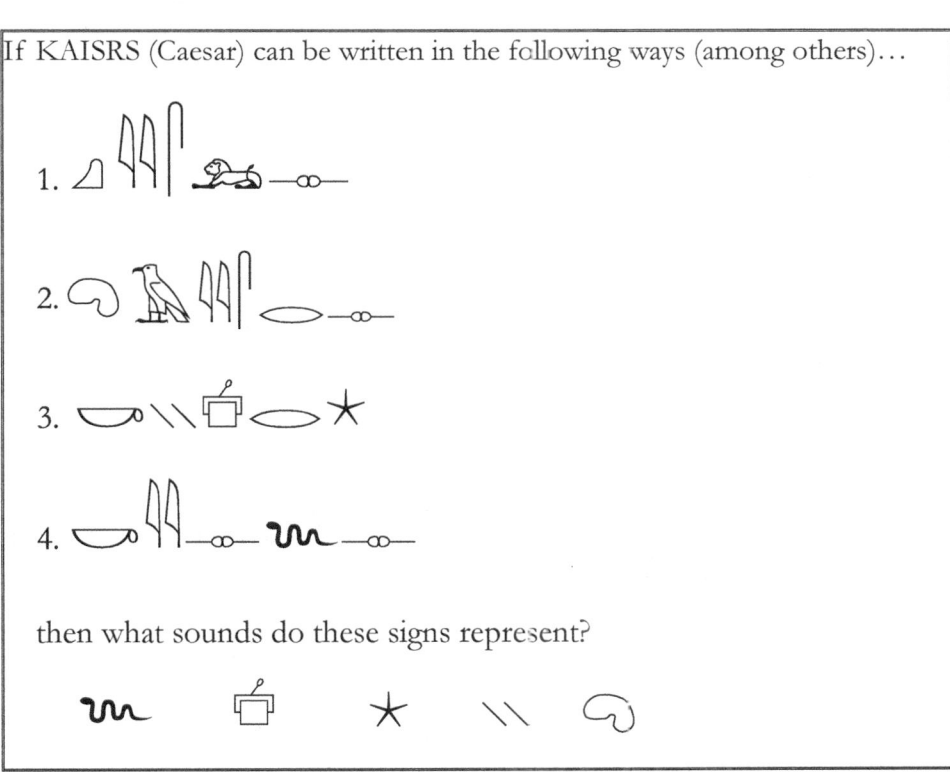

If KAISRS (Caesar) can be written in the following ways (among others)…

1.

2.

3.

4.

then what sounds do these signs represent?

Now try *Autocrator/Autokrator.*

If AUTKRTR (Autocrator) can be written in the following ways...

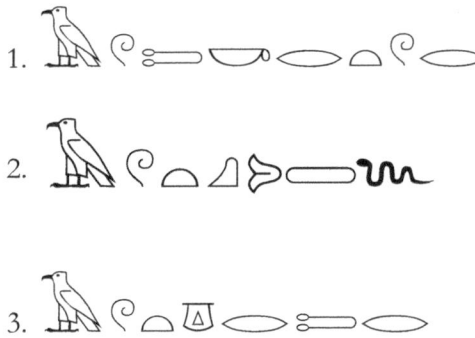

...then what sounds do these signs represent?

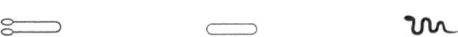

If you did the exercise, you should have no trouble reading the cartouches below. The new hieroglyphs are explained on the next pages, but, I'm sure you are able to figure out their sounds.

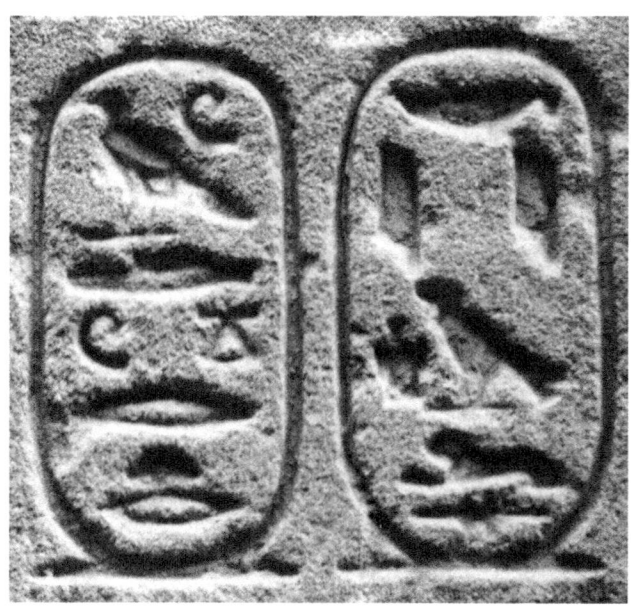

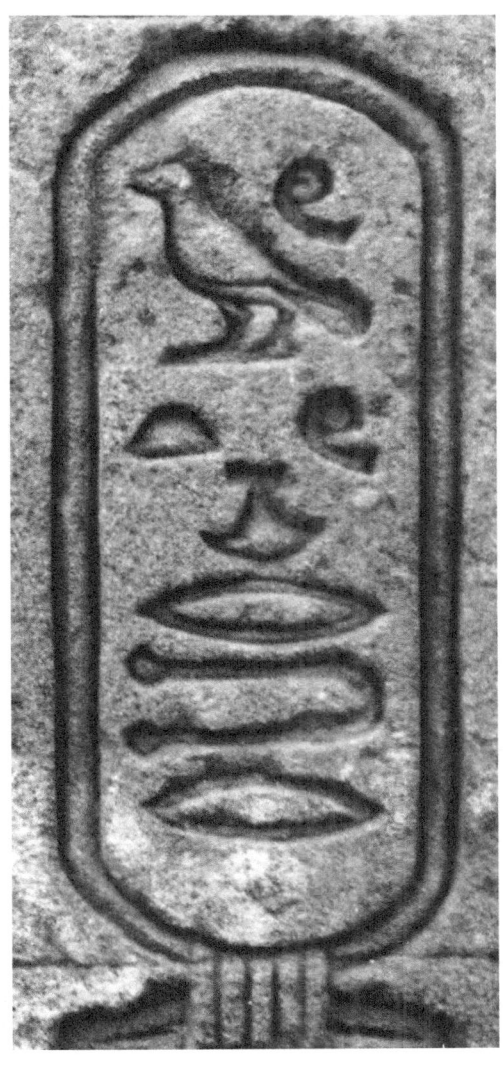

Key to the Exercises

	Sound	Gardiner number	Meaning
	L/R	E23	Lion
	K/G	W11	Jar stand
	S	Aa18	Unidentified object
	N	S3	Red Crown
	M	Aa13	Unidentified object
	U/O	Z7	Rope
	B	R7	Incense burner
	K	N29	Hill
	T/D	D46	Hand
	I/E	D4	Eye
	R	I14	Snake
	S	N14	Star
	Y	Z4	Dual ending

		T	V13	Tether
		T	N18	Sandy Tract
		K	S81*	Head covering
		R	M85**	Flower

* Not listed in **Gardiner**, but cited by **Petty, Hieroglyphic sign list (p 89)** as S81.
** Also omitted from **Gardiner**, cited by **Petty, Hieroglyphic sign list (p 65)** as M85.

D34:1 Caesar Augustus
Imperator Caesar Divi Filius Augustus

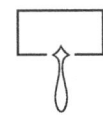

The cartouches of Caesar Augustus are virtually all variations on the *Autocrator* and *Caesar* names we have seen in the preceding exercises. He also used the title /Per Aa/, (O1 + O29) meaning *Great House*. This term came into use in the New Kingdom, and is where we get the title *pharaoh*.

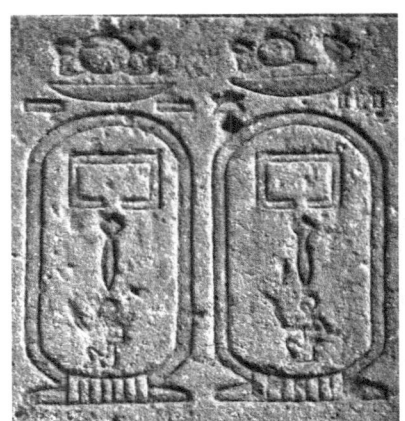

In the photograph, the little seated man following the title is a **DETERMINATIVE**. Although /Per Aa/ in each cartouche is the same, they are surmounted by different late period royal titles.

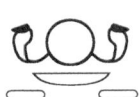
Ra with double *protective cobras.* over /Neb Tawy/, *Lord of the Double Land.*

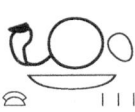
Ra with protective *cobra* and /Sa/ *egg*, meaning *son*, over /Neb Kha-u/, *Son of Ra, Lord of Appearances*

Here is a partial list of the emperors after Caesar Augustus, for whom multiple cartouches exist, numbered according to VON BECKERATH. The "English" spellings and Latin configuration of the names come from SCARRE.

2. **Tiberius** Tiberius Caesar Augustus
3. **Caligula** Gaius Caesar Augustus Germanicus
4. **Claudius** Tiberius Claudius Caesar Augustus Germanicus
5. **Nero** Nero Claudius Caesar Augustus Germanicus
7. **Otho** Imperator Marcus Otho Caesar Augustus
9. **Vespasian** Imperator Caesar Vespasianus Augustus
10. **Titus** Imperator Titus Caesar Vespasianus Augustus
11. **Domitian** Imperator Caesar Domitianus Augustus
12. **Nerva** Imperator Nerva Caesar Augustus
13 **Trajan** Imperator Caesar Divi Nervae Filius Nerva Traianus
14. **Hadrian** Imperator Caesar Traianus Hadrianus Augustus
15. **Antoninus Pius** Imperator Titus Aelius Caesar Hadrianus Antoninus Augustus Pius
16. **Marcus Aurelius** Imperator Caesar Marcus Aurelius Antoninus Augustus
17. **Commodus** Aurelius Commodus Antoninus Augustus

In this section I give what I consider a representative cartouche (written the lazy way, with only front and rear brackets and typing the signs in a line instead of artfully arranging them as the Egyptians would have done), followed by some, not all, "spelling" variations for the main names. I depart from my policy in the first part of *The Field Guide*, in that most of these cartouches are *not* commonly seen on monuments and sculpture. I wish to illustrate the bizarre level of variation in these names, and, mainly, I want to get a better handle on these names myself.

Here are some hieroglyphic variations on the more common names. Note that many of the components of the names above were shared by more than one emperor.

2. Tiberius: Tiberius Caesar Augustus

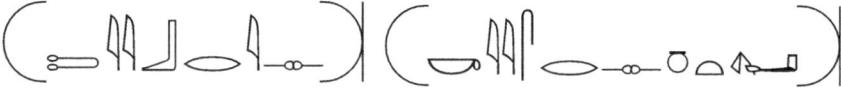

/entykhu/, with its variations, is Augustus rendered into Egyptian.

Here are some variations on *Tiberius*, some used by Tiberius Caesar Augustus (number 2) as well as some used by Claudius, number 4:

3. Caligula: Gaius Caesar Augustus Germanicus. Note that *Caligula* is a nickname meaning *boot*, and is not actually part of the name.

Here is Gaius Caesar Germanicus, with some variations on *Gaius*:

Germanicus was a title originally conferred on emperors who presided over campaigns in Germania, an area in north-central Europe.
Here are some versions of *Germanicus*, used not only by Caligula but by Claudius (number 4), Nero (number 5), and Trajan, number 13.

4. Claudius: Tiberius Claudius Caesar Augustus Germanicus.

This is an example of Tiberius Claudius Caesar, with variations of the name *Claudius*, used also by Nero, number 5:

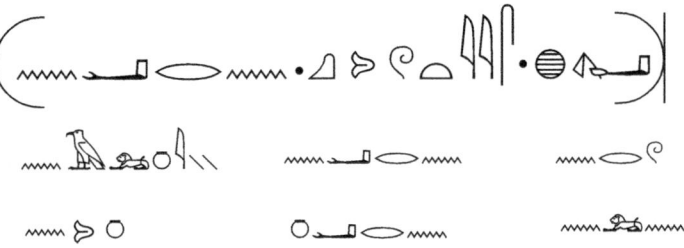

5. Nero: Nero (Neron in Greek) Claudius Caesar Augustus Germanicus

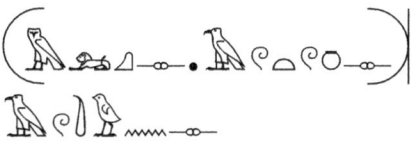

7. Otho: Imperator Marcus Otho Caesar Augustus (seen in genitive case, *Othonis* (GAUTHIER P 77). *Marcus* is used by Marcus Aurelius, number 16, and others not cited here..

9. Vespasian: Imperator Caesar Vespasianus Augustus. *Vespasianus* is also used by Titus, number 10:

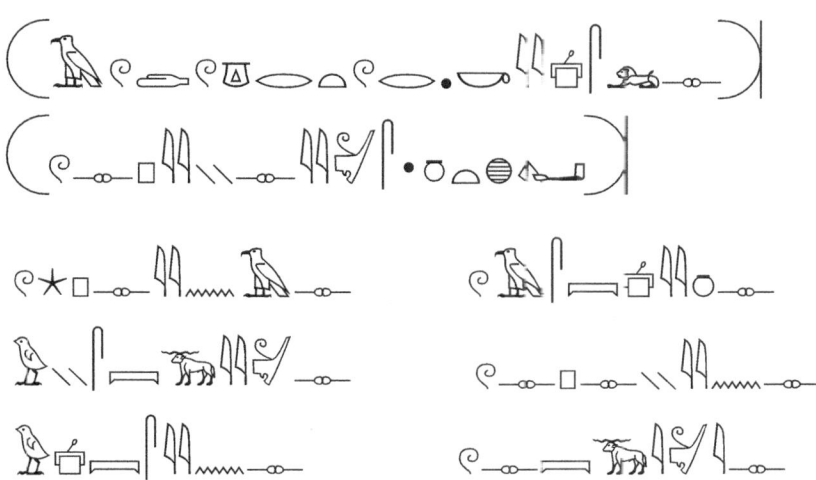

10. Titus Imperator Titus Caesar Vespasianus Augustus. *Titus* is also used by Nerva, 12, and Antoninus Pius, 15)

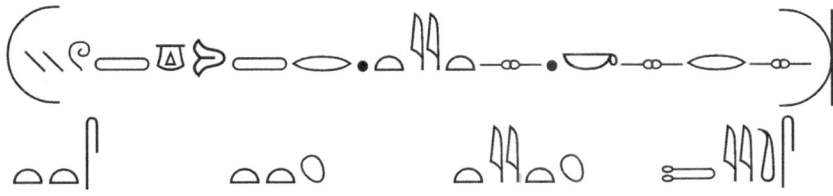

11. Domitian Imperator Caesar Domitianus Augustus. **THRONE NAME** (second line): Hor sa-eset mery-netjeru-nebu (VON BECKERATH P **125**).

Domitian, continued

12. Nerva: Imperator Nerva (Nerouas) Caesar Augustus. *Nerva* is also used by Trajan, number 15

13 Trajan: Imperator Caesar Divi Nervae Filius Nerva Traianus. *Traianus* is also used by Hadrian, number 14)

* Dacicus/Dakikos, after Trajan's Decian victory.

14. Hadrian: Imperator Caesar Traianus Hadrianus Augustus.
Hadrian is used by Antoninus Pius, number 15, as well.

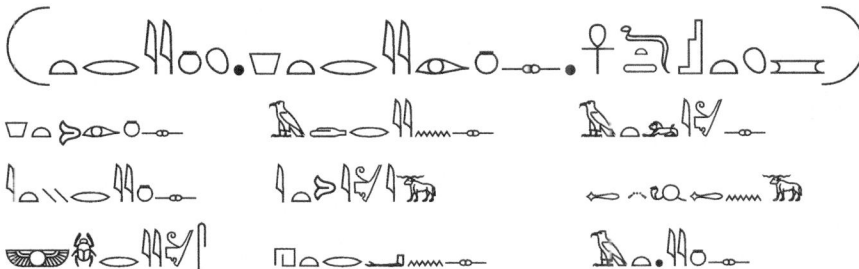

15. Antoninus Pius: Imperator Titus Aelius Caesar Hadrianus Antoninus
Augustus Pius. *Antoninus* is used also by Marcus Aurelius, number 16 and
Commodus, number 17.

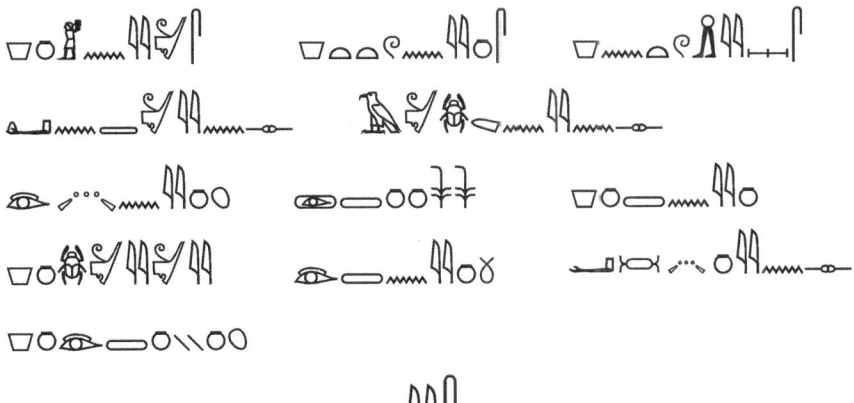

Here are some variations of *Antoninus*.

We get into some tricky business with Antoninus. Just to show that the officials crafting these Roman names were actually thinking in Greek, the terms *Pius* and *Augustus* were not transliterated into hieroglyphs from Latin, but from Greek.

Pius is rendered *Eusebius*, and was used by Caracalla as well.

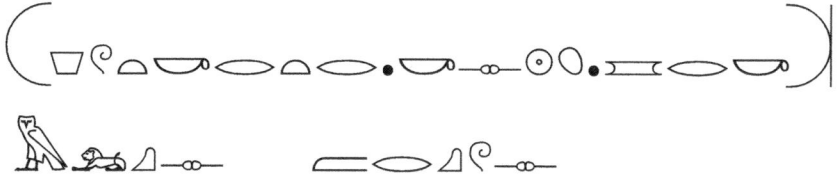

...and *Augustus* is usually translated as *Sebast(os)*.

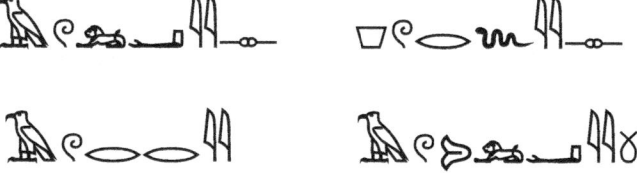

16. Marcus Aurelius: Imperator Caesar Marcus Aurelius Antoninus Augustus. *Aurelius* used also by Commodus, number 17.

Aurelius can be written like this:

17. **Commodus:** (Marcus) Aurelius Commodus Antoninus Augustus

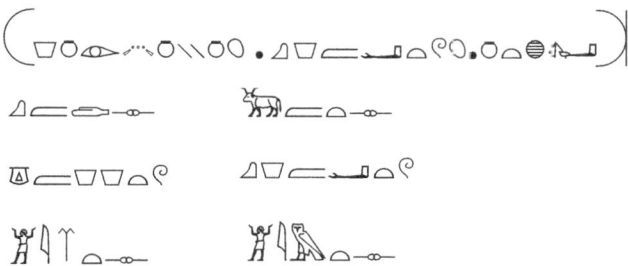

Wennefer

This term means *One who continues to be perfect (***Collier and Manley p 42***)* and refers to the god Osiris. **Wennefer** in a cartouche is often found in conjunction with names or titles of Roman emperors. It is written in two ways, either with a rabbit hieroglyph (E34, actually a *desert hare*), or with what I take to be a stylized flower (not in **Gardiner**).

Wennefer Autocrator Caesar

Photo, left, *Autocrator Caesar*, in two cartouches, with the *flower* version of *Wennefer* in a third. Lower photo, left, three cartouches with *Tiberius Caesar, beloved of Isis, may he live forever; Autocrator*, with the hare version of *Wennefer*.

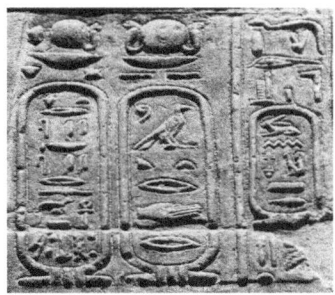

Tiberius Autocrator Wennefer

The signs following *Wennefer* in each case are /Maa Heru/, *true of voice*. In these examples it is written in two different ways (of course!). The first sign, /Maa/, is our familiar /Maat/, written once with the feather and once with the pedastal (A11); /Heru/ is (P8), the oar.

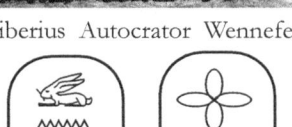

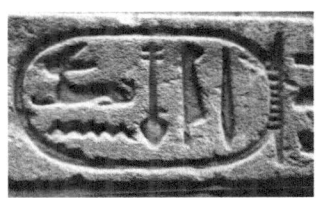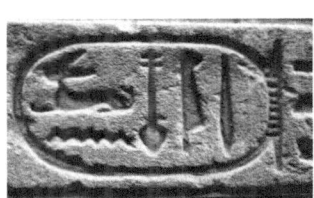

Section II
Cartouche Identification Key

The *Cartouche Identification Key* helps anyone quickly identify almost any cartouche to be found on a monument or statue. No prior knowledge of hieroglyphs is needed. Note that this section includes some less common names and variations not cited earlier in the *Field Guide*.

The *Key* is patterned after a nature field guide to trees, flowers, or birds. In a tree guide, for example, the first page asks you to determine, with the aid of illustrations, whether a tree bears cones and needles, scales, or leaves. If you choose *leaves*, then it next asks you whether the leaves are simple, compound, or fan-shaped. If you choose *fan-shaped*, the guide takes you to the entry for *Ginkgo biloba* (https://www.arborday.org/trees/whattree/). Even with no botanical knowledge, you have identified your tree in two steps. Other trees will take more steps, as you narrow down whether the compound leaves, for instance, are *opposite* or *alternate,* and so on.

How to Use the Key:

The *Cartouche Identification Key* sorts approximately 375 cartouches belonging to about 122 Egyptian royal personages or gods according to what I call *categories*. Each category is represented by one hieroglyph, highlighted in the margin for quick reference. I have chosen these categories as being signs that are unambiguous and easy for any user to recognize, even if the meaning of a given hieroglyph is not immediately apparent. I tend to start with the least common of the signs: thus I avoid using the circular *Ra, sun,* sign, since it occurs in nearly every **THRONE NAME** and is easily mistaken for the round /Kh/ phonetic sign or even the *egg*. I also avoid using signs that occur often in compounds, and personified gods as categories.

Signs that are particularly good discriminators in a given name will be printed in bold script. I use a slash with parentheses to separate alternate, interchangeable signs or groups of signs, and put optional **EPITHETS** in parentheses.

Per the usage throughout the *Field Guide*, the reference number assigned to a cartouche is *D* for *dynasty*, followed the dynasty number, then a sequential number, ending in *B*, for a **BIRTH NAME**, and *T* for a **THRONE NAME**. For example, Ramses II is the third king of the 19th Dynasty, thus **D19:3B** for his **BIRTH NAME**, *Ramses*, and **D19:3T** for the name received when he assumed the throne, *Usermaatra-setepenra*.

Within each dynasty I have chosen to use the numbers assigned by **VON BECKERATH**. This is for consistency and ease of change in the event I add or remove rulers in the future.

In the *Key*, you will be asked whether the cartouche in question contains a given hieroglyph or combination of hieroglyphs. If you find one that matches, you will be directed to a subset of those cartouches, and so on. More instructions and examples will be provided later.

Look at the cartouche you want to identify and ask yourself if it contains one of the signs in *category* number 1. This first *category* contains only one hieroglyph, *three fox skins*, designated F31 by **GARDINER**.

If F31 is part of your cartouche, you are directed to one of eight subcategories, where you will find your identification. If F31 is *not* found in the cartouche, move directly to *category* number 2, and so on. **It is important not to skip ahead. If you don't follow the key in order, it won't work!**

Some tips:

Whenever you try to identify a cartouche, always look for the matching **BIRTH** or **THRONE NAME**, as appropriate. The two names are often, but not always, shown together. There is considerable duplication in both **BIRTH NAMES** and **THRONE NAMES**, so you can only really be sure of your identification when both cartouches are present and match the key.

Shorter cartouches tend to be from earlier dynasties, or earlier in a given dynasty. The builder of the Great Pyramid at Giza went by *Khufu*. The earliest of the eleven *Ramses* names are short and sweet. Their later namesakes' cartouches are much longer and more complicated. The same goes for the Ptolemies (Dynasty 33) and the Roman emperors (Dynasty 34) in the *Field Guide*.

Some very long cartouches may have both **THRONE NAME** and **BIRTH NAME** inside the same cartouche. Try separating them. Occasionally titles and epithets are included inside the cartouches. If you recognize a title, try taking it out and keying the cartouche again. Note that epithets, especially in the New Kingdom, are very changeable.

Let's say you are trying to identify this pair of cartouches:

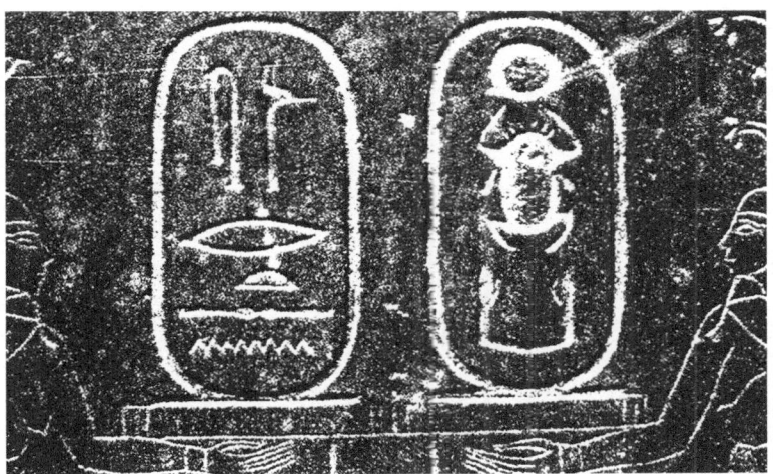

We can start with either of these, but let's start with the one on the right. It has fewer hieroglyphs and they are very distinct

Go to the **ID KEY HOME** spread, (page 212, but look at the example on the next page) where the *categories* are listed and numbered. Look at the *categories* in order, top to bottom. **Do not skip ahead!**

ID KEY

1. ⚝

2. ⚝

3. 🐾   Mammals and parts of mammals, excluding 𓃬

4. ✕

5. 𓏶 ⬅

6. 🪲

7. 🐟

8. ♀

9. ▱

10. ⌐

11. Ⴖ

12. 𓃬

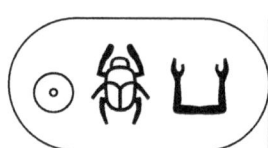

The cartouche in question does not include category 1, ⚝ ,
so skip to category 2.

HOME

13. 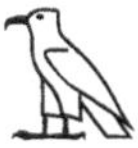 Any bird, at least one bird of any type

14.

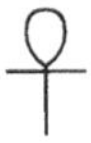

15.

16.

17. 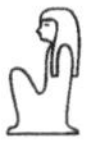 Human figures, anthropomorphic gods

18.

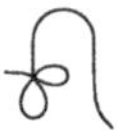

19. 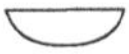 Containers

20. 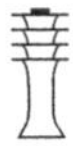 Tall and thin signs

21. 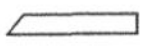 Low, wide signs

Category 2, 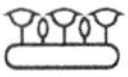 , is not present, either. Likewise, category 3, 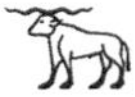 (any mammal or certain parts of mammals, excluding 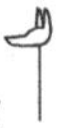 , which is a category in itself. Skip category 4, 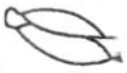 , also.

We finally find what we are looking for in category 5, .

Next step, using the bar in the right margin as a guide, proceed to category 5, the upraised arms.

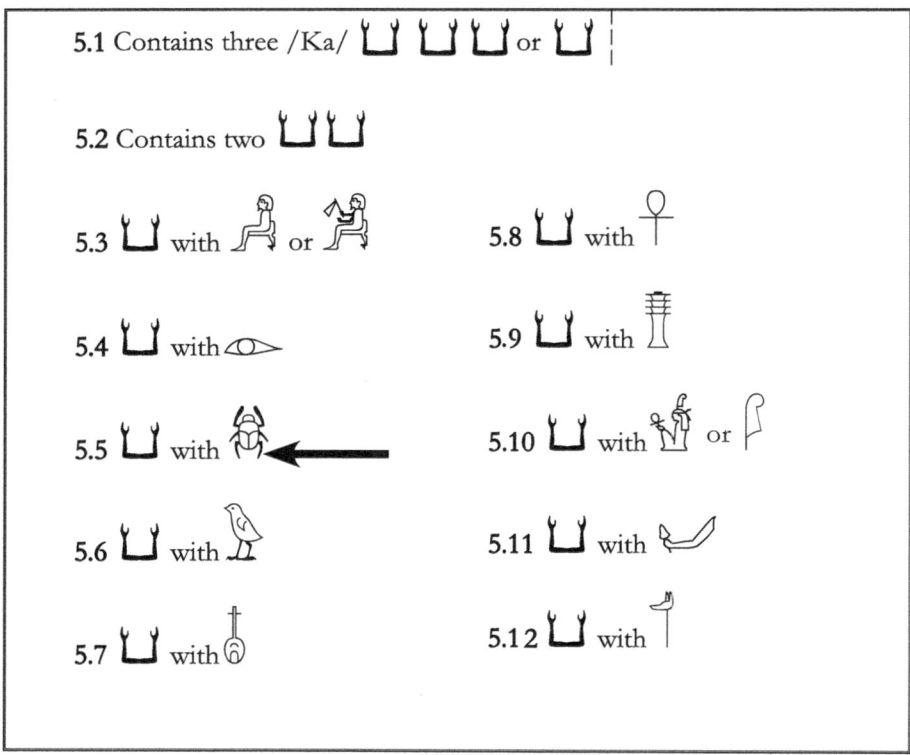

Category 5 includes 12 subcategories. A quick glance shows that our cartouche fits in subcategory 5.5, *upraised arms* with the *beetle*.

Proceeding to subcategory 5.5, we find our cartouche. There are two kings with this **THRONE NAME**. Looking at the adjoining **BIRTH NAME**s, we can identify our cartouche with *Senusret I Kheperkara*.

In the Key, the cartouche you are looking for is always the one in the left column. The one on the right is the associated BIRTH or THRONE NAME.

Remember, the numbers D12:2T and D12:2B refer to *Dynasty 12, the second king,* and *T* for **THRONE NAME** and *B* for **BIRTH NAME**.

Go back to this king in Section I of the *Field Guide* to see another photograph of the cartouches, comments on hieroglyphs found in the names in question, and a **BREAKOUT** of the pronunciation order of the signs.

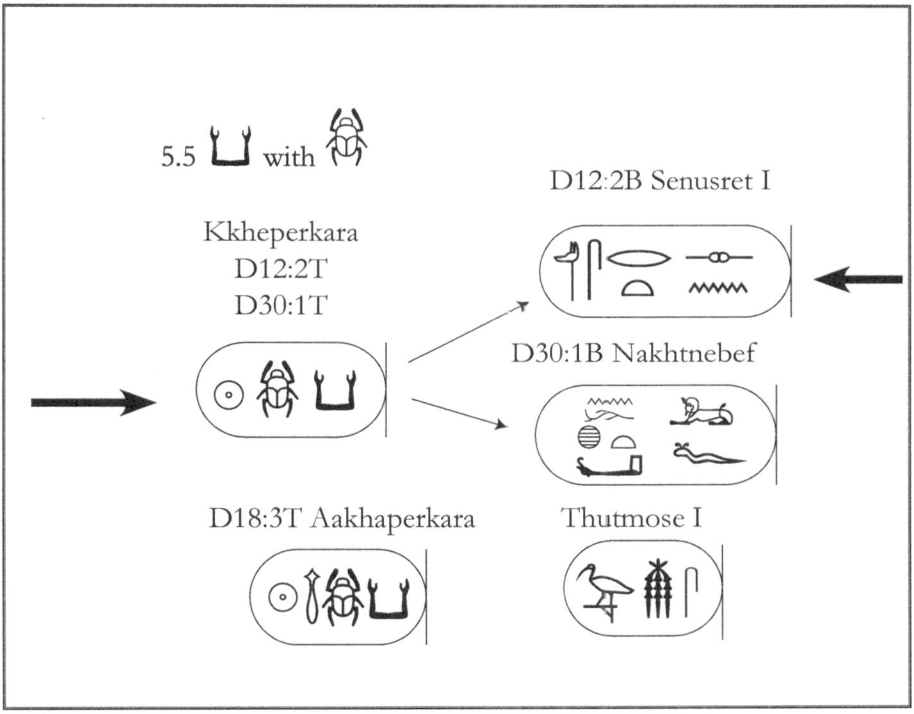

5.5 ⊔ with 🪲

Kkheperkara
D12:2T
D30:1T

⊙ 🪲 ⊔

D12:2B Senusret I

D30:1B Nakhtnebef

D18:3T Aakhaperkara

⊙ 🪲 ⊔

Thutmose I

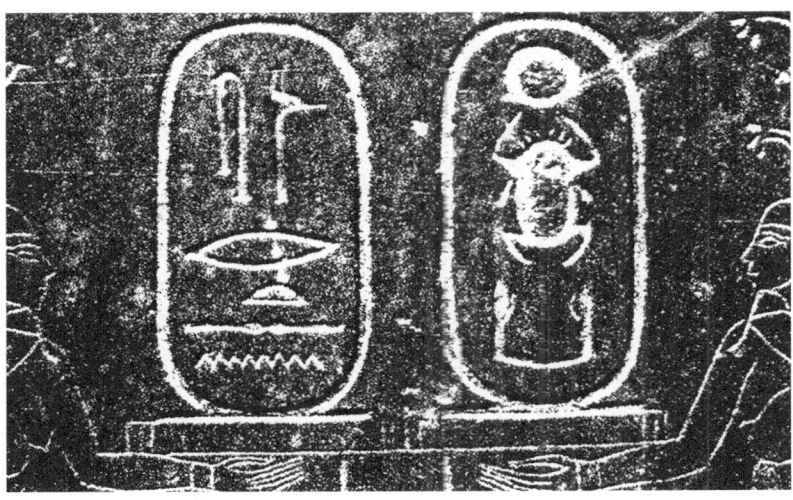

Let's try another pair of mystery cartouches. We can choose either one, but I'm going to go with the one on the left. Scan down the vertical list of *categories*. Yes, there are a lot of them, but, assuming the signs are clear, it should be easy to run down the list until you reach *category 13*, *birds*. As in the last example, *category 13* comprises several *sub-categories*, namely six different types of birds. Even if birds are not your thing, I dare say that most toddlers can tell a chick from an owl from a hawk.

The mystery cartouche contains a hawk, *sub-category 13.4*

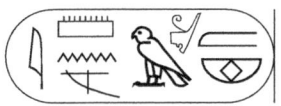 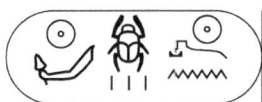

Glance down *category 13.4* until you find the cartouche on the left. I help by highlighting signs to look for. In this case, there is only one hawk cartouche with the alabaster basin. Double check the other cartouche associated with it, and it does indeed include the beetle and arm holding a *wand*. You can be sure you are looking at cartouches of Horemheb Djeserkheperura, fourteenth king of Dynasty 18, in Section I.

Go back to Horemheb, D18:14, in Section I for more details about this pair of cartouches.

As I have mentioned before, the writing of pharaohs' names was never standardized. Signs are added, omitted, or substituted for each other and different gods or place names are included depending on political and religious tides. That is why I highlight important signs which are *likely* to remain constant between different cartouches of the same individual. If those important signs are present, and both cartouches, where you have both, reasonably match, you have solved your riddle.

The *Field Guide* and *Key* do not begin to include every variation. For a much more complete list see *The Names of the Kings of Egypt* by **Johnson and Petty.**

Unfortunately, I am forced to exclude the Romans from the Key. They are much too unruly, although I do include most of the hieroglyphs they used in the sign lists at the end of the book.

Remember, when reading a cartouche in an inscription, read *toward* any animals' or humans' faces, reading toward the *bar* at the end of the cartouche. Most of the time, in using the key, the direction you read is not important, although some categories specify "the first hieroglyph or sign in the cartouche."

Read toward the animals' or gods' faces and toward the bar.

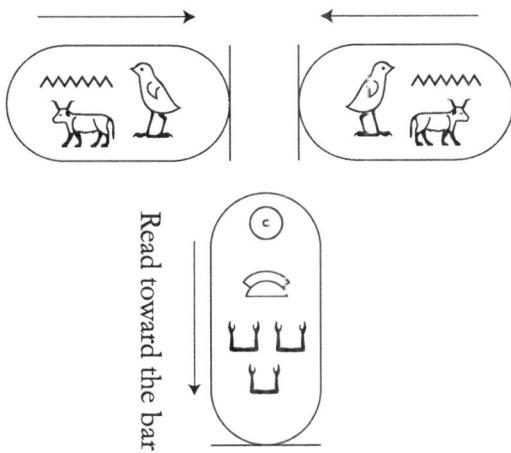

In the Cartouche Identification Key all hieroglyphs are printed from left to right, as in English.

( ) indicate optional signs;

/ separates possible variations

Please remember that every variation of every name is *not* shown.

The *Cartouche Identification Key* begins on the next page.

Cartouche Identification Key
HOME
See instructions on preceding pages

1.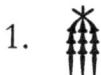

2.

3. Mammals and parts of mammals, excluding

4.

5.

6.

7.

8.

9.

10.

11.

12.

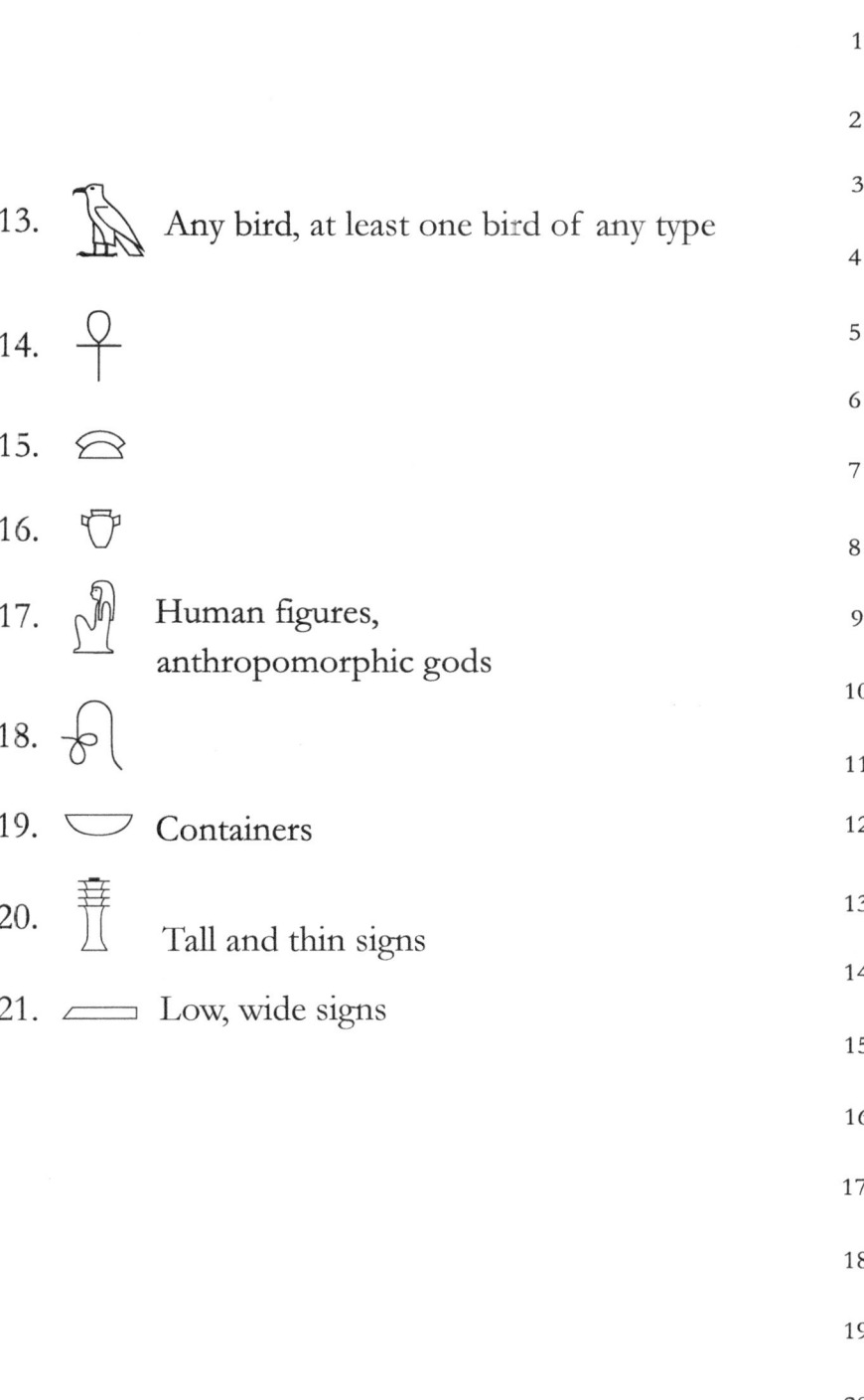

13. Any bird, at least one bird of any type

14.

15.

16.

17. Human figures, anthropomorphic gods

18.

19. Containers

20. Tall and thin signs

21. Low, wide signs

1

2

3

4

5

6

7

8

9

10

11

12

13

14

15

16

17

18

19

20

21

Cartouche Identification Key

1. 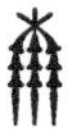 𓏠 /Mos/ or Mes/ (F31) *Three fox skins; birth*. This sign was introduced with D17:15B (Dynasty 17, king number 15, birth name). It is used in many important kings' names.

If the cartouche contains both 𓏠 *and* 𓂀 or 𓂀 go to **1.1**

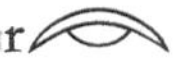

If the cartouche contains both 𓏠 *and* 𓅓 go to **1.2**

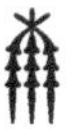

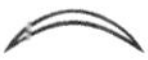

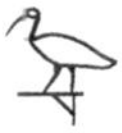

If the cartouche contains both 𓏠 *and* 𓏌 go to **1.3**

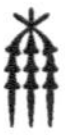

If the cartouche contains both 𓏠 *and* ☉ or 𓀭 go to **1.4**

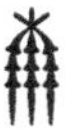

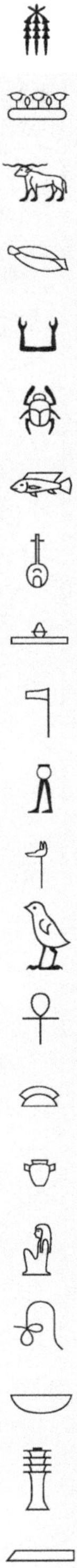

1 𓏠
2 𓋞
3 𓃝
4 𓆟
5 𓏌
6 𓆣
7 𓆜
8 𓊽
9 𓈖
10 𓌉
11 𓀔
12 𓅡
13 𓅆
14 ☥
15 𓄿
16 𓏙
17 𓂡
18 𓆓
19 𓎯
20 𓊽
21 𓇯

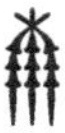

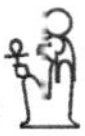

1.1   The cartouche contains both 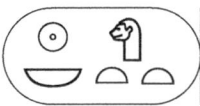 *and*  or  the *crescent moon*.

D18:1B Ahmose

D18:1T Nebpehtyra

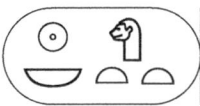

D26:5B Ahmose Sineit

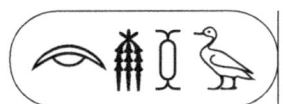

D26:5T Khnemibra

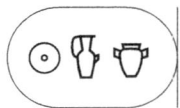

D18:1 Queen Ahmose-Nefertari

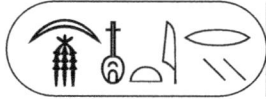

1.2 The Cartouche contains both [glyph] *and* [glyph]

The *ibis on a standard* (G26) represents the *god Thoth*, and is used in the names of the four kings of the 18th Dynasty called Thutmose. All were fond of epithets and titles in their cartouches. Only the most common of these are given, in parentheses. Hopefully you will also have access to their throne names in order to distinguish them from one another.

Some of these epithets are given in the Section I of the *Field Guide*.

D18:3B Thutmose I

D18:3T Aakheperkara

D18:4B Thutmose II

D18:4T Aakheperenra

D18:6B Thutmose III

D18:6T Menkheperra

or

or

or

1 [glyph]

2 [glyph]

3 [glyph]

4 [glyph]

5 [glyph]

6 [glyph]

7 [glyph]

8 [glyph]

9 [glyph]

10 [glyph]

11 [glyph]

12 [glyph]

13 [glyph]

14 [glyph]

15 [glyph]

16 [glyph]

17 [glyph]

18 [glyph]

19 [glyph]

20 [glyph]

21 [glyph]

D18:8B   Thutmose IV

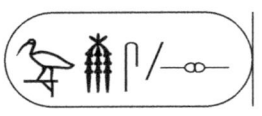

or

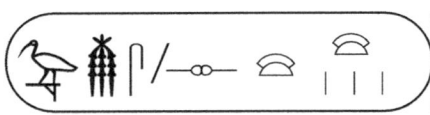

D18:8T Menkheperura

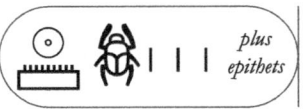

1.3   The Cartouche contains both *and* *upraised arms.*

Kamose D17:15B

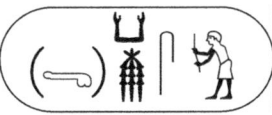

D17:15T Wadjkheperra

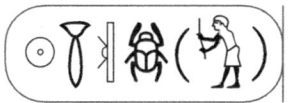

1.4 The Cartouche contains both 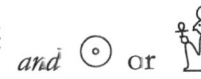 *and* ☉ or

The sun disk and the hawk-headed god wearing the sun disk on his head both represent *Ra, the sun god*. This *Ra* is the first syllable of *Ramses (Ramessu)*, meaning *Born of Ra*. (Note that the sun god may be standing, striding, or sitting).

There were eleven Ramseses, but fortunately most of them were very creative in modifying their cartouches to differentiate among themselves.

Although Ramses II, Ramses the Great, reigned for 66 years, in terms of number of cartouches I have documented, Ramses III is a very close second (86 and 82 respectively). If you figure out that you are looking at a Ramses cartouche, I suggest you look at Ramses II and III in the first part of the book (D19:3 and D20:2) to see if one of these is your man. As always, a birth name, in this case *Ramses*, combined with a throne name will give you the most accurate identification.

The final /ses/ or /su/ in these names can be written with seemingly any combination of the following:

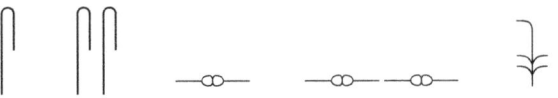

Proceed to the next page to "key out" these Ramseses.

1

2

3

4

5

6

7

8

9

10

11

12

13

14

15

16

17

18

19

20

21

1.4 The Cartouche contains both 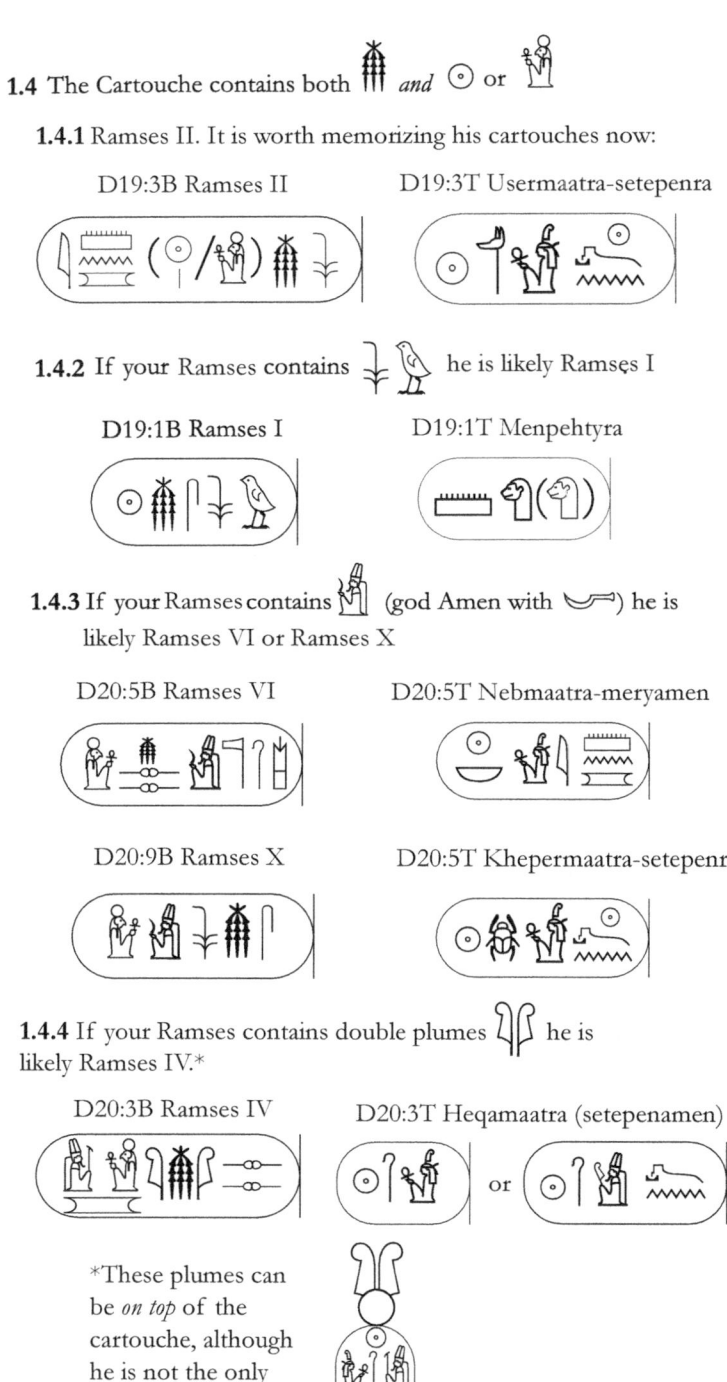 *and* ☉ or 🧍

1.4.1 Ramses II. It is worth memorizing his cartouches now:

D19:3B Ramses II   D19:3T Usermaatra-setepenra

1.4.2 If your Ramses contains 🐦 he is likely Ramses I

D19:1B Ramses I   D19:1T Menpehtyra

1.4.3 If your Ramses contains 🧍 (god Amen with 〰) he is likely Ramses VI or Ramses X

D20:5B Ramses VI   D20:5T Nebmaatra-meryamen

D20:9B Ramses X   D20:5T Khepermaatra-setepenra

1.4.4 If your Ramses contains double plumes 🪶 he is likely Ramses IV.*

D20:3B Ramses IV   D20:3T Heqamaatra (setepenamen)

or

*These plumes can be *on top* of the cartouche, although he is not the only pharaoh to do that.

1.4.5 If your Ramses contains 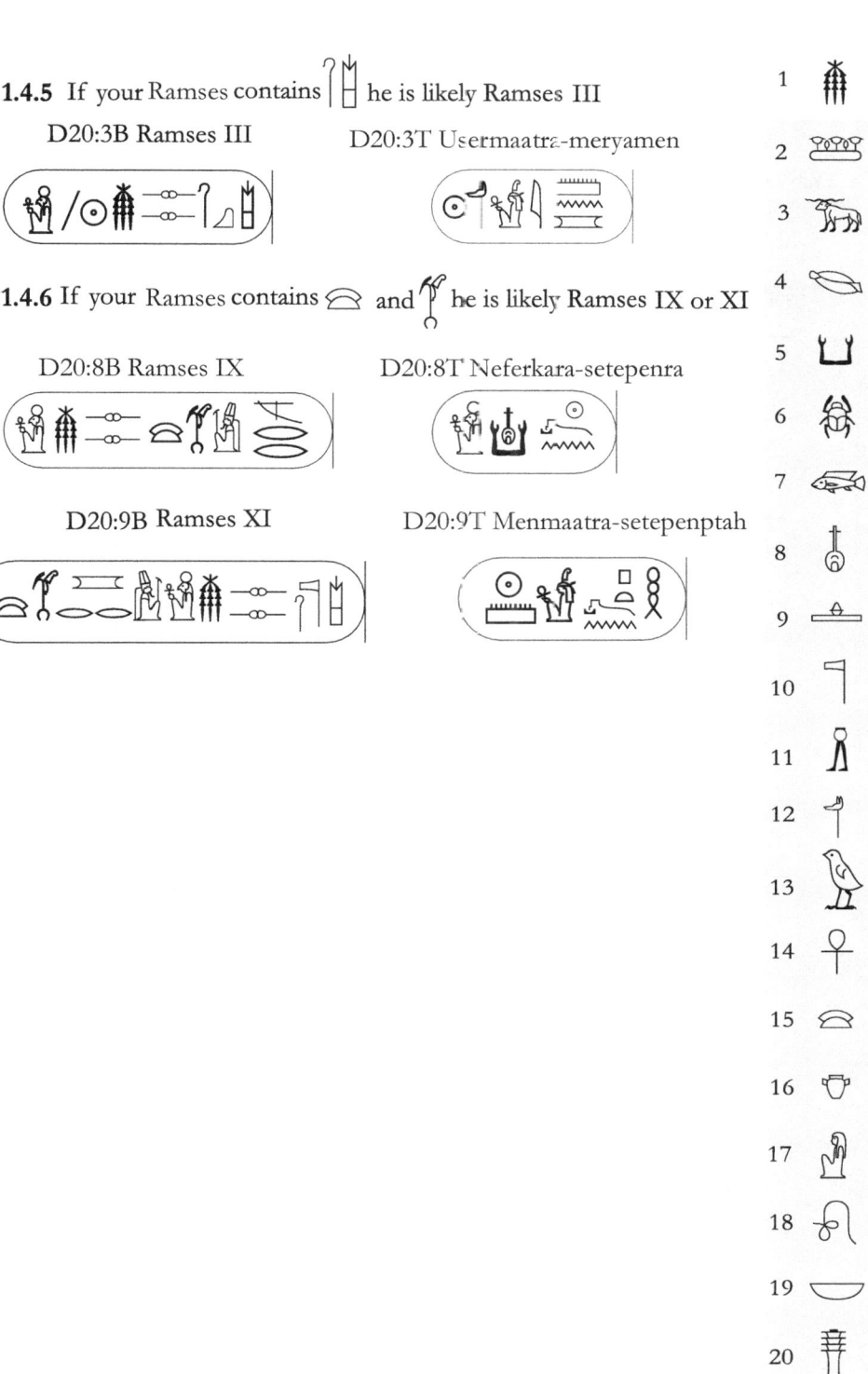 he is likely Ramses III

D20:3B Ramses III

D20:3T Usermaatra-meryamen

1.4.6 If your Ramses contains ⌒ and 𓀭 he is likely Ramses IX or XI

D20:8B Ramses IX

D20:8T Neferkara-setepenra

D20:9B Ramses XI

D20:9T Menmaatra-setepenptah

1

2

3

4

5

6

7

8

9

10

11

12

13

14

15

16

17

18

19

20

21

2. 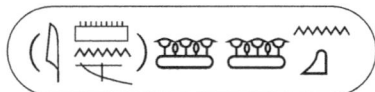 /Sh/ (M8)   *Pool with lotus flowers (or papyrus umbels) and buds.*
This sign was introduced with Sheshonq I D22:1B. Used phonetically.

> **2.1** Contains two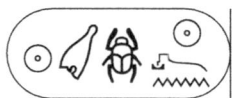

D22:1B Sheshonq (meryamen) I   D22:1T Hedjkheperra-setepenra

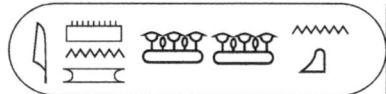   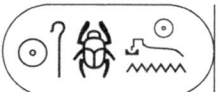

D22:3B Sheshonq (meryamen) II   D22:3T Heqakheperra-setepenra

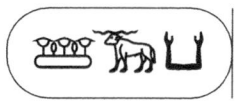

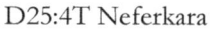
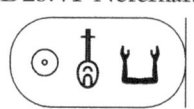

> **2.2** Contains one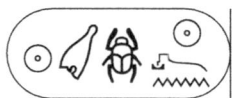

D25:4B Shabaka   D25:4T Neferkara

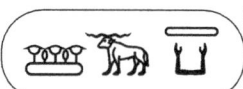   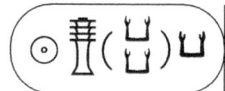

D25:5B Shabitko   D25:5T Djedka(u)ra

1

3. 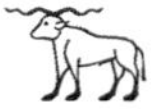 Any mammal, certain parts of mammals, excluding .   2

3

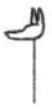

If the cartouche contains 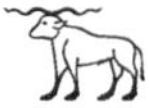 go to **3.1**   4

5

If the cartouche contains 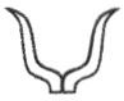 or 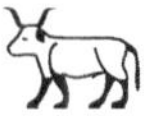 go to **3.2**   6

7

If the cartouche contains 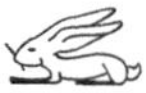 go to **3.3**   8

9

If the cartouche contains 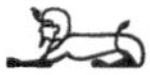 (sphinx) go to **3.4**   10

11

If the cartouche contains 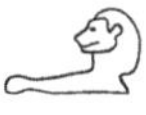 go to **3.5**   12

13

If the cartouche contains 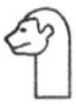 go to **3.6**   14

15

If the cartouche contains 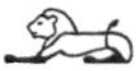 go to **3.7**   16

17

For 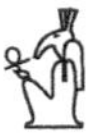 see **17.2**   18

19

20

21

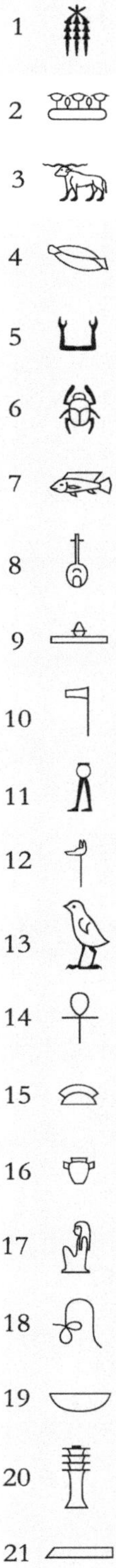

3.1 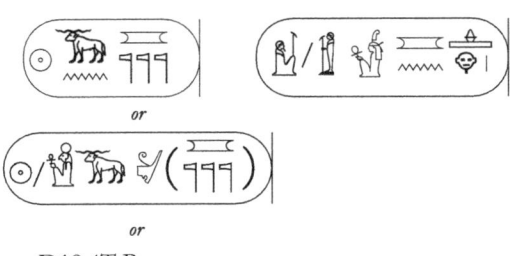 /Ba/ (E11) *Ram, god Khnum*

D19:4T Baenra-merynetjeru   D19:4B Merenptah-hetephermaat

or

or

D19:4T Baenra-meryamen

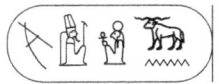

D19:3 Queen Bintanath

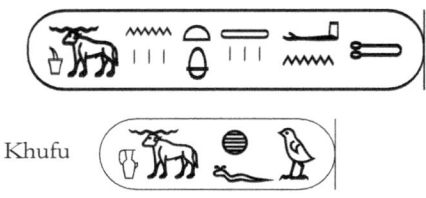

D4:2 Khufu

3.2 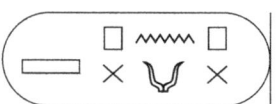 /Wep/ (F13) *Ox horns, open*

or   /Ba/ (E1) Bull, ox; *Bull, ox; ka* aspect of the soul

D25 Divine Adoratrice Shepenwepet

D26:2B Nekau II   D26:2B Wahibra

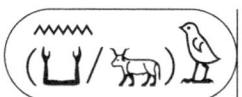   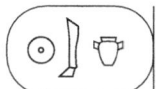

3.3 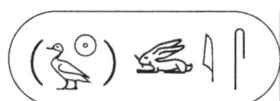 /Wen/ (E34) *Desert hare; exist, become*

D5:9B Unas

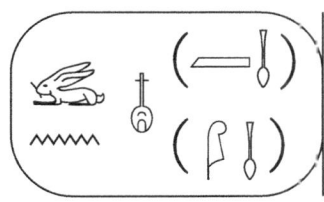

Wennefer (an epithet of Osiris), often used in connection with names and titles of Roman emperors. Can contain *True of Voice*, /Makheru/ included below in parentheses.

Wennefer (makheru)

3.4 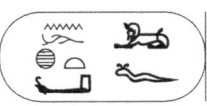 /Neb/ *Sphinx* (not in **Gardiner**) Used rather uniquely by this king as an alternate writing of ⬭ (V30), the *basket*, meaning *lord, master*, or *all*. Not to be confused with the *lion*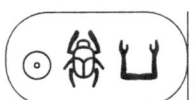

D30:1B Nakhtnebef   D30:1T Kheperkara

1

2

3

4

5

6

7

8

9

10

11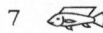

12

13

14

15

16

17

18

19

20

21

3.5 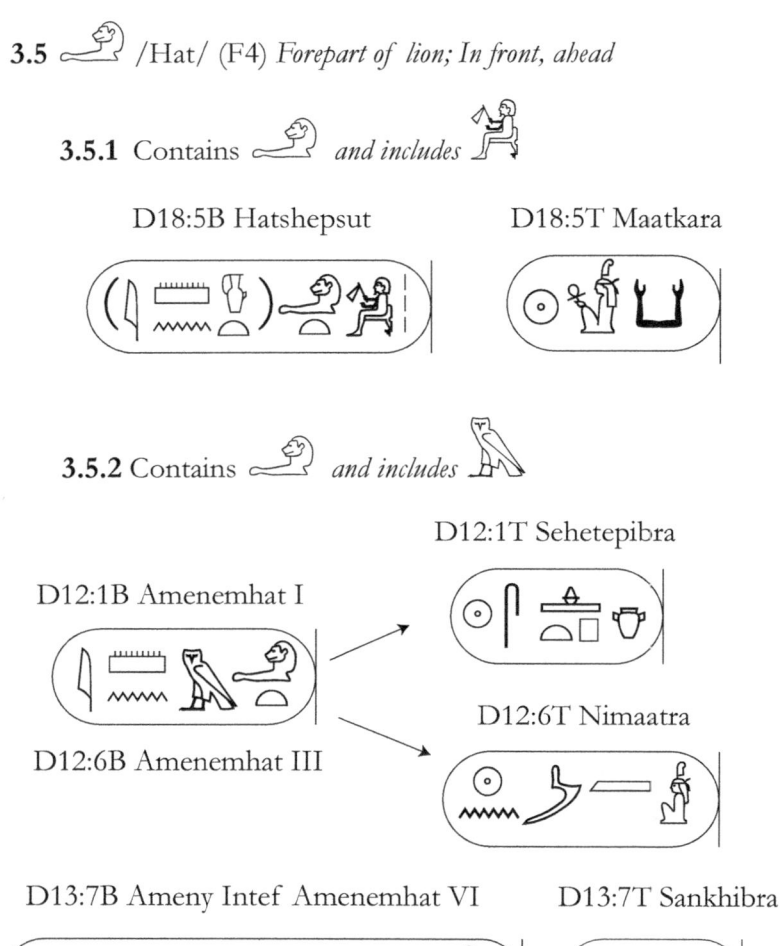 /Hat/ (F4) *Forepart of lion; In front, ahead*

1

2

3

3.6   /Peht(y) (F9) *Head of leopard; strength*

4

D18:1T Nebpehtyra

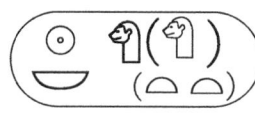

D18:1B Ahmose I

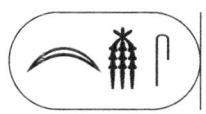

5

D19:1T Menpehtyra

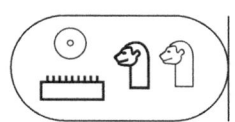

D19:1B Ramses I

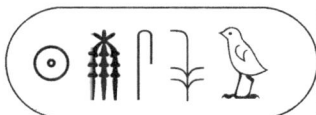

6

7

8

9

10

11

12

13

14

15

16

17

18

19

20

21

3.7 🦁 /L, R/ (E23) *Lion.* Used phonetically only.

If the cartouche contains 🦁 *and starts with* ⬭ go to **3.7.1**

If the cartouche contains 🦁 *and starts with* 🦅 go to **3.7.2**

If the cartouche contains 🦁 *and starts with* △ go to **3.7.3**

If the cartouche contains 🦁 *and* 👁, go to **3.7.4**

If the cartouche contains 🦁 *and starts with* 🏺 *or* 🔨, go to **3.7.5**

If the cartouche contains 🦁 *and starts with* ☐ ⌒ go to **3.7.6**

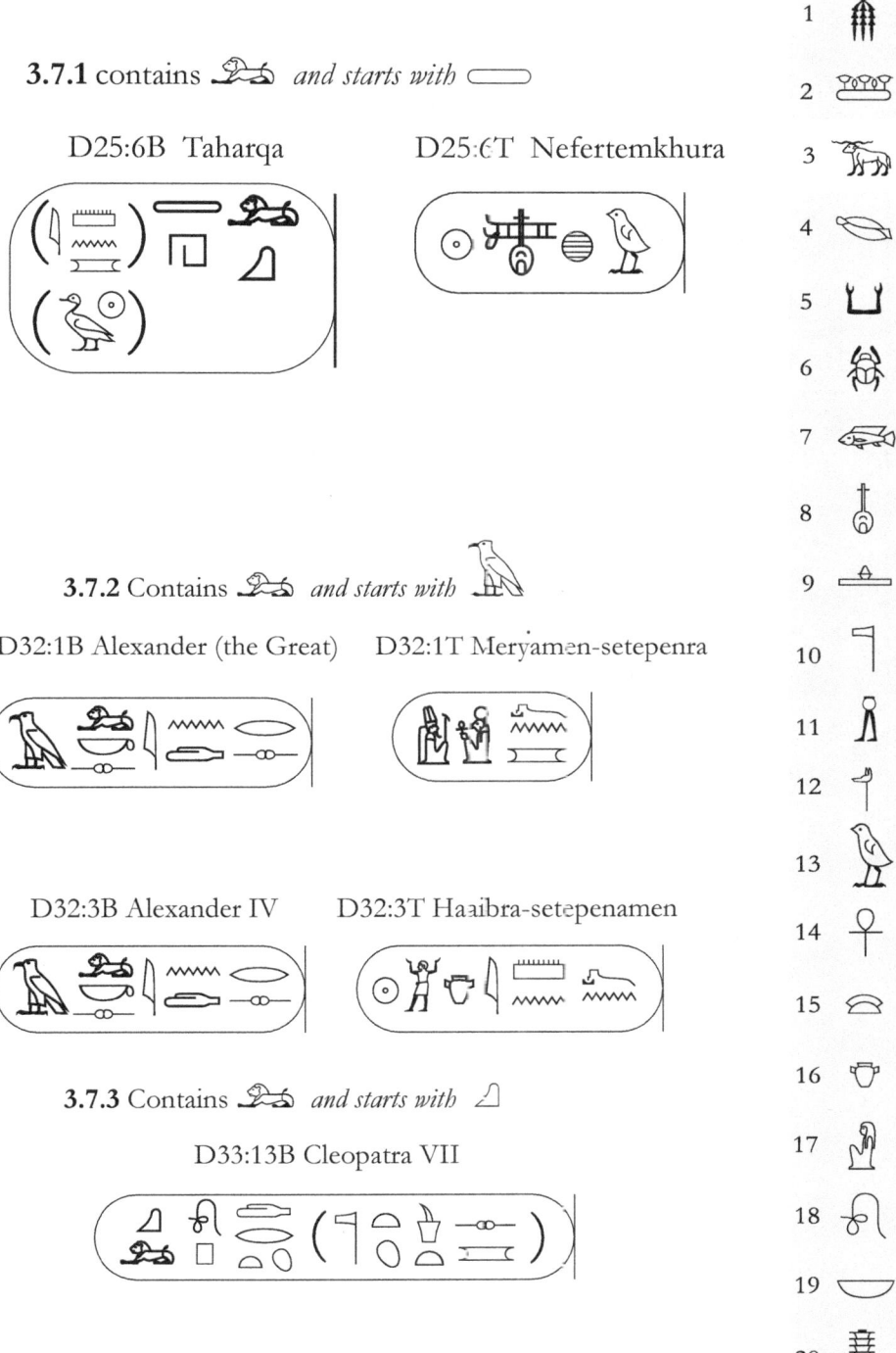

3.7.1 contains 🦁 *and starts with* ⬭

D25:6B Taharqa

D25:6T Nefertemkhura

3.7.2 Contains 🦁 *and starts with* 🦅

D32:1B Alexander (the Great)

D32:1T Meryamen-setepenra

D32:3B Alexander IV

D32:3T Haaibra-setepenamen

3.7.3 Contains 🦁 *and starts with* △

D33:13B Cleopatra VII

1
2
3
4
5
6
7
8
9
10
11
12
13
14
15
16
17
18
19
20
21

3.7.4 Contains 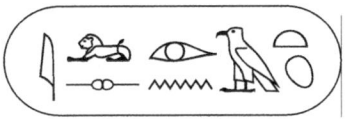 *and*

D33 Queen Arsinoe

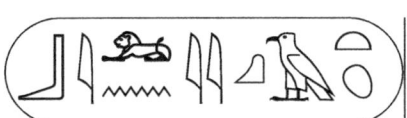

3.7.5 If the cartouche contains 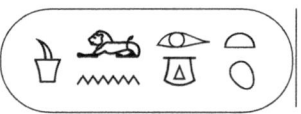 *and starts with* or

D33 Queen Berenice

or

3.7.6 Contains 🐾 *and starts with* ☐ ◠.

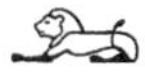

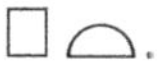

These are the Ptolemies (☐◠ ...), of whom there were fifteen. Twelve had cartouches.

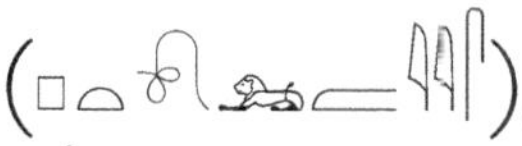

I will not include the throne names here for most of the Ptolemies, as they are so unwieldy. Those names are found in the next section. Remember, variations and exceptions abound!

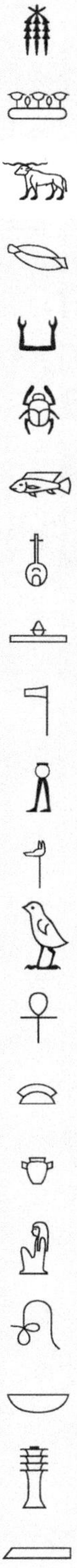

1

2

3

4

5

6

7

8

9

10

11

12

13

14

15

16

17

18

19

20

21

3.7.6.1 *Ptolemy* without embellishements

D33:1T

D33:1B Ptolemy I

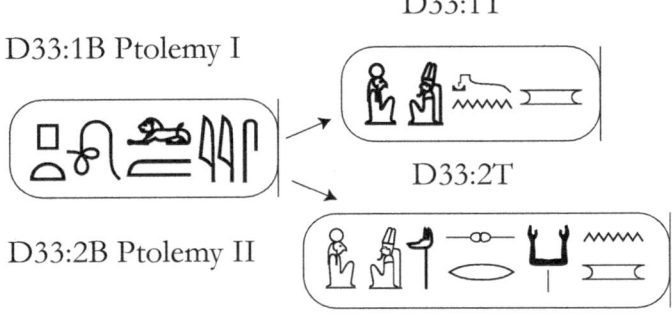

D33:2T

D33:2B Ptolemy II

3.7.6.2 Ends in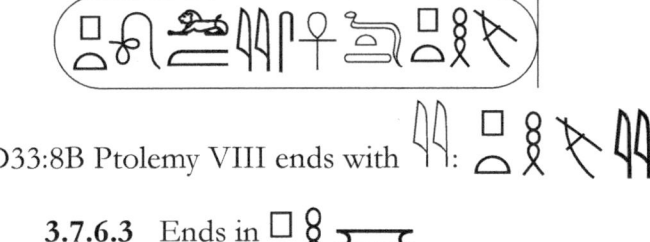

D33:3B Ptolemy III; D33:5B Ptolemy V; D33:6B Ptolemy VI

D33:8B Ptolemy VIII ends with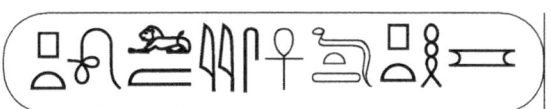

3.7.6.3 Ends in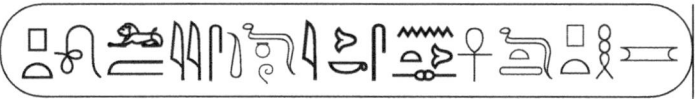

D33:9B Ptolemy IX;

D33:10B Ptolemy X Alexander contains the name
Alexander inside the cartouche. It is in bold print.

or, another of several possible ways to write *Alexander:*

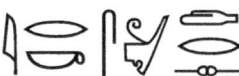

3.7.6.4 includes ⌐⌐ near the end

D32:4B Ptolemy IV

D32:12B Ptolemy XII

D32:15B Ptolemy XV (note new /M/ in P*tolemy*)

3.7.6.5 D32:15B is Ptolemy Caesarion. He includes the name *Caesar* inside his cartouches (except when he doesn't, as in the cartouche above!) In the Roman tradition, he writes *Caesar* different ways and hides it in different parts of the cartouche, or writes it in a separate cartouche althogether.

D32:15B Ptolemy XV

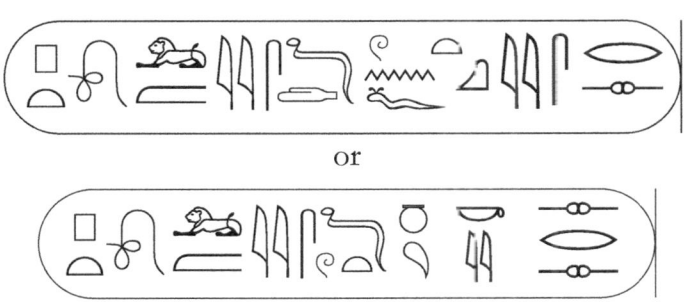

or

1

2

3

4

5

6

7

8

9

10

11

12

13

14

15

16

17

18

19

20

21

4. ⬤ /Iwa/ (F44) *Thigh of beef on the bone, heir.*
All but two of the throne names of the Ptolemies contain this sign.
While it is technically classified under *Parts of Mammals,* what it is
is not obvious– it looks more (to my eyes) like a hamburger, or maybe
a flying saucer. Or a dried fish...

It is used, rarely, in other names to mean *son (of).*

I do not give the birth names of the Ptolemies in this section. They are
found in the section immediately preceding this one.

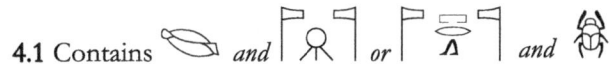

4.1 Contains ⬤ *and* or *and*

D33:6T Iwaennetjerwyper-setepen ptahkhepri Irmaaten amenra
(Ptolemy VI)

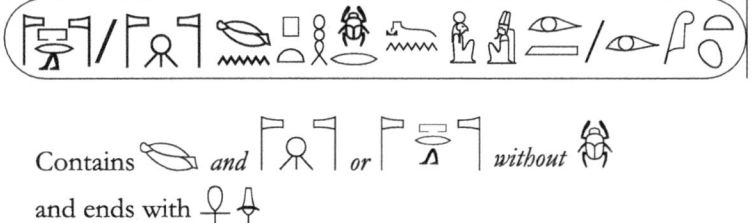

Contains ⬤ *and* or *without*
and ends with

D33:8T Iwaennetjerwyra setepenptah Irmaatenra
sekhemankhamen (Ptolemy VIII)

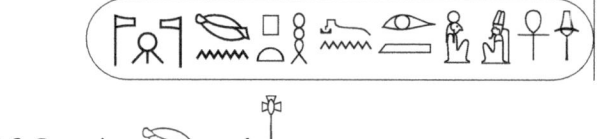

4.2 Contains ⬤ *and*

D33:9T Iwaennetjermenkh netjeretmeretmutes nedjetsetepenptah Irmaatenra sekhemankhamen (Ptolemy IX)

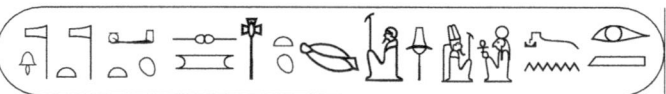

4.3 Contains 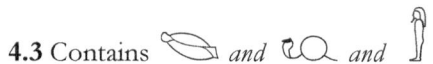 *and* *and*

D33:10T Iwaennetjermenkh netjeretmenkhetsatra setepenptah
Irmaatenra senenankhenamen
(Ptolemy X)

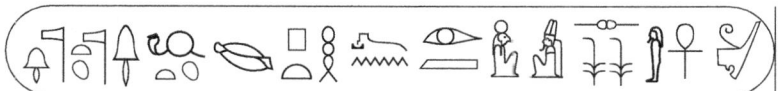

4.4 Contains 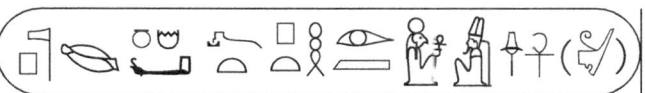 *and*

D33:12T Iwaenpanetjernehem setepenptah Irmaatenra
sekhemankhamen (Ptolemy XII)

D33:13cT Iwapanetjer entynehem Sepetenptah
Irmaatenra Sekhemankhamen
(Ptolemy XV)

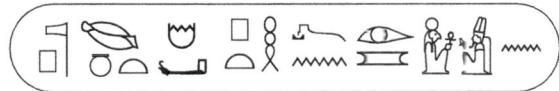

1 　

2 　

3 　

4 　

5 　

6 　

7 　

8 　

9 　

10 　

11 　

12 　

13 　

14 　

15 　

16 　

17 　

18 　

19 　

20 　

21

4.5 Other cartouches with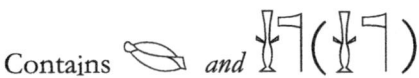

Contains 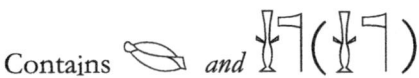 *and*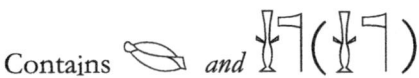

D33:3T Iwaennetjerwysenwy sekhemankhra setepamen
(Ptolemy III)

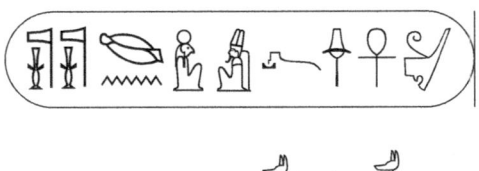

Contains 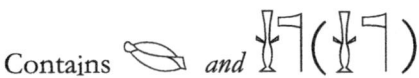 *and*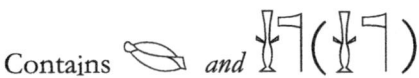

D33:4T Iwaennetjerwymenkhwy seteptah userkara-sekhemankham
(Ptolemy IV)

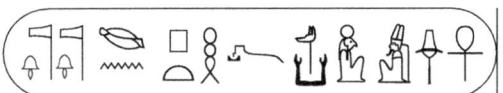

D33:5T Iwaennetjerwy merwytu setepptah userkara sekhemankh
(Ptolemy V)

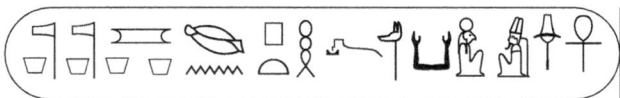

1

5 Contains /Ka/ (D28) *upraised arms; the Ka aspect of the soul.*

2

3

5.1 Contains three /Ka/

4

5

5.2 Contains two

6

5.3 with or

5.8 with

7

8

5.4 with

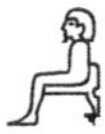

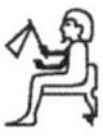

5.9 with

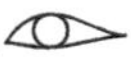

9

5.5 with

5.10 with or

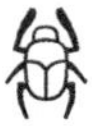

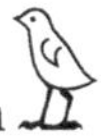

10

11

5.6 with

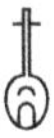

5.11 with

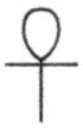

12

5.7 with

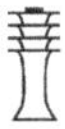

5.12 with

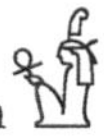

13

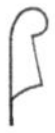

14

15

16

17

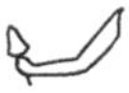

18

19

20

21

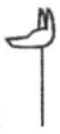

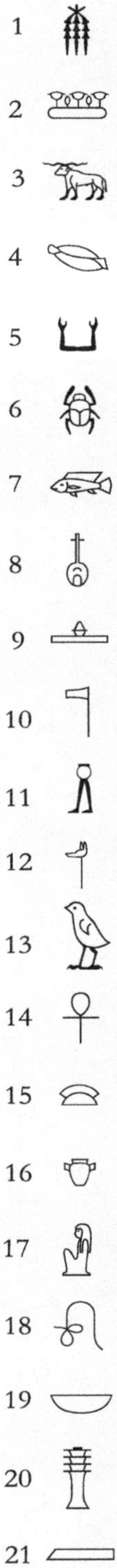

5.1 Contains three /Ka/ 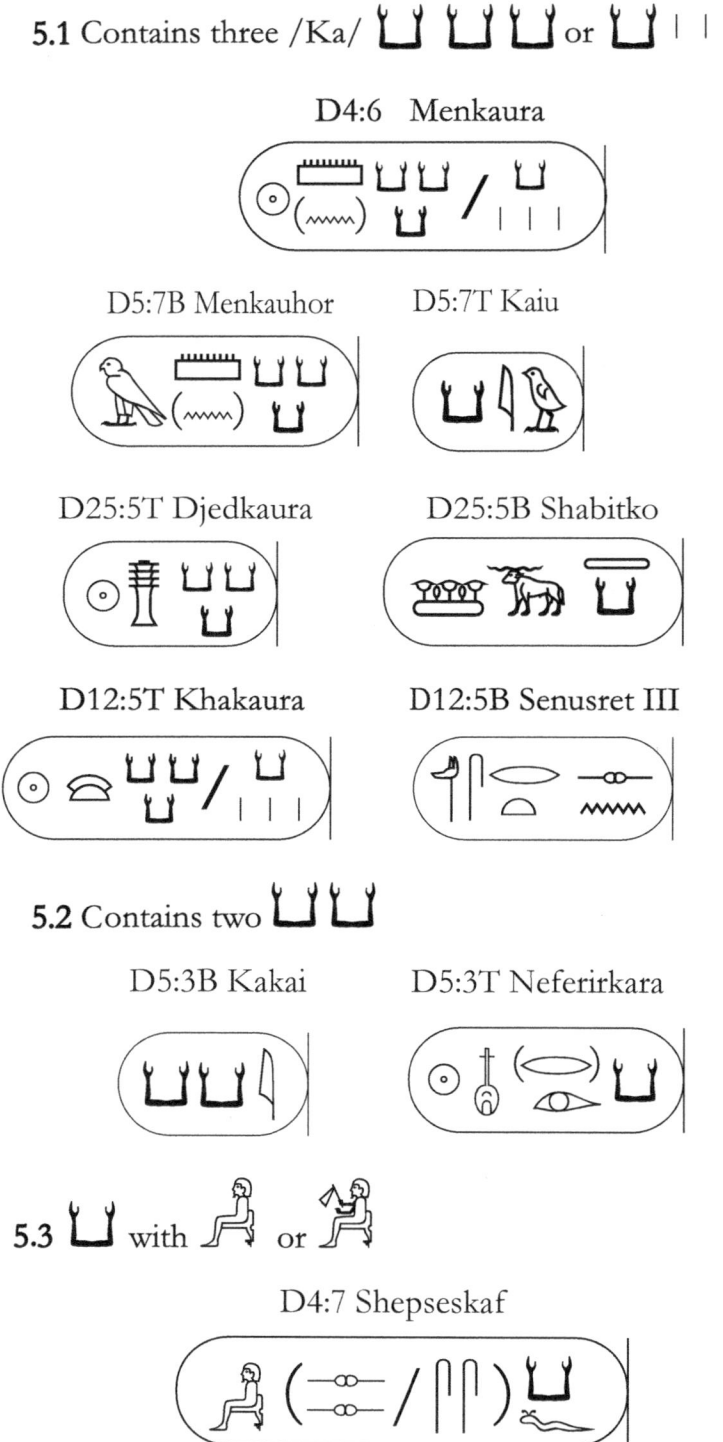 or

D4:6   Menkaura

D5:7B Menkauhor   D5:7T Kaiu

D25:5T Djedkaura   D25:5B Shabitko

D12:5T Khakaura   D12:5B Senusret III

5.2 Contains two

D5:3B Kakai   D5:3T Neferirkara

5.3 with   or

D4:7 Shepseskaf

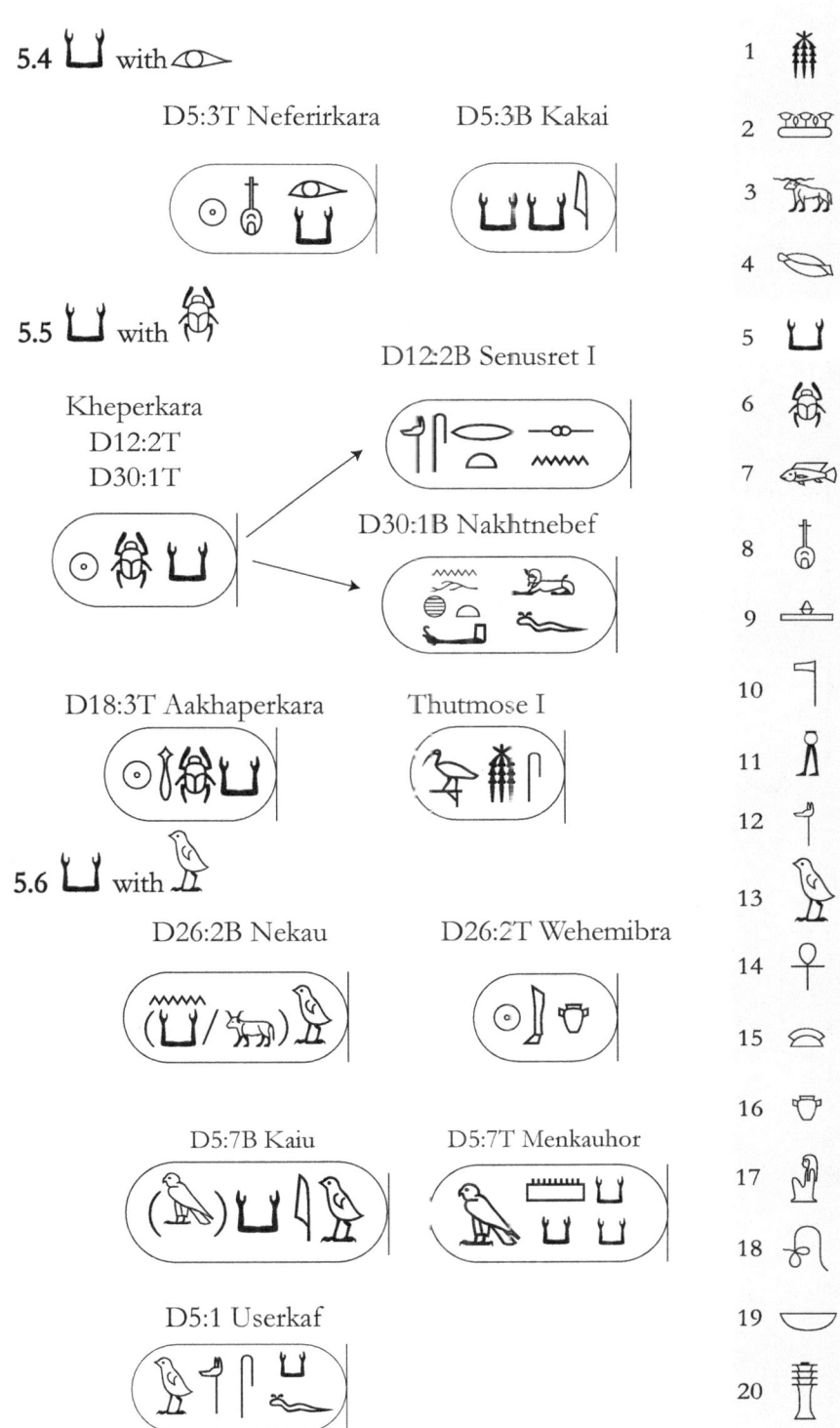

5.4 ⊔ with ⟨○⟩

D5:3T Neferirkara   D5:3B Kakai

5.5 ⊔ with 🪲

D12:2B Senusret I

Kheperkara
D12:2T
D30:1T

D30:1B Nakhtnebef

D18:3T Aakhaperkara   Thutmose I

5.6 ⊔ with 🐦

D26:2B Nekau   D26:2T Wehemibra

D5:7B Kaiu   D5:7T Menkauhor

D5:1 Userkaf

1
2
3
4
5
6
7
8
9
10
11
12
13
14
15
16
17
18
19
20
21

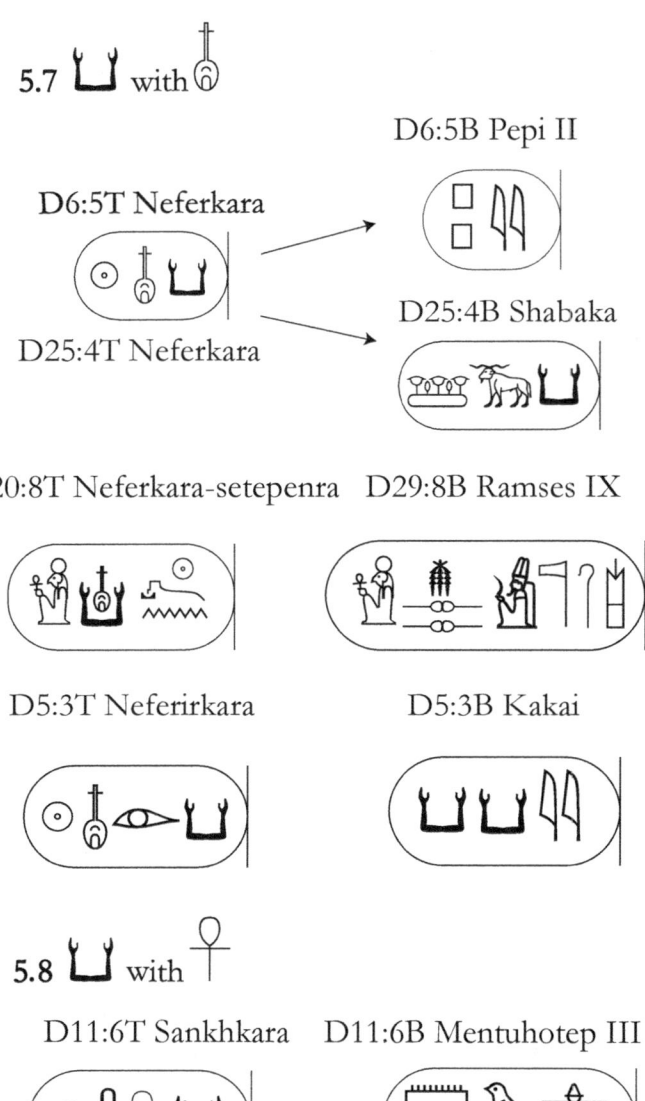

5.7 ⊔ with 🜊

D6:5B Pepi II

D6:5T Neferkara

D25:4B Shabaka

D25:4T Neferkara

D20:8T Neferkara-setepenra   D29:8B Ramses IX

D5:3T Neferirkara   D5:3B Kakai

5.8 ⊔ with ☥

D11:6T Sankhkara   D11:6B Mentuhotep III

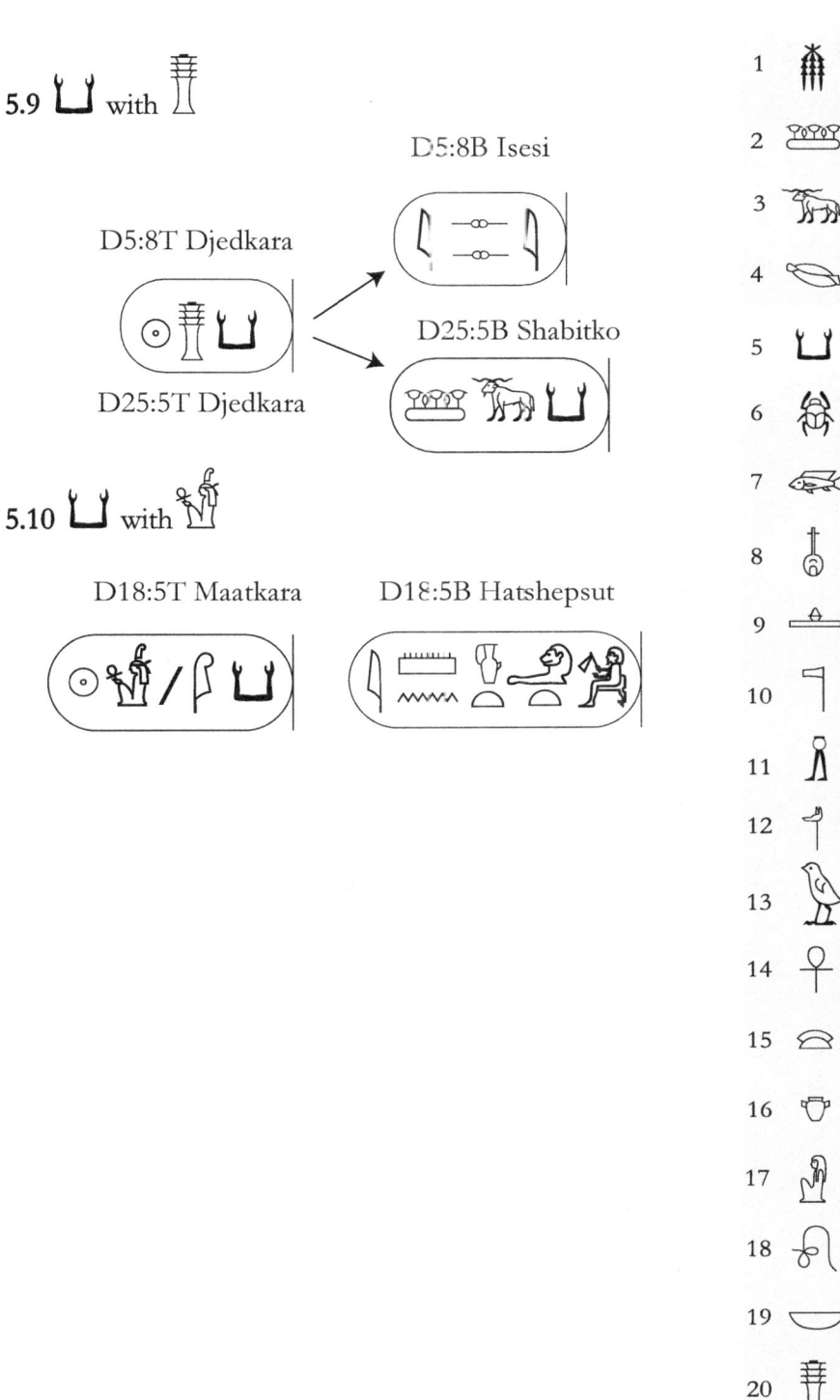

5.9 with

D5:8B Isesi

D5:8T Djedkara

D25:5T Djedkara

D25:5B Shabitko

5.10 with

D18:5T Maatkara

D18:5B Hatshepsut

1
2
3
4
5
6
7
8
9
10
11
12
13
14
15
16
17
18
19
20
21

6 Contains 🪲 /Kheper/ *Dung beetle; become*

6.1 Contains two 🪲 and 👁

6.2 Contains 🪲 *and* ▭

6.8 Contains 🪲 *and* 〰

6.3 Contains 🪲 *and* 🍶 (*not* 🍶)

6.9 Contains 🪲 *and* ⌣

6.4 Contains 🪲 *and* 🚩

6.10 Contains 🪲 *and* 🍾

6.5 Contains 🪲 *and* 𓏏

6.11 Contains 🪲 *and* 𓀭

6.6 Contains 🪲 *and* ⌒

6.12 Contains 🪲 *and* 𓉴

6.7 Contains 🪲 *and* 🔑

6.13 Contains 🪲 *and* 𓌙

6.14 Contains 🪲 *and* 𓄿

6.1 Contains two 🪲 and 👁

D18:13T Kheperkheperura-irmaat   D18:13B Ay

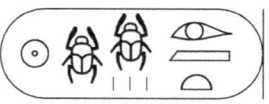   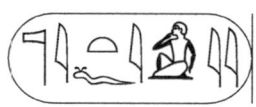

Watch out for extra signs (epithets)
in Dynasty 18 names.

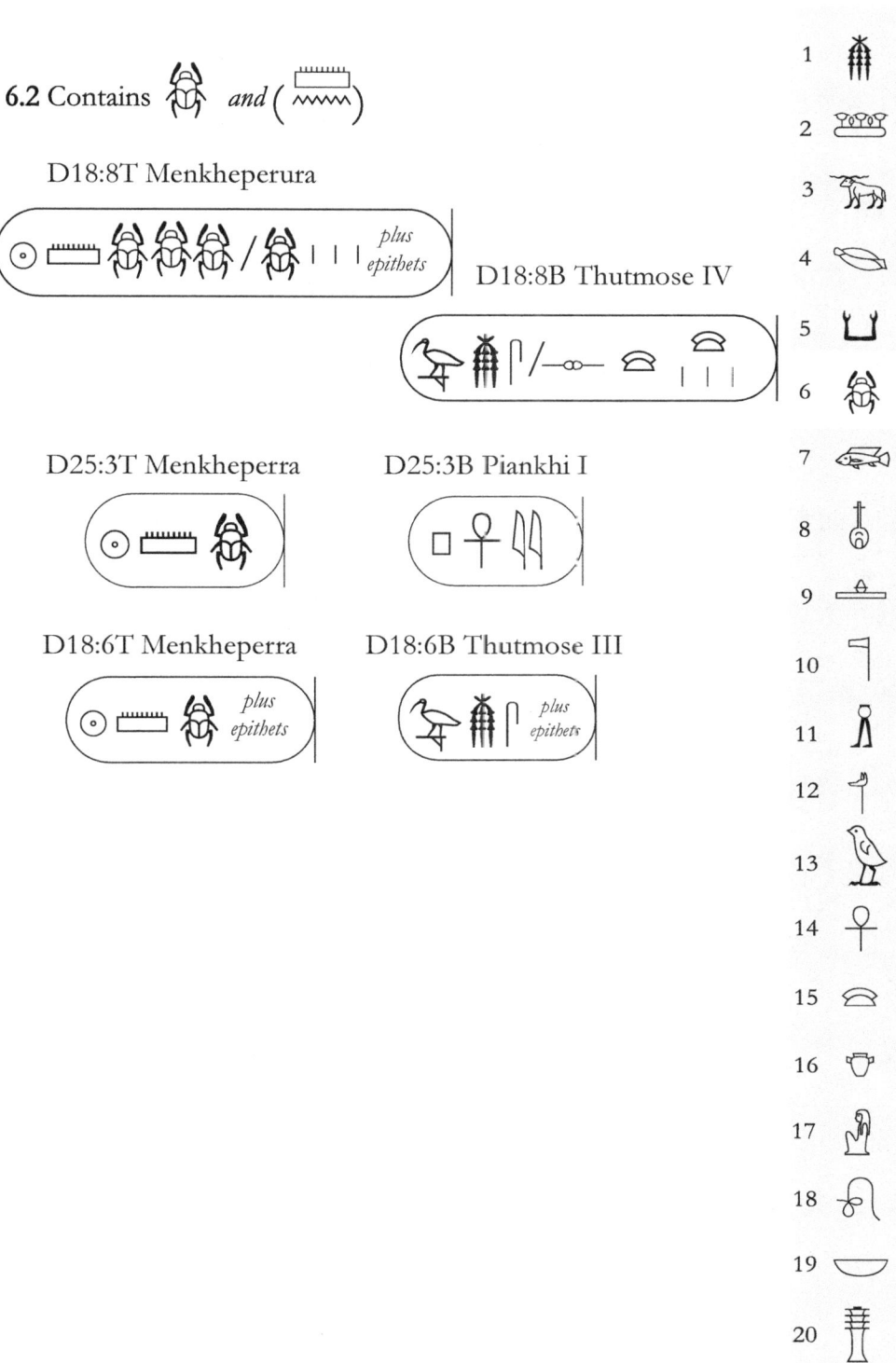

6.2 Contains 🪲 *and* (〰️)

D18:8T Menkheperura

D18:8B Thutmose IV

D25:3T Menkheperra

D25:3B Piankhi I

D18:6T Menkheperra

D18:6B Thutmose III

plus epithets

1
2
3
4
5
6
7
8
9
10
11
12
13
14
15
16
17
18
19
20
21

6.3 Contains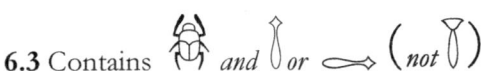

D18:4T Aakheperenra

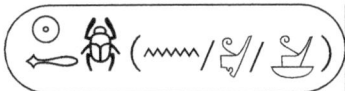

D18:4B Thutmos II

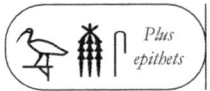

D18:7T Aakheperura

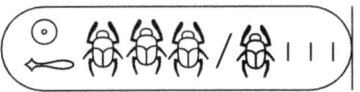

D18:7B Amenhotep II

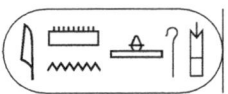

D21:3T Aakheperra-setepenamen

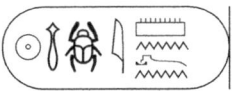

D21:3B Pasebakhaenniut I

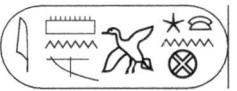

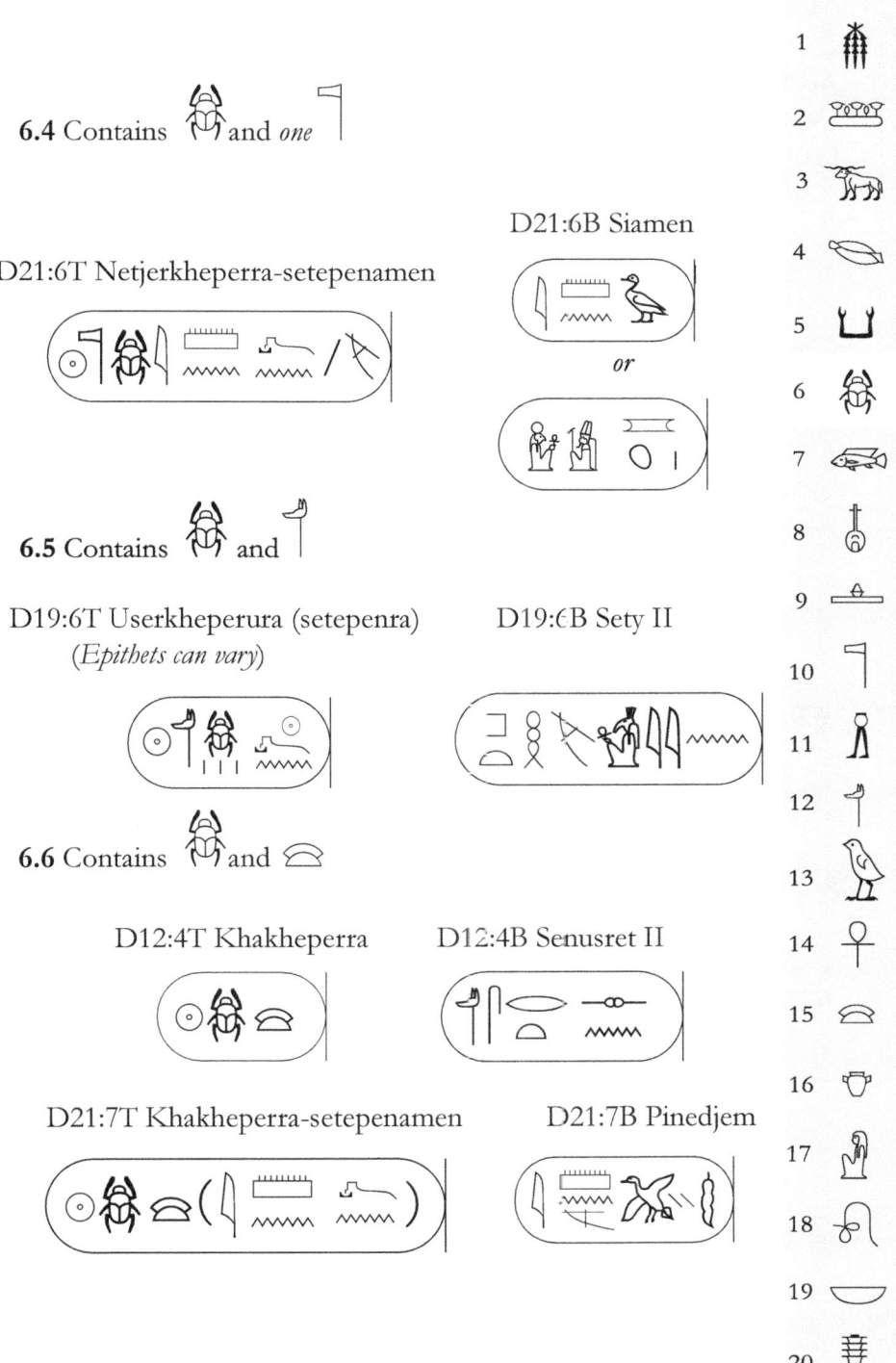

6.4 Contains 🪲 and *one* 🚩

D21:6T Netjerkheperra-setepenamen

D21:6B Siamen

or

6.5 Contains 🪲 and 🚩

D19:6T Userkheperura (setepenra)
(*Epithets can vary*)

D19:6B Sety II

6.6 Contains 🪲 and ⌒

D12:4T Khakheperra

D12:4B Senusret II

D21:7T Khakheperra-setepenamen

D21:7B Pinedjem

1
2
3
4
5
6
7
8
9
10
11
12
13
14
15
16
17
18
19
20
21

6.7 Contains 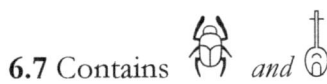 *and*

D18:10T Neferkheperura-waenra   D18:10B Akhenaten

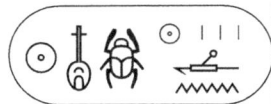   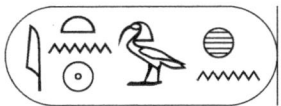

6.8 Contains 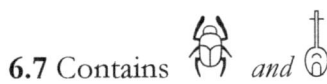 *and*

D18:14T Djeserkheperura-setepenra   D18:14B Horemheb

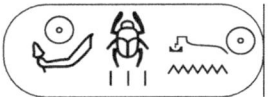   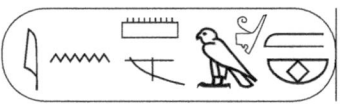

6.9 Contains 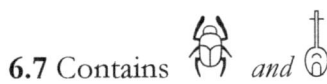 *and*

D18:12T Nebkheperura   D18:12B Tutankhamen

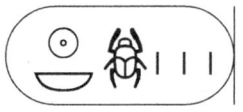   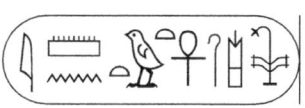

6.10 Contains 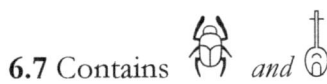 *and*

D17:15T Wadjkheperra   D17:15B Kamose

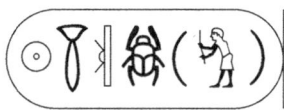   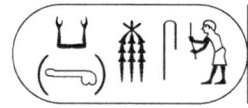

6.11 Contains 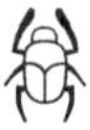 *and*

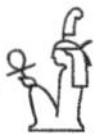

D20:9T Khepermaatra-setepenra 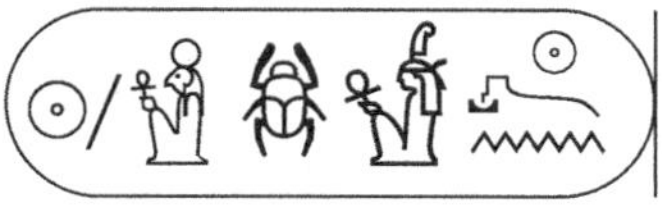   D20:9B Ramses X

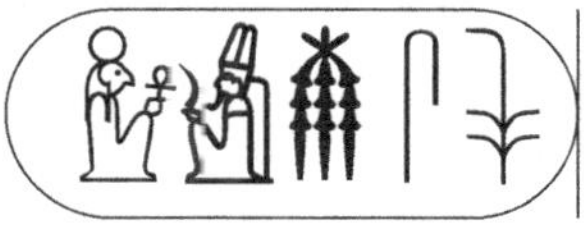

6.12 Contains 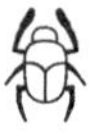 *and*

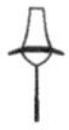

D22:2T Sekhemkheperra.-setepenra 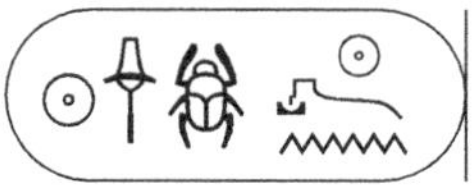   D22:2B Osorkon I

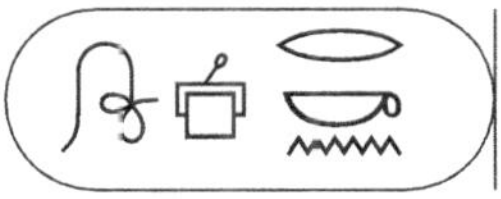

6.13 Contains 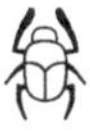 *and*

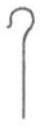

D22:3T Heqakheperra-setepenra 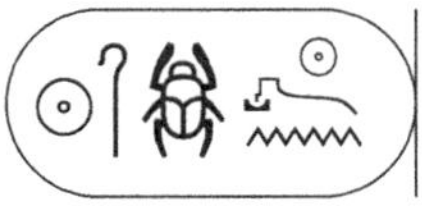   D22:3B Sheshonq II (meryamen)

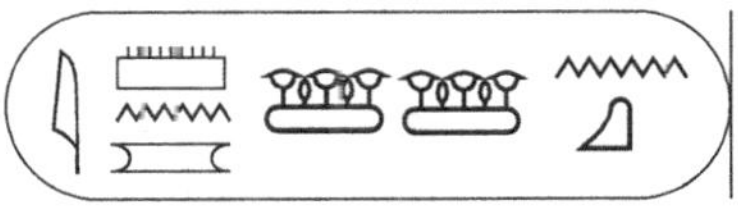

6.14 Contains 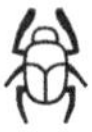 *and*

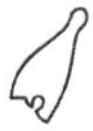

D22:1T Hedjkheperra-setepenamen 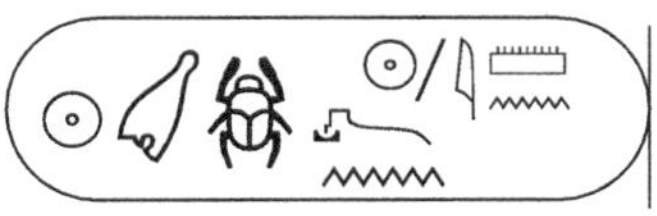   D22:1B Sheshonq I (meryamen)

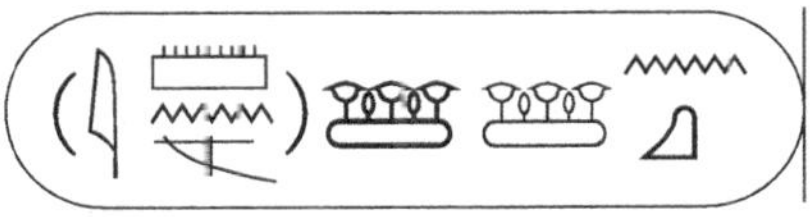

1

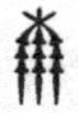

2

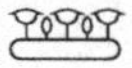

3

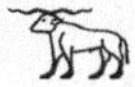

4

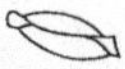

5

6

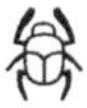

7

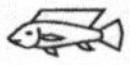

8

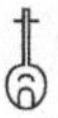

9

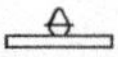

10

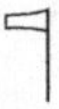

11

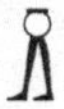

12

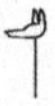

13

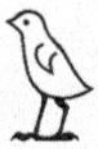

14

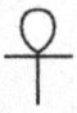

15

16

17

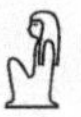

18

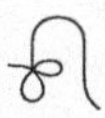

19

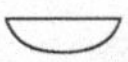

20

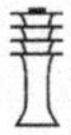

21

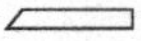

7 Contains 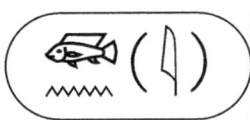 /N/ (K1) *tilapia fish*

D5:6B Ini   D5:6T Niuserra

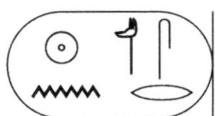

8 Contains 🜊 /Nefer/ (F35) *Heart and trachea; beautiful, good*

8.1 Contains multiple 🜊

8.2 Contains 🜊 *and* 🝙   8.4 Contains 🜊 *and* 🦅

8.3 Contains 🜊 *and* 🐦   8.5 Contains 🜊 *and* ✤

8.1 Contains multiple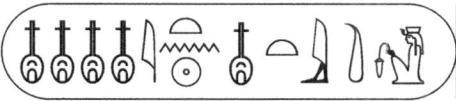

D18:10 Queen Neferneferuaten-Nefertiti

D18:5 Princess Neferura

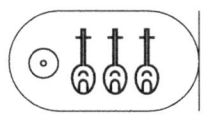

D12:6 Princess Neferuptah

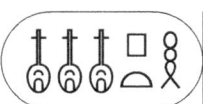

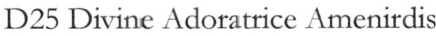

D25 Khaneferumut   D25 Divine Adoratrice Amenirdis

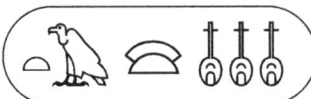   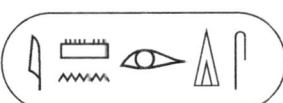

1   𓋿

2   𓏥

3   𓃀

4   𓆱

5   𓎡

6   𓆣

7   𓆟

8   𓏏

9   𓈖

10   𓏲

11   𓀀

12   𓆓

13   𓅂

14   𓋹

15   𓈎

16   𓎺

17   𓁐

18   𓋴

19   𓏌

20   𓊽

21   𓂧

8.2 Contains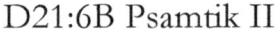

D21:6T Neferibra   D21:6B Psamtik II

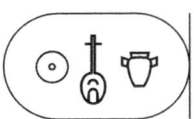   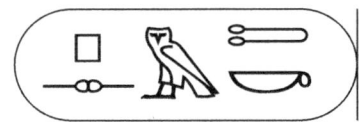

8.3 Contains

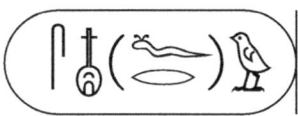

D4:1 Sneferu

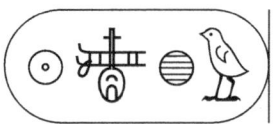

D25:6T Nefertemkhura   D25:6B Taharqa

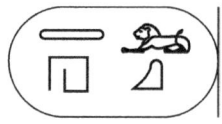

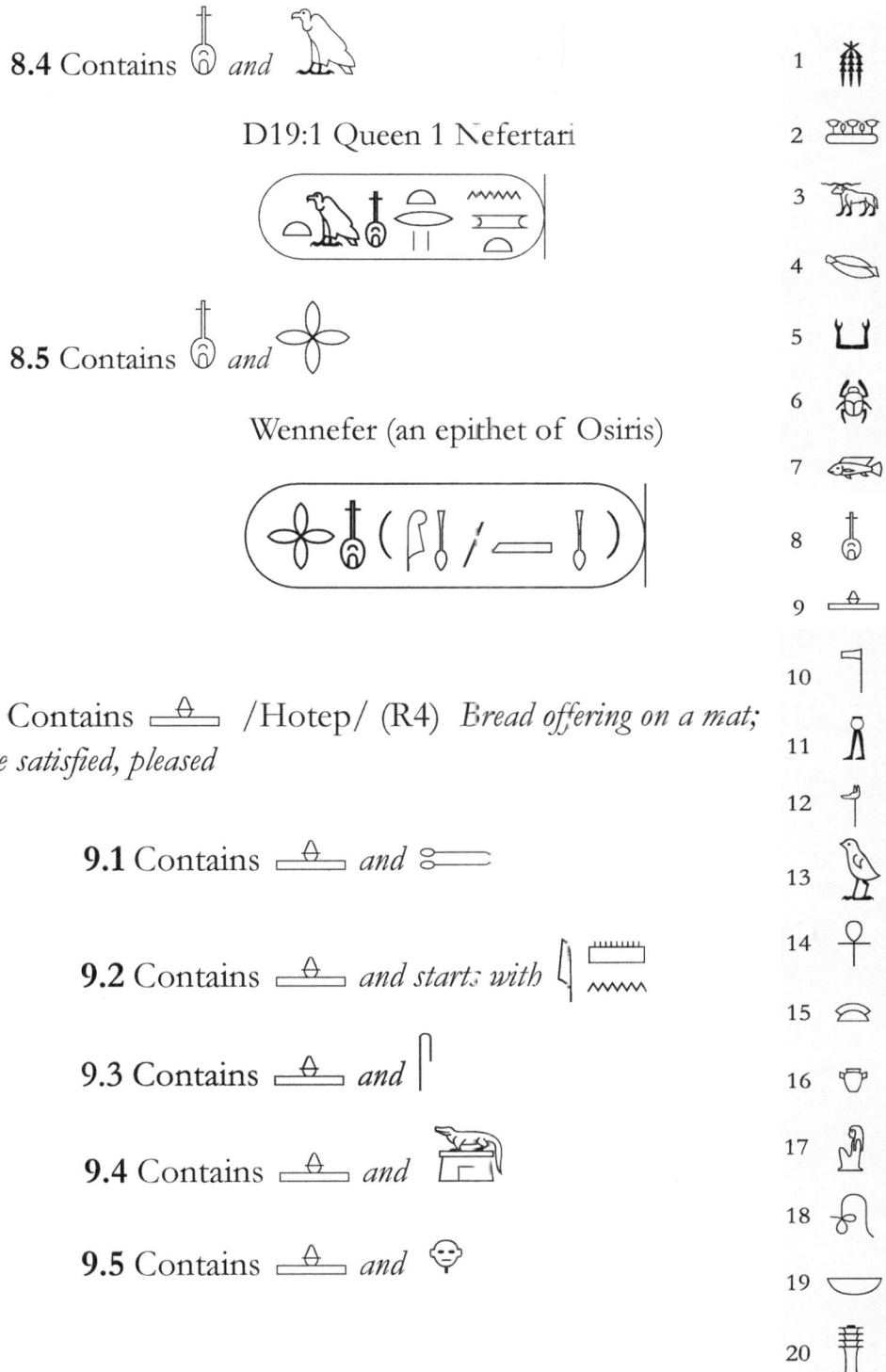

8.4 Contains 🔱 *and* 🦅

D19:1 Queen 1 Nefertari

8.5 Contains 🔱 *and* ✳

Wennefer (an epithet of Osiris)

9 Contains ⟳ /Hotep/ (R4) *Bread offering on a mat; be satisfied, pleased*

9.1 Contains ⟳ *and* ⟾

9.2 Contains ⟳ *and starts with* ⟜

9.3 Contains ⟳ *and* ⌐

9.4 Contains ⟳ *and* 🐊

9.5 Contains ⟳ *and* 😊

1

2

3

4

5

6

7

8

9

10

11

12

13

14

15

16

17

18

19

20

21

9.1 Contains 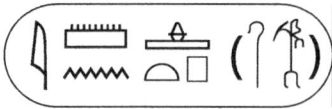 *and*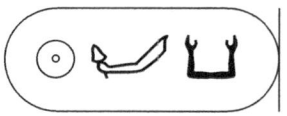

D11:5T Nebhepetra

D11:5B Mentuhotep II

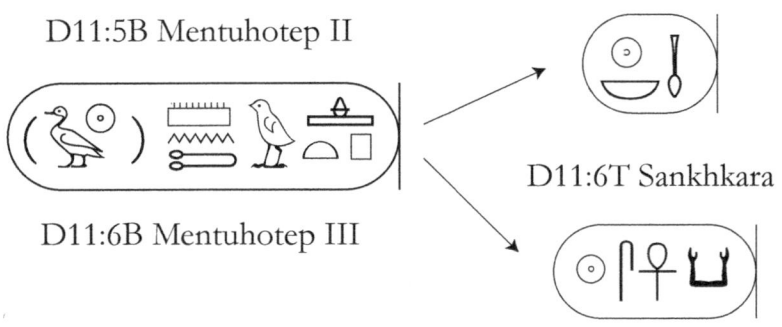

D11:6B Mentuhotep III

D11:6T Sankhkara

Once again, Dynasty 18 names
have many variations and epithets. Not all are
included in the Field Guide.

9.2 Contains 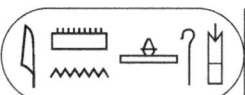 *and starts with* 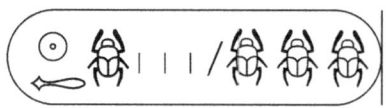 .

D18:2B Amenhotep I   D18:2T Djeserkara

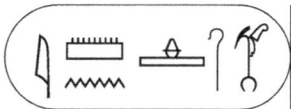

D18:7B Amenhotep II   D18:7T Aakheperura

D18:9B Amenhotep III   D18:9T Nebmaatra

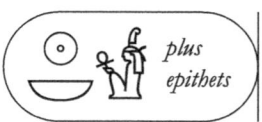

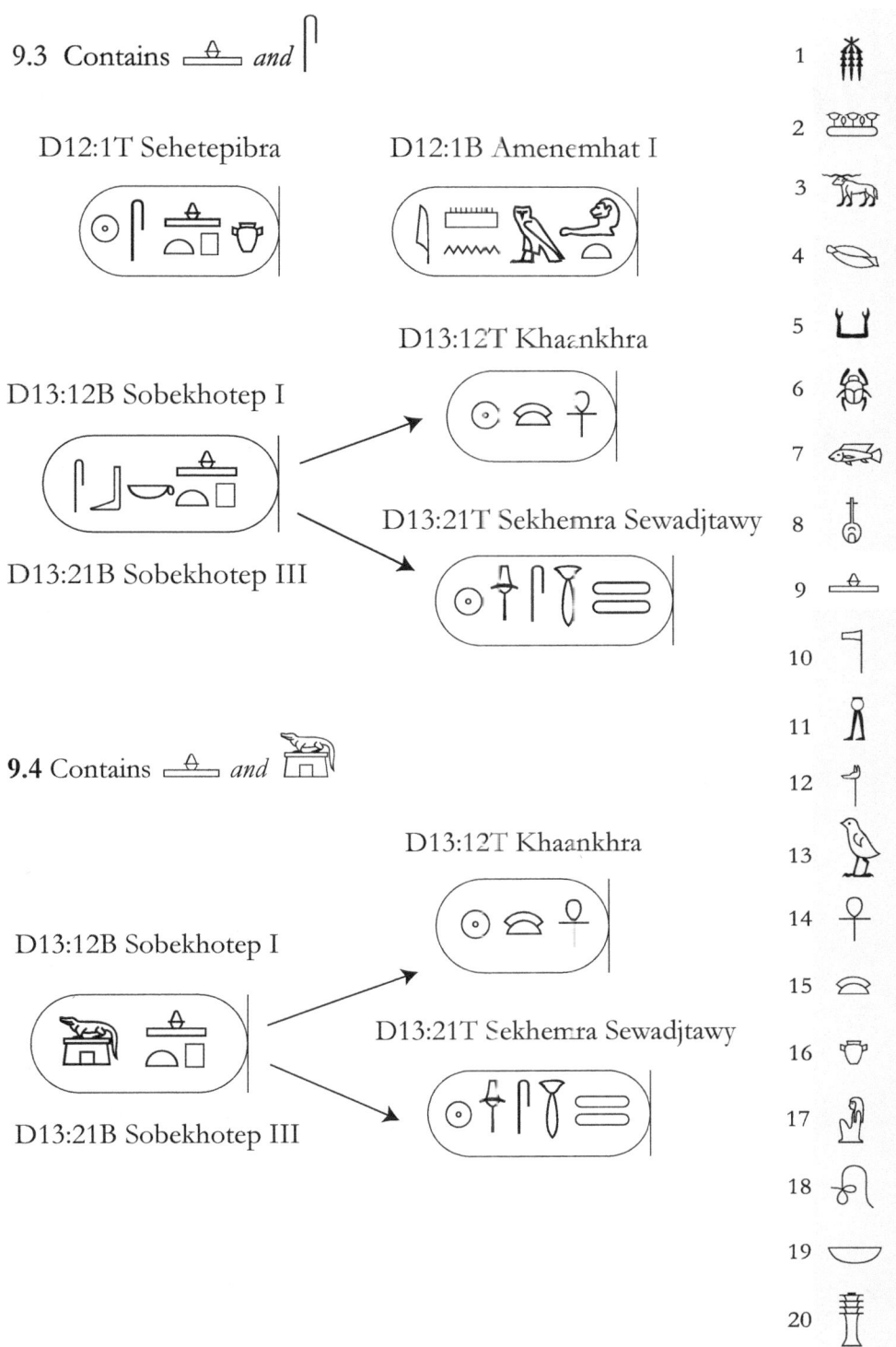

9.3 Contains ⚊ and ❘

D12:1T Sehetepibra   D12:1B Amenemhat I

D13:12B Sobekhotep I

D13:12T Khaankhra

D13:21B Sobekhotep III

D13:21T Sekhemra Sewadjtawy

9.4 Contains ⚊ and 🐊

D13:12B Sobekhotep I

D13:12T Khaankhra

D13:21T Sekhemra Sewadjtawy

D13:21B Sobekhotep III

1
2
3
4
5
6
7
8
9
10
11
12
13
14
15
16
17
18
19
20
21

9.5 Contains 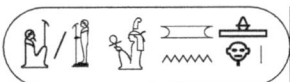 *and*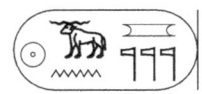

    D19:4B Merenptah-hetephermaat   D19:4T Baenra-merynetjeru

 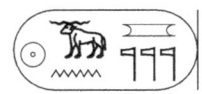

or

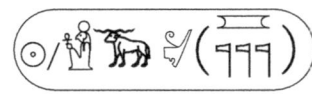

10 Contains 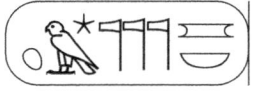 /Netjer/ (R8) *Temple banner; god, divine*

    10.1 Contains (three)

      D34:11T Horsieset-Merynetjeru   D34:11B Domitianus

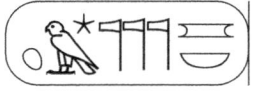 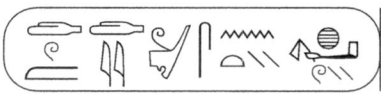

    10.2 Contains (two)

    D18:13B (Itnetjer-)Ay Netjerheqawaset D18:13T Kheperkheperura

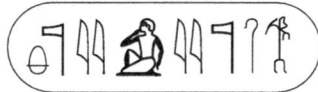 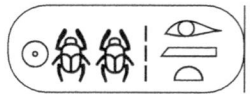

    10.3 Contains a single

      D25 Divine Adoratrice Amenirdis

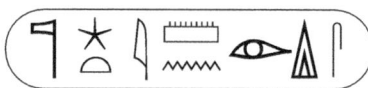

    D20:11B Hemnetjer-tepyenamen D20:11T Herihor-siamen

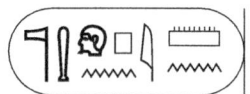 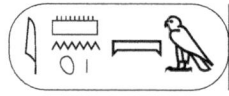

11 Contains 𓈖 /In/ (W25) *pot with legs*

D11:2B Intef I
D11:4B Intef III *(not in Field Guide)*

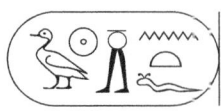

D11:3B Intef II

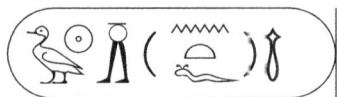

1	𓏴
2	𓋥
3	𓃾
4	𓆭
5	𓎶
6	𓆣
7	𓆛
8	𓋹
9	𓃀
10	𓏏
11	𓈖
12	𓄿
13	𓅂
14	𓋹
15	𓂋
16	𓎼
17	𓃰
18	𓆑
19	𓎡
20	𓊽
21	𓈒

12 Contains ⌐ /User/ (F12) *Canine head on a staff; power*

    12.1 Contains ⌐ as the first sign in the cartouche

    12.2 Contains ⌐ and starts with ◠ (𓅃)

    12.3 Contains ⌐ and starts with 𓇳

    12.4 Contains ⌐ *and* 𓏤

    12.5 Contains ⌐ *and* contains 𓄿 | | |

    12.6 Contains ⊙ ⌐ 𓊽

    ⊙ or 𓁛 (Ra) + ⌐ + a version of Maat: 𓁦 / 𓏤 / ⟹

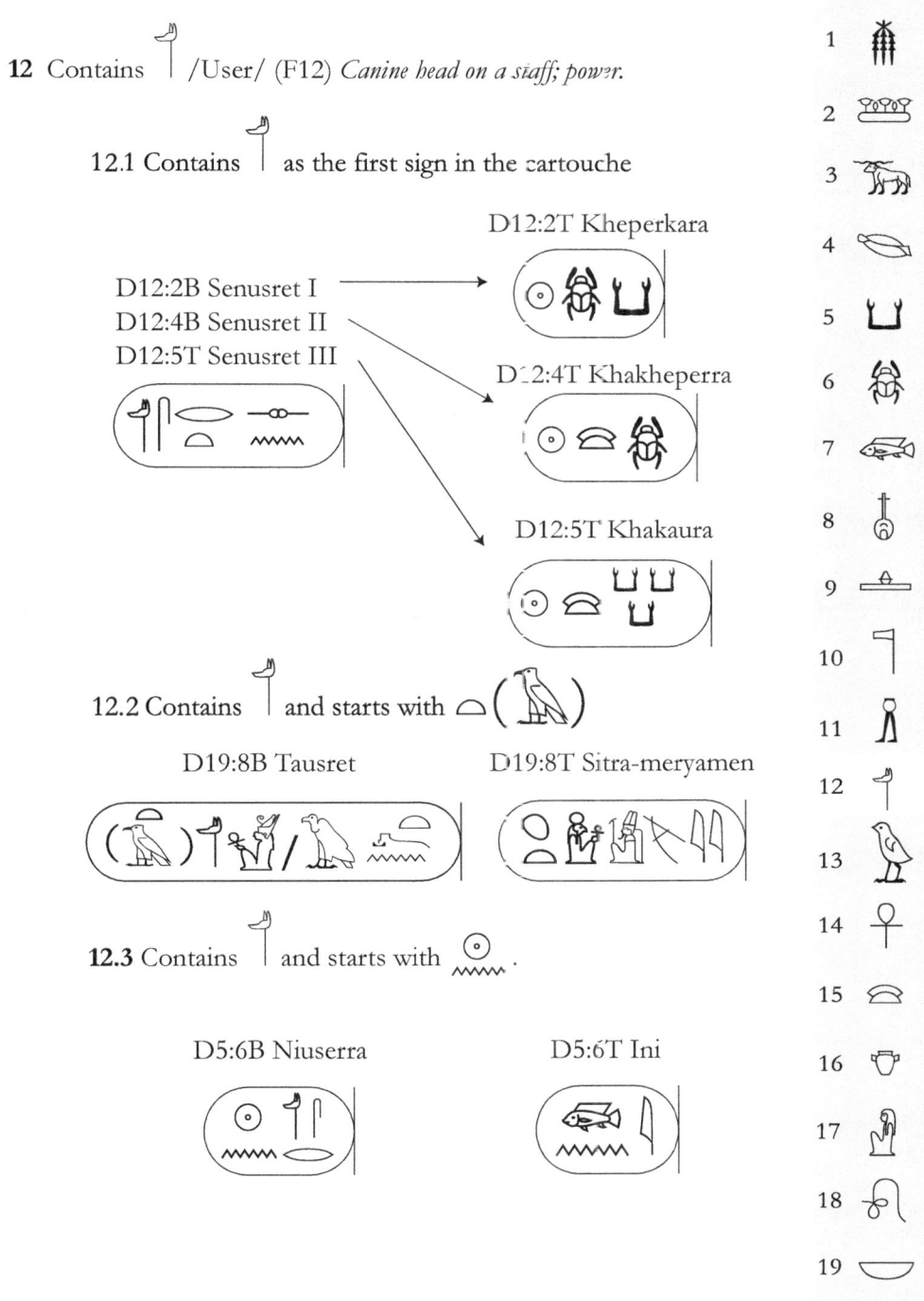

12 Contains ⸾ /User/ (F12) *Canine head on a staff; power.*

12.1 Contains ⸾ as the first sign in the cartouche

D12:2T Kheperkara

D12:2B Senusret I ⟶
D12:4B Senusret II
D12:5T Senusret III

D12:4T Khakheperra

D12:5T Khakaura

12.2 Contains ⸾ and starts with ⌒ (𓅀)

D19:8B Tausret   D19:8T Sitra-meryamen

12.3 Contains ⸾ and starts with ☉.

D5:6B Niuserra   D5:6T Ini

1
2
3
4
5
6
7
8
9
10
11
12
13
14
15
16
17
18
19
20
21

12.4 Contains 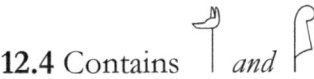 *and*

D22:5T Usermaatra-setepenamen

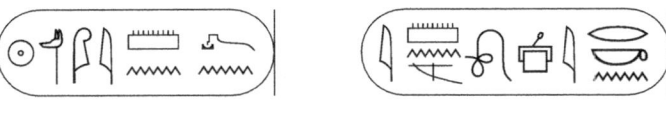

12.5 Contains 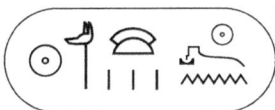 *and*

D20:1T Userkhaura setepenra   D20:1B Setnakht

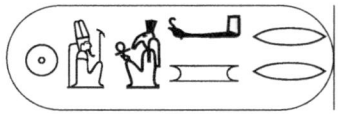

12.6 Contains the phrase /User-Maat-Ra/:

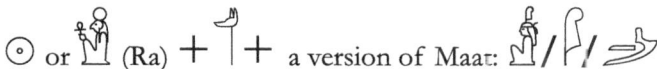 a version of Maat:

This phrase, *The justice of Re is Powerful* **(Clayton p 146)**, begins the throne names of at least ten pharaohs of Dynasties 19 - 23. This name is obviously complicated. Luckily the *User, power,* sign remains constant. *Ra* can be written with the *sun disk* or a *falcon-headed god* wearing that same *sun disk* on his head. *Maat,* however, can be written with any of the three hieroglyphs listed above.

D19:3T Usermaatra-setepenra

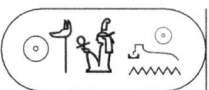

D19:3B Ramses II

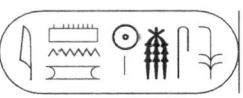

D20:2T Usermaatra-meryamen

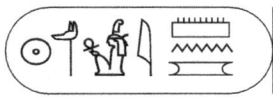

D20:2B Ramses III

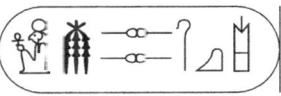

D22:5T Usermaatra-setepenamen

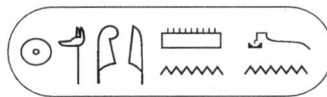

D22:5B Osorkon II

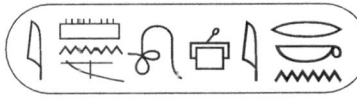

1

2

3

4

5

6

7

8

9

10

11

12

13

14

15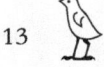

16

17

18

19

20

21

13 Contains at least one bird:

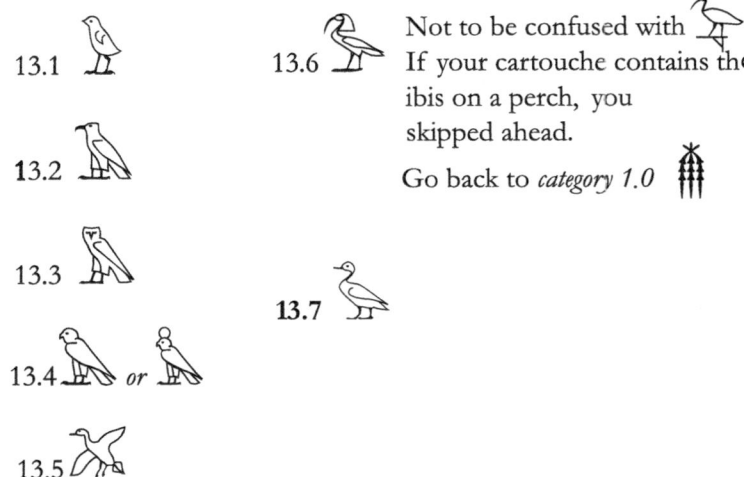

13.1

13.2

13.3

13.4 *or*

13.5

13.6 Not to be confused with
If your cartouche contains the
ibis on a perch, you
skipped ahead.

Go back to *category 1.0*

13.7

The combination /Sa Ra/, the royal title meaning *Son of Ra*, is normally found *outside* a cartouche, not technically being part of a king's name. That said, it was sometimes included inside the cartouche. If you come across this combination of signs, omit them and start going through the *Key* from the beginning.

Here are a few examples of this, with references to where they are listed in the key.

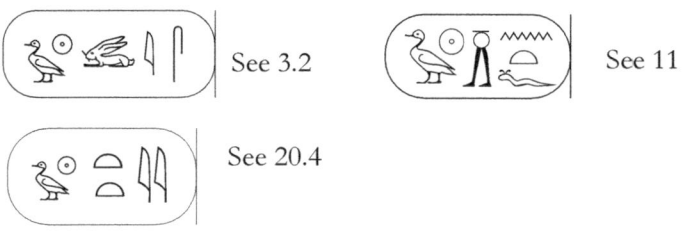

See 3.2

See 11

See 20.4

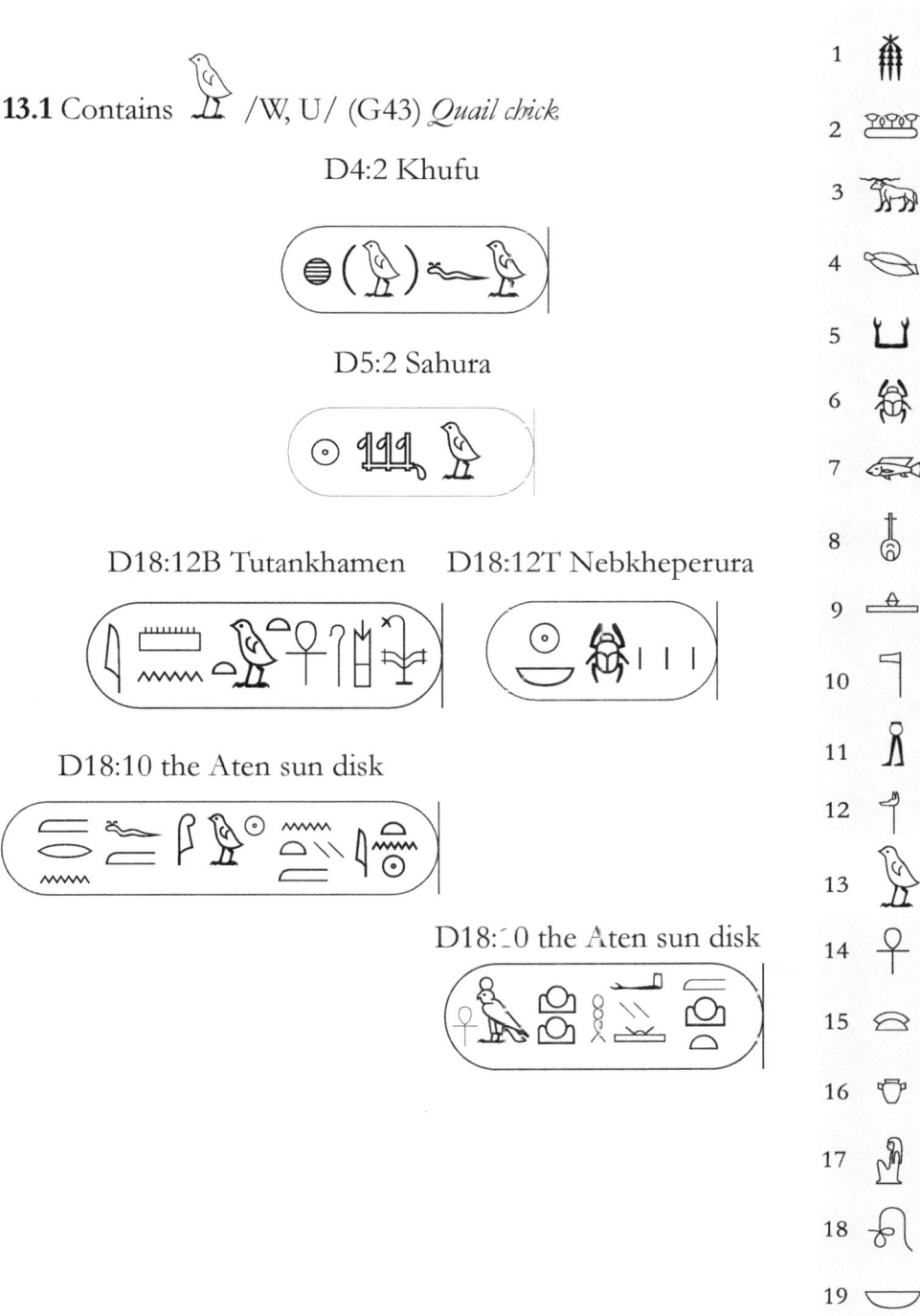

13.1 Contains /W, U/ (G43) *Quail chick*

D4:2 Khufu

D5:2 Sahura

D18:12B Tutankhamen   D18:12T Nebkheperura

D18:10 the Aten sun disk

D18:10 the Aten sun disk

1
2
3
4
5
6
7
8
9
10
11
12
13
14
15
16
17
18
19
20
21

13.2 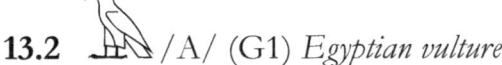 /A/ (G1) *Egyptian vulture*

13.2.1 Contains 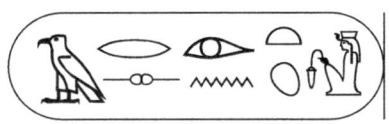 *and* ⌒◯⌐

D33 Queen Arsinoe

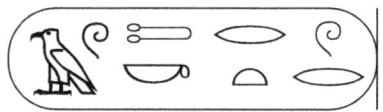

13.2.2 Begins with

Autocrator, title of Roman emperors, is spelled many different ways but usually starts with these two characters.

13.3 Contains

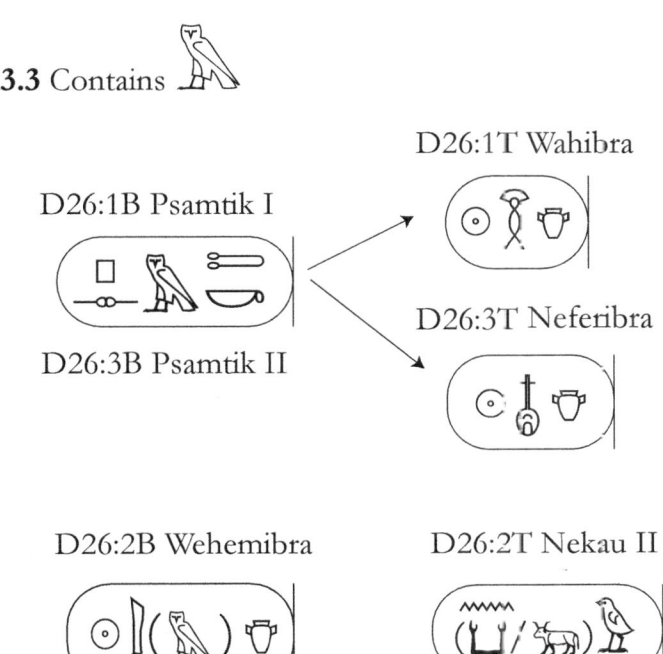

D26:1B Psamtik I

D26:1T Wahibra

D26:3B Psamtik II

D26:3T Neferibra

D26:2B Wehemibra

D26:2T Nekau II

1

2

3

4

5

6

7

8

9

10

11

12

13

14

15

16

17

18

19

20

21

13.4 Contains 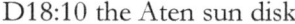 /Hor/ (G5) *Falcon; god Horus or* 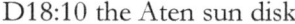 /Ra-Horakhti/ (G9) *Falcon with sun disk; god Horus on the Horizon.*

D18:10 the Aten sun disk   D18:10 the Aten sun disk

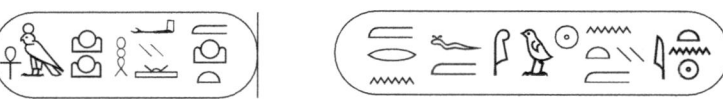

D30:3B Nakhthorheb   D30:3T Snedjemibra

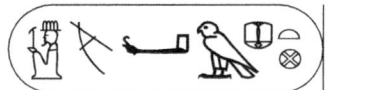

D18:14B Horemheb   D18:14T Djeserkheperura

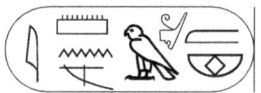
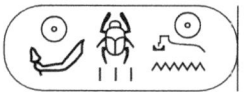

D20:11B Herihor-siamen   D20:11T Hemnetjer tepyenamen

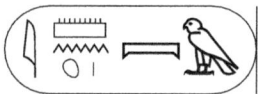
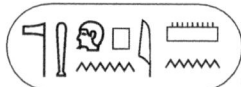

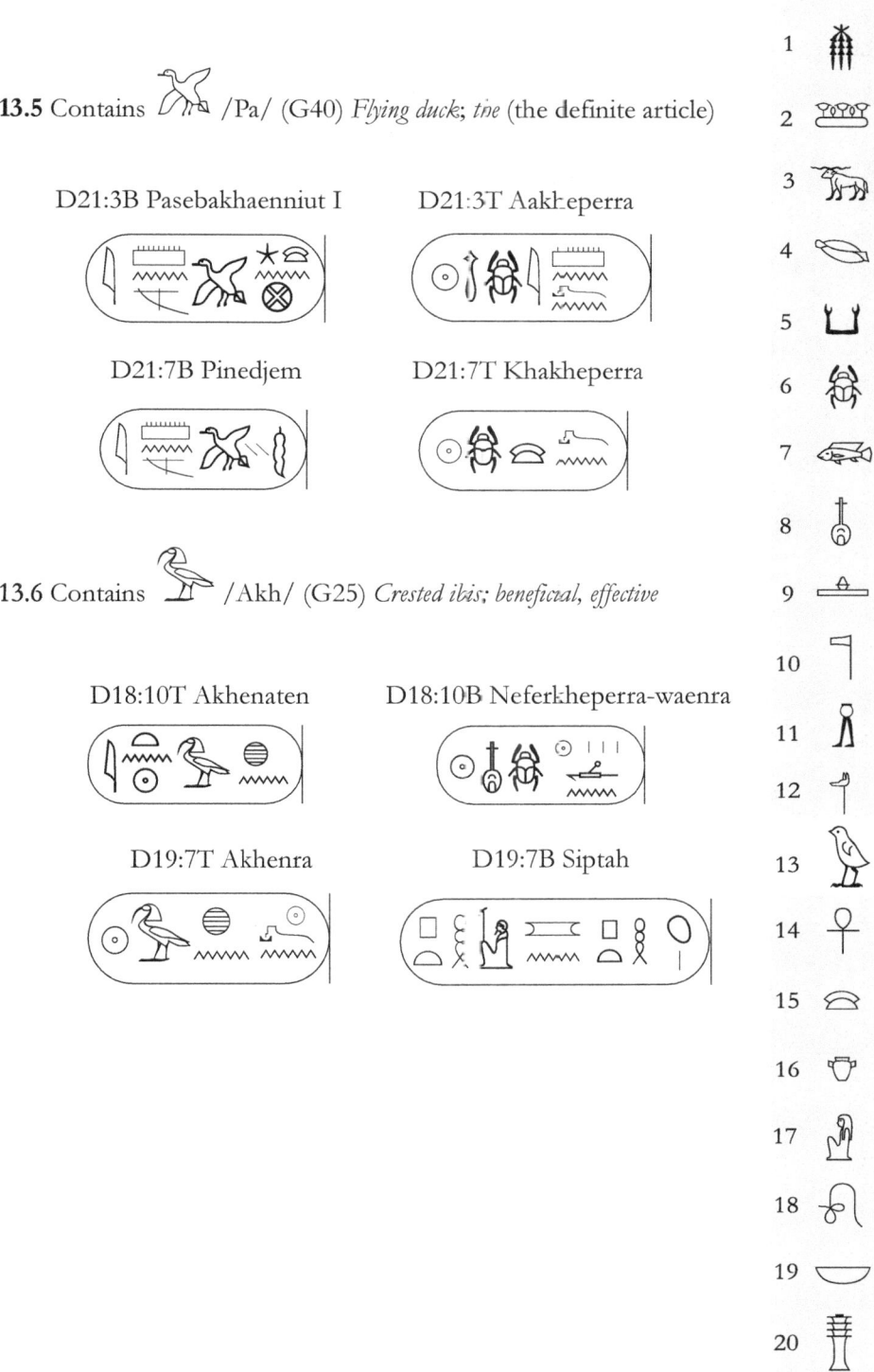

13.5 Contains /Pa/ (G40) *Flying duck; the* (the definite article)

D21:3B Pasebakhaenniut I   D21:3T Aakheperra

D21:7B Pinedjem   D21:7T Khakheperra

13.6 Contains /Akh/ (G25) *Crested ibis; beneficial, effective*

D18:10T Akhenaten   D18:10B Neferkheperra-waenra

D19:7T Akhenra   D19:7B Siptah

1

2

3

4

5

6

7

8

9

10

11

12

13

14

15

16

17

18

19

20

21

13.7 Contains 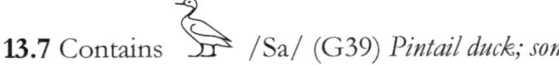 /Sa/ (G39) *Pintail duck; son*

D18:6 Queen Sitiah/Ahsat

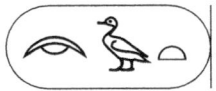

D21:6B Siamen

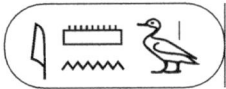

D21:6T Netjerkheperra

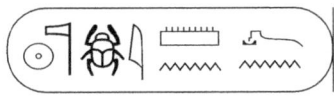

D19:8T Sitra Meryamen

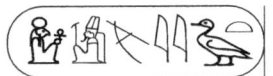

D18:8B Tausret

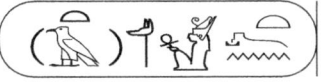

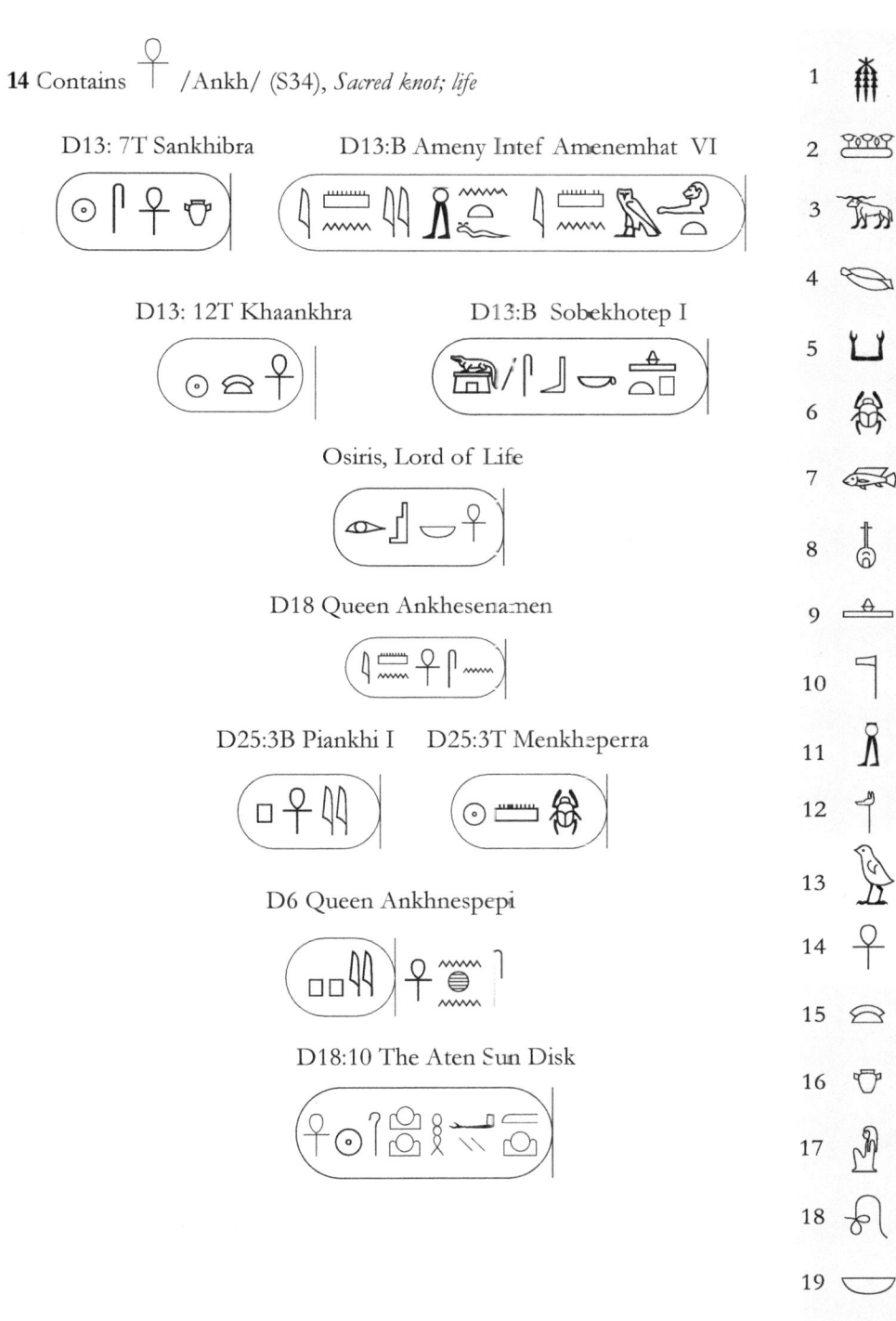

14 Contains /Ankh/ (S34), *Sacred knot; life*

D13: 7T Sankhibra

D13:B Ameny Intef Amenemhat VI

D13: 12T Khaankhra

D13:B Sobekhotep I

Osiris, Lord of Life

D18 Queen Ankhesenamen

D25:3B Piankhi I   D25:3T Menkheperra

D6 Queen Ankhnespepi

D18:10 The Aten Sun Disk

1
2
3
4
5
6
7
8
9
10
11
12
13
14
15
16
17
18
19
20
21

15 Contains 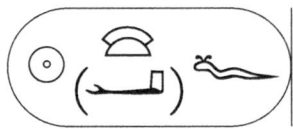 /Kha/ (N28) *Sun rising behind hills; appear, shine*

D4:4 Khafra

D13:pB Menkhaura   D13pT Seshib

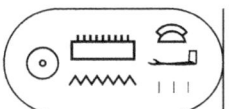   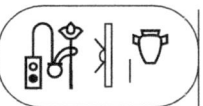

16 Contains /Ib/ (F34) *Heart; mind, understanding, will*

D26:1B Psamtik I

D26:1T Wahibra

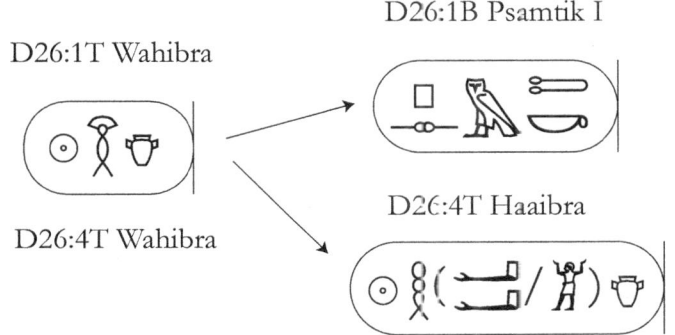

D26:4T Wahibra

D26:4T Haaibra

D26:4T Haaibra

D26:4B Wahibra

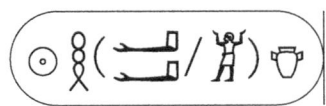   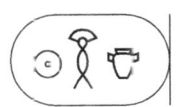

D26:2T Wehemibra

Nekau II

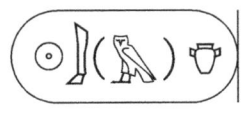   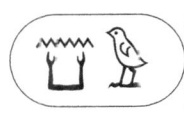

or

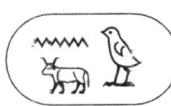

D13:12B Seshib

D13:12T Menkhaura

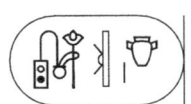   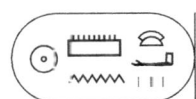

1

2

3

4

5

6

7

8

9

10

11

12

13

14

15

16

17

18

19

20

21

16 Contains 🏺, continued

D30:3T Snedjemibra

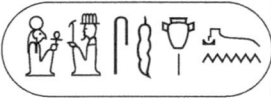

D30:3B Nakhthorheb

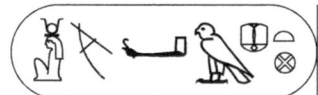

D26:4 Haaibra

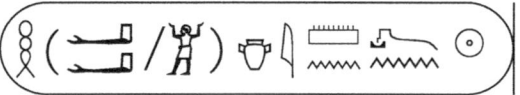

D32:3B Alexander IV

D12:1T Sehetepibra

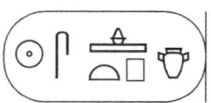

D30:3B Amenemhat I

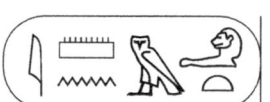

D25:5T Khnemibra

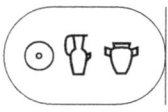

D25:5B Ahmose Sineit

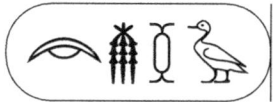

17 Contains *human figures* or **ANTHROPOMORPHIC** *gods*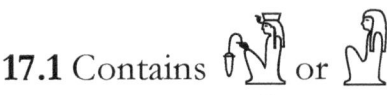

  17.1 Contains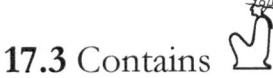

  17.2 Contains

  17.3 Contains

  17.4 Contains

  17.5 Contains two seated gods facing each other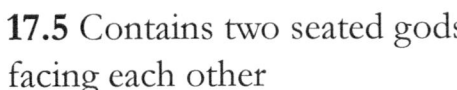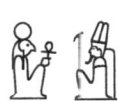

1

2

3

4

5

6

7

8

9

10

11

12

13

14

15

16

17

18

19

20

21

17.1 Contains 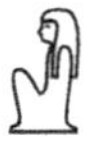 /Silent/ (B1) *Woman, or* 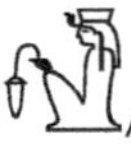 /Silent/ (B7) *Queen*

D18:9 Queen Tiy

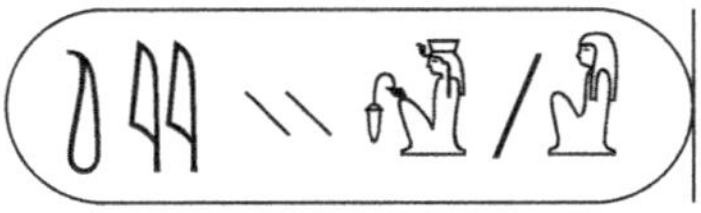

17.2 Contains 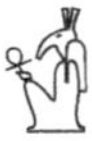 /Set/ (Cx4) *God Seth*

D20:1B Setnakht   D20:1T Userkhaura

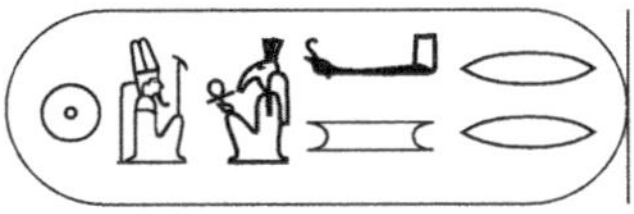

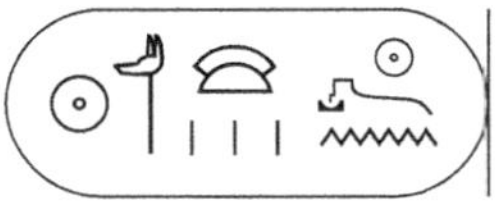

D19:2B Sety I 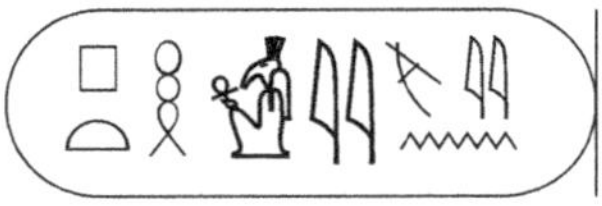   D19:2T Menmaatra

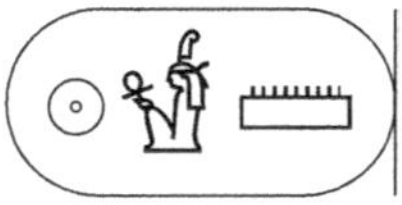

D19:6B Sety II 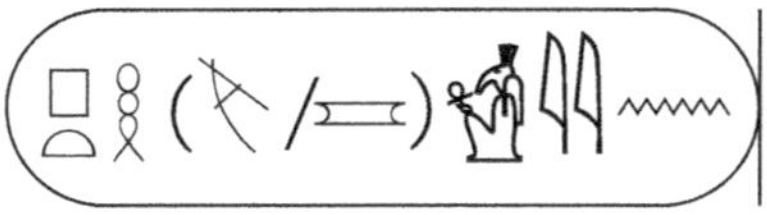   D19:6T Userkheperura

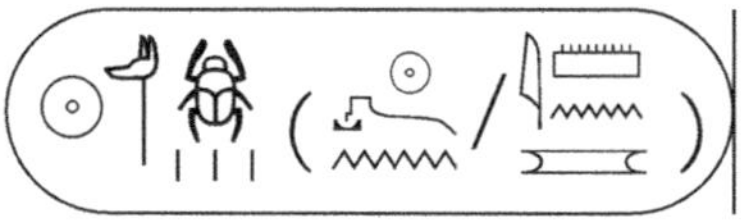

17.3 Contains /Usir/ (C83, not in Gardiner)
God Osiris

D19:2B Sety I   D19:2T Menmaatra

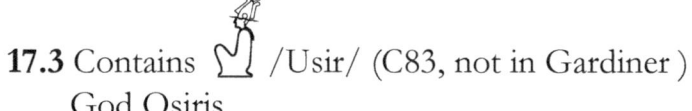

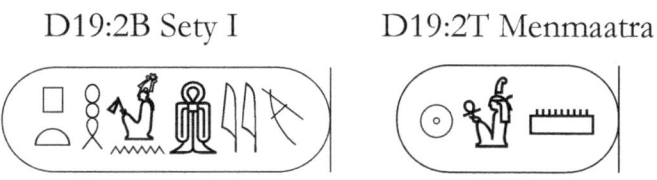

17.4 Contains ⬚ /Maat/ (Cx1) *Goddess Maat*, wearing or holding feather; *truth, justice, order*

17.4.1 Contains ⬚ and ⬚

D19:2T Menmaatra   D19:2B Sety I

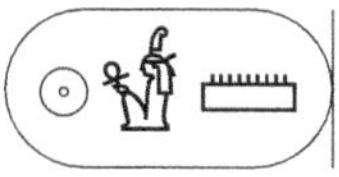

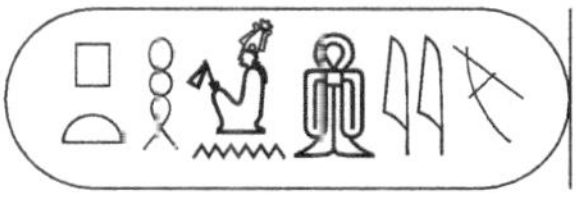

D20:10T Menmaatra-setepenptah 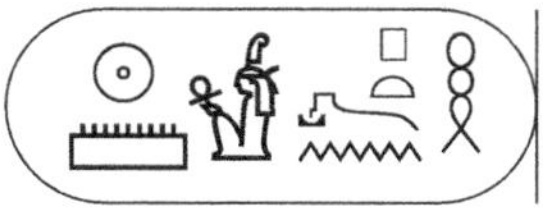   D20:10B Ramses XI

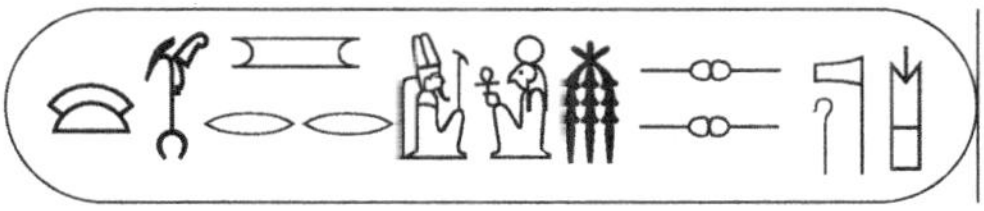

17.4.2 Contains ⬚ and ⬚

D18:9T Nebmaatra   D18:9B Amenhotep III

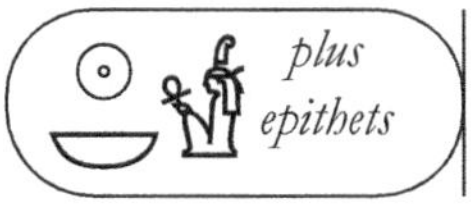

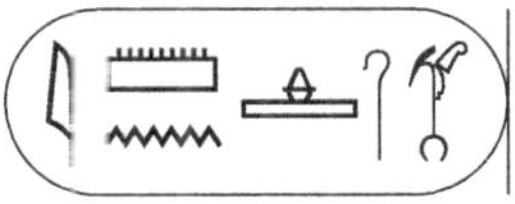

plus epithets

D20:5T Nebmaatra 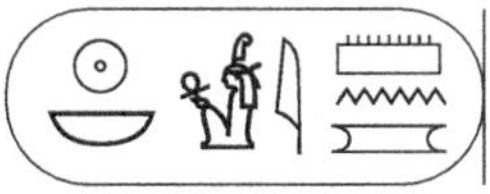   D20:5B Ramses VI

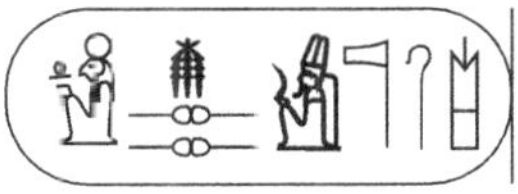

17.4.3 Contains ⬚ and ⬚

D20:3T Heqamaatra   D20:3B Ramses IV

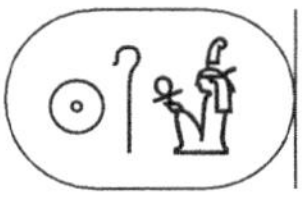

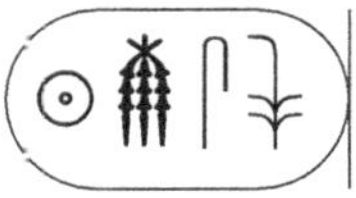

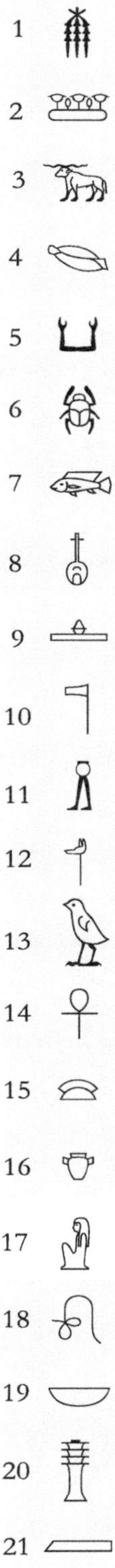

1
2
3
4
5
6
7
8
9
10
11
12
13
14
15
16
17
18
19
20
21

17 Two gods facing each other

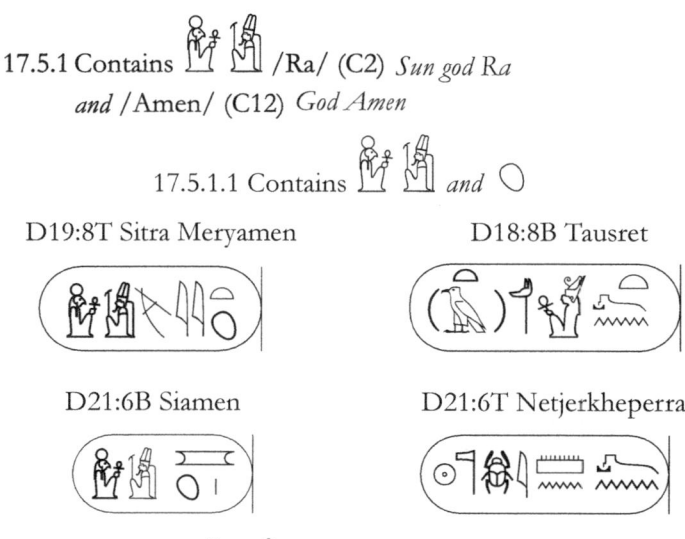

17.5.1 Contains ⸏ ⸏ /Ra/ (C2) *Sun god Ra*
and /Amen/ (C12) *God Amen*

17.5.1.1 Contains ⸏ ⸏ *and* ◯

D19:8T Sitra Meryamen   D18:8B Tausret

D21:6B Siamen   D21:6T Netjerkheperra

17.5.1.2 Contains ⸏ ⸏ *and both* ⸏ *and* ⸏

D32:1B Alexander the Great

D32:1T Setepenra-meryamen

D33:1B Ptolemy I

D33:1T Setepenra-meryamen

17.5.2 *Two Amens* facing each other

D21:6B Siamen   D21:6T Netjerkheperra-setepenamen

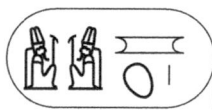   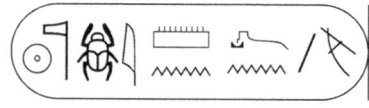

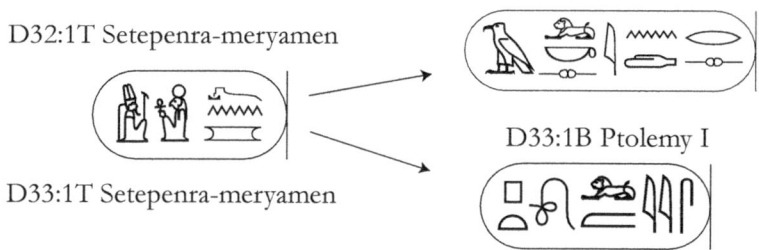

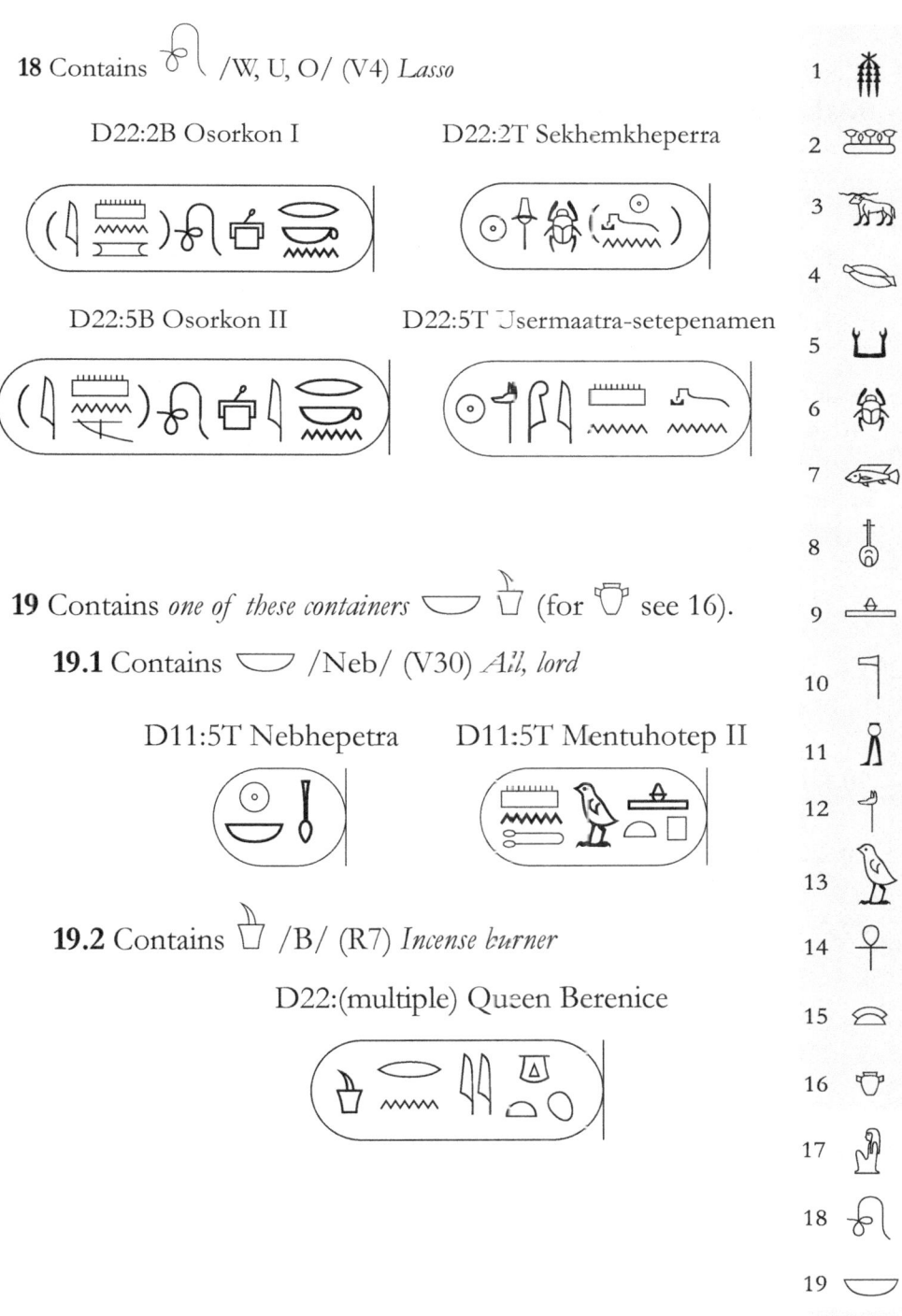

18 Contains /W, U, O/ (V4) *Lasso*

D22:2B Osorkon I

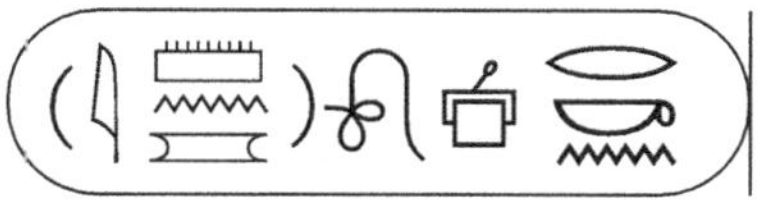

D22:2T Sekhemkheperra

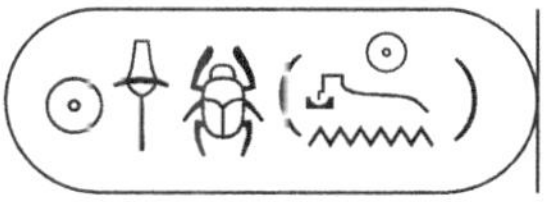

D22:5B Osorkon II

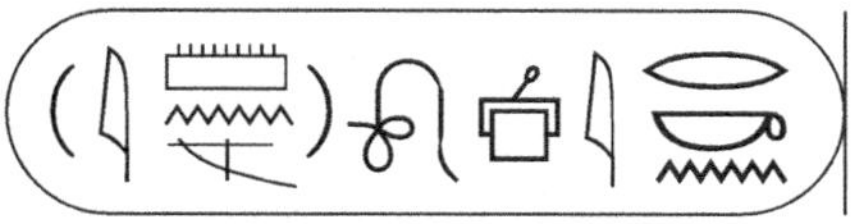

D22:5T Usermaatra-setepenamen

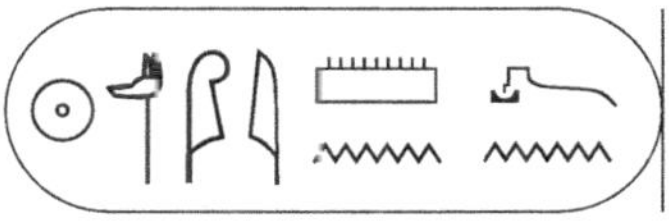

19 Contains *one of these containers* (for see 16).

19.1 Contains /Neb/ (V30) *All, lord*

D11:5T Nebhepetra

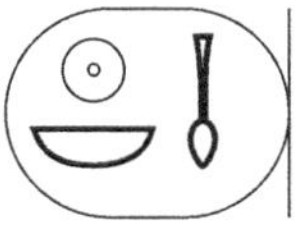

D11:5T Mentuhotep II

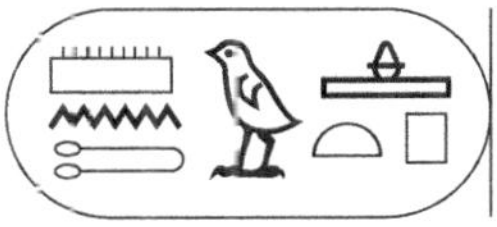

19.2 Contains /B/ (R7) *Incense burner*

D22:(multiple) Queen Berenice

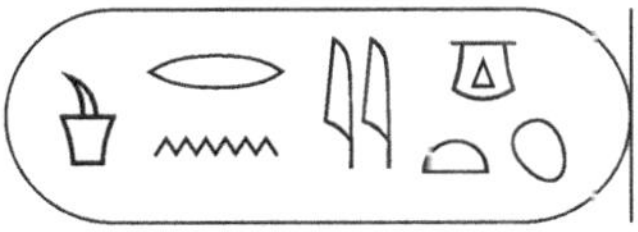

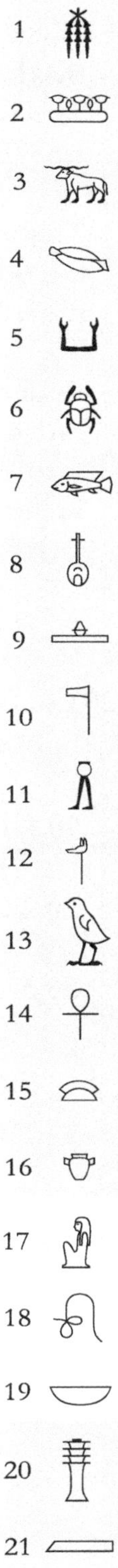
1
2
3
4
5
6
7
8
9
10
11
12
13
14
15
16
17
18
19
20
21

Note: I freely acknowledge that the next two *categories*, "tall and thin hieroglyphs" and "low and wide hieroglyphs" are forced. This is how I have decided to deal with the debris remaining from classifying all the other cartouches to this point.

This would be a good time to take my earlier advice and try to key out the *corresponding* cartouche of a pair, birth or throne name, if available.

If all else fails, by this point you should be able to just *read* your cartouche and look it up in the index or in a web browser.

Remember, there are hundreds of cartouches that are not included in the *Field Guide*.

20 Contains tall and thin hieroglyphs:

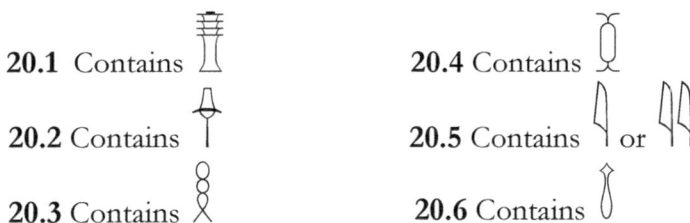

20.1 Contains

20.2 Contains

20.3 Contains

20.4 Contains

20.5 Contains ⁣ or

20.6 Contains

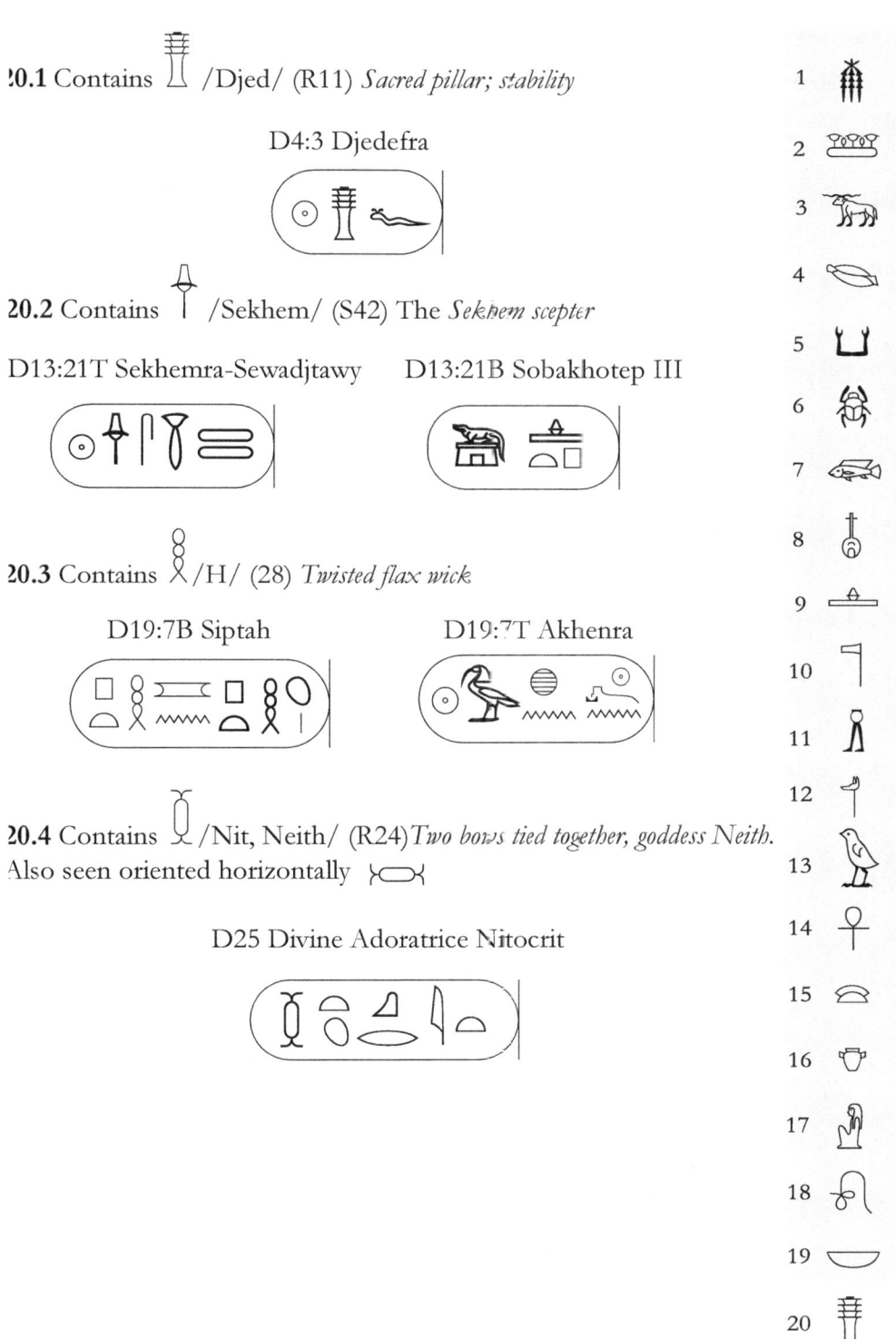

20.1 Contains 𐎤 /Djed/ (R11) *Sacred pillar; stability*

D4:3 Djedefra

20.2 Contains 𐎤 /Sekhem/ (S42) The *Sekhem scepter*

D13:21T Sekhemra-Sewadjtawy   D13:21B Sobakhotep III

20.3 Contains 𐎤 /H/ (28) *Twisted flax wick*

D19:7B Siptah   D19:7T Akhenra

20.4 Contains 𐎤 /Nit, Neith/ (R24)*Two bows tied together, goddess Neith.*
Also seen oriented horizontally

D25 Divine Adoratrice Nitocrit

1

2

3

4

5

6

7

8

9

10

11

12

13

14

15

16

17

18

19

20

21

20.5 Contains 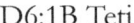 /I/ or /Y/ Reeds

D6:1B Teti

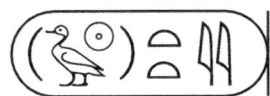

D6:3B Pepy I   D6:3T Meryra

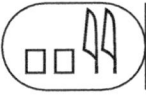   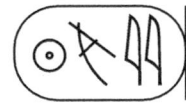

D6:5B Pepy II   D63:T Neferkara

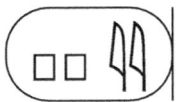   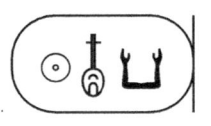

D6:3T Meryra   D6:3B Pepy I

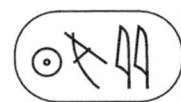   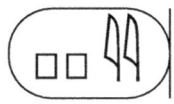

D25 Divine Adoratrice Amenirdis

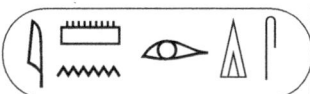

D5:8B Isesi   D5:8T Djedkara

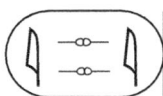   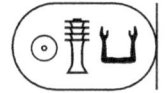

D18:10 the Aten sun disk

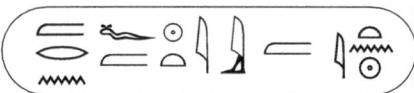

D19:3 Queen Merit-Amen

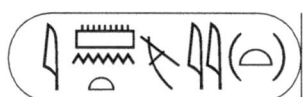

D32:1B Alexander the Great   D32:1T Meryamen setepenra

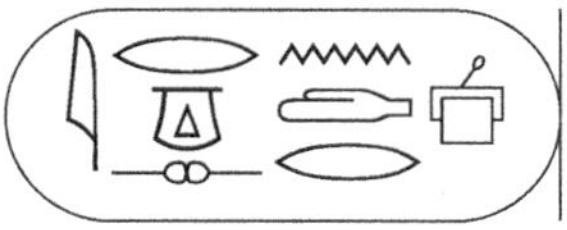

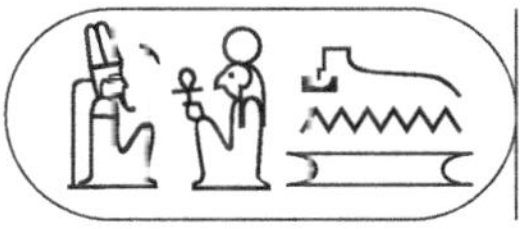

20:6 Contains ⌀ /Aa/ (O29) *Architectural column; great*
Also seen oriented horizontally.

Per-Aa (*Great House, Pharaoh*), Generic term used
during and after the New Kingdom

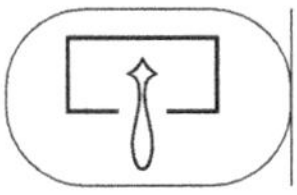

21 Contains low, wide hieroglyphs

   21.1 Contains ⬜ /Maat/ (Aa11) *Statue base?;*
Truth, Justice

     D12:6T Nimaatra   D12:6B Amenemhat III

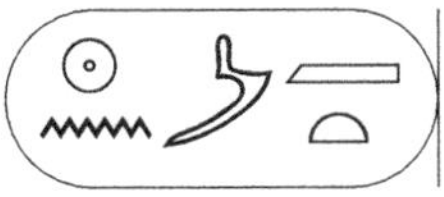

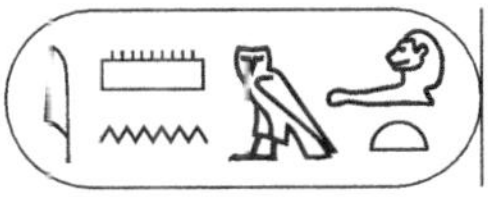

   21.2 Contains ⬭ , see 20.4.

   21.3 Contains ⬅ , see 20.6.

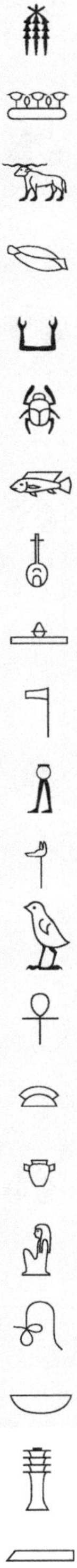

1

2

3

4

5

6

7

8

9

10

11

12

13

14

15

16

17

18

19

20

21

Important Principles

Arrangement of Hieroglyphs: The Egyptians liked to fill the space in a pleasing way. They wrote hieroglyphs so they would fill an imaginary rectangle. See D4:1, pharaoh number one of the Fourth Dynasty.

The letter e: When a vowel isn't explicitly written in Egyptian, we insert an *e* to make a word easier to pronounce. The consonantal skeleton of *Nefer*, for instance, is NFR. We supply the *e*'s so we can comfortably say it. See example in D4:1.

Honorific Transposition: When a cartouche contains the name of a god, the Egyptians always "bump the god up to first class," to the front of the cartouche, regardless of where the god's name is pronounced in the pharaoh's name. See D4:3.

Plurals: In Egyptian, three signs together denote plural. Phonetically, an/U (oo)/ sound is added to the word. Thus, /Ka-u/, with three /Ka/s, is plural *spirits* or *souls*. Instead of repeating the hieroglyph three times, three strokes can be added behind the sign. See D4:6, D18:2.

The presence of a cartouche does not mean the tomb or artifact belongs to the ruler named in the cartouche. It is important to note that while a pharaoh's cartouche may be seen on the wall of a tomb, sarcophagus or on other item, that does *not* mean that the tomb or object belonged to that king. Officials who worked under one or more pharaohs often included the names of those monarchs in their résumés on the walls of their own tombs. Furthermore, they tended to include pharaohs' names, inside cartouches, in their children's names. See D6:1 Meriteti.

Effaced names, usurped monuments: We saw how some pharaohs, or at least their supporters, hacked out the names of gods who were out of favor, or removed others' cartouches entirely. Common candidates for being hacked out of inscriptions are the god Set/Seth, Queen Hatshepsut, and anything containing the name of the god Amen. See D13:21, D18:10, D19:2B. Some also *added* their names to those of existing pharaohs, on temples and sarcophagi.

Both cartouches are often required for positive identification of a ruler: There are 11 kings named Ramses; 15 Ptolemies; several Amenemhats, among other examples. Whenever possible, check the associated BIRTH or THRONE NAME along with any cartouche you are trying to read. See D6:3B and D6:5B, Pepi I and II.

Combined Cartouches: Occasionally a ruler's THRONE NAME and BIRTH NAME, and even royal titles, are combined into one cartouche. If a cartouche seems excessively long, try dividing it up. See D12:2.

Alternate Phonetics: Names of Greco-Roman rulers, not being in the Egyptian language, had to be written phonetically. To give these phonetically spelled-out names some pizazz, those pharaohs, or their designated "name-spellers," tried very hard to come up with original ways to write those names. If you have not had special training, or done a lot of close study yourself, these names can be unintelligible. See Roman emperors Dynasty 34.

List of Royal Names

The following list includes the names of the royal personages whose cartouches are described in Section I, Cartouches of Ancient Egyptian Royalty. It includes BIRTH NAMES and THRONE NAMES, both what I call *the Egyptian version*, (the name where the syllables seem to correspond most closely with the actual hieroglyphs), as well as Greek and other versions of the names. Names of Roman emperors are also included.

Each name is followed by an alphanumeric sequence describing where to find it in the *Field Guide*. For instance, D11:6B refers to Dynasty 11, pharaoh number 6, BIRTH NAME. D11:6T, refers to the same pharaoh's THRONE NAME.

For standardization's sake, the numbers, where possible, are those assigned by VON BECKERATH.

Note that although technically the ancient Egyptian dynasties only number up to 31, for indexing purposes I have assigned D32-D34 to the Macedonian Kings, Ptolemies, and Roman emperors.

Aakheperenra D18:4T
Aakheperkara D18:3T
Aakheperra-setepenamen D21:3T
Aakheperura D18:7T
Acherres D18:13B
Ahmose I D18:1B
Ahmose Nefertari, Queen D18
Ahmose-Sineit D26:5B
Ahmosis D18:1B
Ahsat, Queen D18
Akhenaten D18:10B
Akhenra D19:7T
Alexander I, Ptolemy X D33:10B
Alexander I the Great, Alexandros D32:1B
Alexander IV D32:3B
Alexander II D32:3B
Alexander III of Macedonia D32:1B
Amenemhat I D12:1B; Amenemhat III D12:6B

Amenhotep I D18:2B; Amenhotep II D18:7B; Amenhotep III D18:9B; Amenhotep IV D18:10B
Amenirdis I, II Divine Adoratrice D25
Amenophis D18:2B; D18:7B; D18:9B
Ameny Intef Amenemhat VI D13:7B
Ammanemes D12:1B; Ammenemes D12:6B
Ammenephthes D19:4T
Amosis D26:5B
Ankhesenamen, Queen D18
Ankhnes neferibra, Divine Adoratrice, D26
Ankhnespepi D6
Antef D11:2; D11:3
Antoninus: Pius Imperator Titus Aelius Caesar Hadrianus
        Antoninus Augustus Pius. Romans 15
Apries D26:4B
Armesis D18:14B
Arsinoe, Queens D33
Ay D18:13B
Baenra-meryamen/-merynetjeru D19:4T
Berenice, Queens D33
Bicheres D4:7
Bintanath Queen D19
Caesar Augustus, Romans 1
Caesarion D33:13cB
Caligula: Gaius Caesar Augustus Germanicus. Romans 3
Chefren D4:4
Cheops D4:2
Claudius: Tiberius Claudius Caesar Augustus Germanicus
        Romans 4
Cleopatra, Queens D33
Cleopatra VII, Queen D33:13B
Commodus: Aurelius Commodus Antoninus Augustus.
        Romans 17
Djedefra D4:3
Djedkara D25:5T; D5:8T
Djedkaura D25:5T
Djehutymes D18:3B; D18:4B; D18:6B
Djeserkara D18:2T
Djeserkheperura D18:14T

Domitian: Imperator Caesar Domitianus Augustus. Romans 11
Epiphanes (Ptolemaios)
Euergetes I (Ptolemaios) D33:3B; Euergetes II (Ptolemaios)
D33:9B
Gaius: Caesar Augustus Germanicus (Caligula)
Haaibra D26:4T
Haaibra-setepenamen D32:3T
Hadrian: Imperator Caesar Traianus Hadrianus Augustus.
                    Romans 14
Haremheb D18:14B
Hedjkheperra D22:1T
Hemnetjer-tepyenamen D20:11T
Heqakheperra D22:3T
Heqamaatra D20:3T
Herihor-siamen D20:11B
Horemheb D18:14B
Ikhnaten D18:10B
Ini D5:6B
Intef I D11:2; Intef II D11:3
Inyotef D11:2; D11:3
Isesi D5:8B
Iwaennetjermenkh netjeretmenkhetsatra setepenptah
Irmaatenra senenankhenamen D33:10T
Iwaennetjermenkh netjeretmeretmutes nedjetsetepenptah
Irmaatenra sekhemankhamen D33:9T
Iwaennetjerwymenkhwy-setepptah-userkara-sekhemankhamen
D33:4T
Iwaennetjerwymerwytu-setepptah-userkara-sekhemankhamen
D33:5T
Iwaennetjerwyper-setepenptah Khepri Irmaatenamenra D33:6T
Iwaennetjerwyperwy setepenpta Irmaatenra-sekhemankhamen
D33:8T
Iwaennetjerwysenwy-sekhemankhra-setepamen D33:3T
Iwaenpanetjer entynehem setepenptah Irmaatenra
sekhemankhamen D33:12T
Iwapanetjer entynehem Sepetenptah Irmaatenra
Sekhemankhamen D33:13cT
Kaiu D5:7B
Kakai D5:3B

Kamose D17:15B
Khaankhra D13:12T
Khafra D4:4
Khakaura D12:5T
Khakheperra D12:4T; D21:7T
Kheperkara D12:2T; D30:1T
Kheperkheperura D18:13T
Khepermaatra D20:9T
Khufu D4:2
Knemibra D26:5T
Maatkara D18:5T
Marcus Aurelius: Imperator Caesar Marcus Aurelius Antoninus
        Augustus. Romans 16
Mencheres D4:6; D5:7T
Menephtes D19:7T
Menkauhor D5:7T
Menkaura D4:6
Menkhaura D13-pT
Menkheperra D18:6T
Menkheperra D25:3T; D18:8T
Menmaatra D19:2T
Menmaatra setepenptah D20:10T
Menpehtyra D19:1T
Mentuhotep II D11:5B; Mentuhotep III D11:6B
Mentuhotpe D11:5B; D11:6B
Merenptah D19:4B
Meritamen Queen D19
Meryamen-setepenra D32:1T; D33:1T
Meryra D6:3T
Montuhotep II D11:5B Montuhotep III D11:6B
Mycerinus D4:6
Nakhthorheb D30:3B
Nakhtnebef D30:1B
Nebhepetra D11:5T
Nebkheperura D18:12T
Nebmaatra D18:9T
Nebmaatra-Meryamen D20:5T
Nebpehetra D11:5T
Nebpehtyra D18:1T

Necho D26:2B
Nectanebes D30:1B
Nectanebo I D30:1B
Neferkara D6:5T
Neferibra D26:3T
Neferirkara D5:3T
Neferkara D6:5T; D25:4T
Neferkara-setepenra D20:8T
Neferkheperura-waenra D18:10T
Neferneferuaten-Nefertiti, Queen D18:10
Nefertari, Queen D19
Nefertemkhura D25:6T
Neferuptah, Princess D12
Neferura Princess D18:5
Nekau II D26:2B
Nephercheres D5:3T
Nero: Nero Claudius Caesar Augustus Germanicus. Romans 5
Nerva: Nerva Imperator Caesar Augustus. Romans 12
Netjerkheperra D21:6T
Nimaatra D12:6T
Nitiqret, Divine Adoratrice D26
Nitocris, Divine Adoratrice D26
Nitocrit, Divine Adoratrice D26
Niuserra D5:6T
Onnos D5:9B
Osorkon I D22:2B; Osorkon II D22:5B
Osorthon I D22:2B; Osorthon II D22:5B
Otho: Imperator Marcus Otho Caesar Augustus. Romans 7
Othoes D6:1
Pasebakhaenniut I D21:3B
Pepi I D6:3B; Pepi II D6:5B
Pepy I D6:3B; Pepy II D6:5B
Philadelphus (Ptolemaios) D33:2B
Philometor (Ptolemaios) D33:6T
Philopator (Ptolemaios) D33:4B
Phiops D6:3B; Phiops II D6:5B
Phios D6:3B
Piankhi I D25:3B
Pinedjem D21:7B

Piyi, Piye D25:3B
Psammetichus D26:1B; D26:3B
Psammuthis D26:1B; D26:3B
Psamtik I D26:1B; Psamtik II D26:3B
Psinaches D21:6B
Psusennes I D21:3B
Ptolemaios Epiphanes D33:5B
Ptolemaios Euergetes I D33:3B
Ptolemaios Euergetes II D33:8B
Ptolemaios Neos Dionysos D33:12B
Ptolemaios Philadelphus D33:2B
Ptolemaios Philometor D33:6B
Ptolemaios Philopator D33:4B
Ptolemaios Soter I D33:1B
Ptolemaios Soter II D33:9B
Ptolemy I D33:1B
Ptolemy II D33:2B
Ptolemy III D33:3B
Ptolemy IV D33:4B
Ptolemy V D33:5B
Ptolemy VI D33:6B
Ptolemy VIII D33:8B
Ptolemy IX D33:9B
Ptolemy X D33:10B
Ptolemy XII D33:12B
Ptolemy XV D33:13cB
Radjedef D4:3
Ramses, Ramessu, Ramesses I D19:1B
Ramses, Ramessu, Ramesses II D19:3B
Ramses, Ramessu, Ramesses III D20:2B
Ramses, Ramessu, Ramesses IV D20:3B
Ramses, Ramessu, Ramesses VI (Amenherkhepshef-
Netjerheqaiunu) D20:5B
Ramses, Ramessu, Ramsesses IX (Khaemwaset-Mereramen)
D20:8B
Ramses, Ramessu, Ramesses X (Amenherkhepshef) D20:9B
Ramses, Ramessu, Ramesses XI (Khaemwaset-merreramen-
netjerheqaiunu D20:10B
Rathures D5:6T

Ratoises D4:3
Saba D25:4B
Sabacon D25:4B
Sahura D5:2
Sankhibra D13:7T
Sankhkara D11:6T
Sebekhotpe D13:12B; D13:21B
Sebichos D25:5B
Sehetepibra D12:1T
Sekhemkheperra D22:2T
Sekhemrasewadjtawy D13:21T
Sena'a-ib D13-14:?B
Senedjemibra D30:3T
Senusret I D12:2B; Senusret II D12:4B; Senusret III D12:5B
Senwosre D12:2B, D12:4B, D12:5B
Sepheres D5:2
Seshib D13:pB
Sesonchis D22:1B, D22:3B
Sesostris D12:2B, D12:4B. D12:5B
Sethos D19:2B, D19:6B
Setnakht D20:1B
Setnekhtes D20:1B
Sety I, Seti I D19:2B,
Sety II , Seti II D19:6B
Shabaka, Shabako, Shabakon D25:4B
Shabitka, Shabitko D25:5B
Shepenupet, Divine Adoratrice D25
Shepenwepet I, II, Divine Adoratrice D25
Shepseskaf D4:7
Sheshonq, Shoshenq I D22:1B; Sheshonq, Shoshenq II D22:3B
Siamen D21:6B
Siptah, Siptahs D19:7B
Sitiah, Queen D18
Sitra-Meryamen D19:8T
Sneferu, Snefru, Snofru D4:1
Sobekhotep I or II D13:12B, Sobekhotep III D13:21B
Soris D4:1
Soter I (Ptolemaios) D33:1B
Soter II (Ptolemaios) D33:8B

Suphis D4:2; D4:4
Taharqa D25:6B
Tancheres D5:8T
Tarcus D25:6B
Tausret, Tausert, Queen D19:8B
Teti D6:1B
Thutmose, Thutmosis I D18:3B; Thutmose,
Thutmosis II D18:4B; Thutmose, Thutmosis III D18:6B;
Thutmose, Thutmosis IV D18:8B
Tiberius: Tiberius Caesar Augustus. Romans 2
Titus: Imperator Titus Caesar Vespasianus Augustus.
Romans 10
Tiye, Queen D18
Trajan: Imperator Caesar Divi Nervae Filius Nerva Traianus.
        Romans 13
Tutankhamen D18:12B
Tutankhaten D18:12B
Twosre, Tawosret, Queen D19
Uaphres D26:4B
Unas D5:9B
Usercheres D5:1
Userkaenra-Meryamen D33:2T
Userkaf D5:1
Userkhaura-Setepenra D20:1T
Userkheperura D19:6T
Usermaatra-Meryamen D20:2T
Usermaatra-setepenamen D22:5T
Usermaatra-setepenra D19:3T;
Userten D12:2B, D12:4B, D12:5B
Vespasian: Imperator Caesar Vespasianus Augustus. Romans 9
Wadjkheperra D17:15T
Wahibra D26:1T
Wahibra D26:4B
Wehemibra D26:2T
Wenis D5:9B

Sign List, Gardiner Order

Each entry shows the Gᴀʀᴅɪɴᴇʀ number, the hieroglyph, the pronunciation, the definition, and the citation, namely with which pharaoh the sign was introduced in the *Field Guide*. A reminder, as an example: D4:2 is the second king in Dynasty 4. *B* and *T* refer to the ʙɪʀᴛʜ ɴᴀᴍᴇ and the ᴛʜʀᴏɴᴇ ɴᴀᴍᴇ respectively. Sign numbers containing *x* were assigned by Pᴇᴛᴛʏ. This list is not intended to show the complete range of uses or pronunciations of each sign.

Note that section *Aa* is found at the *end* of Gᴀʀᴅɪɴᴇʀ's sign list.

Aa: Unclassified

Aa1 ⊜ /Kh/, Unidentified. D4:2

Aa8 ⊢┼┼┤/N/ *Irrigation channels,* in Greco-Roman names.

Aa11 ⊂══⊃ /Maat/ *Pedestal for a statue; Maat, truth, virtue.* D12:6T

Aa13 ⊂══⊃/M/ Unknown object. D18:10T

Aa18 ⛉/S/ in Greco-Roman and other foreign names and titles. Unknown object. D22:2B

Aa27 ⳨/Nedjet/ Unknown object. D33:9B

A: Mankind

A2 𓀁(Silent), *Man with hand to mouth, eat, speak.* D18:13T

A17 𓀔 /A?/ *young, child,* in Greco-Roman names.

A24 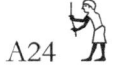 (silent here), *man striking with a stick; strong, victorious.* D17:15B

A28 /K / in Greco-Roman names.

A31 /T/ *Man averting face,* in Greco-Roman names.

A50, A51 /Sheps/ *Seated person holding flail; noble person.* D4:7; D18:5

A53 /silent/ *Mummy; image, statue.* D33:10B

B Women

B1 /silent/ *Woman.*

B7 /silent/ *Queen.* Queen Tiye. D18

C Personified gods Note that several hieroglyphs representing gods are not included in **Gardiner**, including the following

/Usir/ *God Osiris.* D19:2B

/Mut/ *Goddess Mut.* D19:8B.

Cx2 (**Payne**) /Anhur/ *God Onouris.* D30:3B

C2 /Ra/ *Sun god Ra.* D12:3B

C7 🗿/Set/ *God Set or Seth.* D19:2B

C9 🗿/Hathor/*Goddess Hathor*, or **DETERMINATIVE** for a *goddess.* D33:4B

C10 🗿/Maat/*Seated goddess Maat wearing a feather headdress; truth, justice, order.* D18:5T

C12 🗿/Amen/*God Amen (Amun).* D12:1B

Cx8 **(PAYNE)** 🗿Amen-her-khepshef/*Amen (Amun) with his scimitar.* D21:5B

C19 🗿/Ptah/ *God Ptah.* D19:4B

C19a **(PETTY)** 🗿/Ptah/ *God Ptah.* D19:4B

D Human body parts

D1 🗿/Tep/ *Human head, first, principal.* D20:11T

D2 🗿/Her/ *Face; in, at, through, to.* D19:4B

D4 🗿/Ir/ *Eye; see, make, do.* D5:3T

D6 🗿 D8 🗿 *Eye.* /I or A/ in Greco-Roman names.

D21 ⬭ /R/ *Mouth.* D4:1

D28 𓂉 *Upraised arms; spirit, soul.* D4:6. /K/ in Greco-Roman names.

D36 ⟶ /A/ (Hebrew *Ayin*, Arabic *Ain*), *Elbow, forearm and hand.* D13

D37 ⟶ /T/ *Arm and hand offering bread, give,* in Greco-Roman names.

D39 ⟶ /Mut?/ *Arm and hand offering jar of liquid, offer .* D33:9T

D40 ⟶ /Nakht/ *Arm with stick; strong, victorious.* D20:1B

D43 ⟶ /Khu/ Roman title /enty-khu/ ⬭ ⟶ is *Augustus.*

D45 ꙮ /Djeser/ *Hand with nehbet wand; holy, clear.* D18:2T

D46 ⬭ /D/ *Hand.* /T/ in Greco-Roman names. D33:13B

D52 ⬭ /silent/ *Male genitals; male.* D17:15B

D53 ⬭ /D/ *Male genitals emitting liquid ,* in Greco-Roman names.

D58 ⬭ /B/ *Leg or foot.* D13:12B

D61 𓂦 /Sah/ *Toes; approach.* D5:2

E: Mammals

E1 /Ka/ *Bull; Ka aspect of the soul.* D26:2B
/K/ in Greco-Roman names.

E10 /Ba/ *Ram; Ba aspect of the soul.* Queen Bintanath D19
/B/ or /S/ in Greco-Roman names.

E23 /R, L/ *Lion.* D25:6B

E34 /Wen, Un/ *Desert hare, exist.* D5:9B

F: Parts of Mammals

F4 /Hat/ *Forepart of lion; in front.* D12:1B

F9 /Pehty/ *Leopard's head; strength.* D18:1T

F10 *Head and neck of bovine animal.* /R/ in Greco-Roman names.

F12 /User/ *Canine head on staff; strong, wealthy.* D5:1

F13 /Wep/ *Bull horns; open.* Divine Adoratrice Shepenwepet, D25

F23 /Khepesh/ *Foreleg of bull, power, strength.* D18:6B

F25 /Wehem/ *Leg and hoof of ox; repeat.* D26:2T

F31 ![F31 sign] /Mos/Mes/ *Fox-tail apron; give birth, be born.* D17:15B

F34 ![F34 sign] /Ib/ *Heart.* D12:1T

F35 ![F35 sign] /Nefer/ *Heart and windpipe; good, beautiful, perfect.* D4:1

F44 ![F44 sign] /Iwa/ *Joint of meat; heir.* D33:3T

G. Birds

G1 ![G1 sign] /A/ *Egyptian vulture,* phonetic. D32:1B

G5 ![G5 sign] /Hor/ *Falcon, god Horus.* D5:7BT

G9 ![G9 sign] /Ra-Horakhti/ *Falcon with sun disk; god Ra-Horakhti, Ra on the Horizon.* D18:10T

G14 ![G14 sign] *Vulture; goddess Mut, mother.* Queen Nefertari, D19 (/N/ in Roman names (Nervo)

G17 ![G17 sign] /M/ *Owl.* D12:1B

G25 ![G25 sign] /Akh/ *Crested ibis; beneficial, beautiful.* D18:10B

G26 ![G26 sign] /Thut, Djehuty/ *Ibis on a standard; god Thoth.* D18:3B

G29 ![G29 sign] /Ba/ G29 *Stork; Ba aspect of the soul.* /B/ in Greco-Roman names.

G36 /Wer/ *Swallow; great.* Queen Tiye, D18

G39 /Sa/ *Pintail duck; son.* D5:9

G40 /Pa, Pi/ *Flying duck; the, this.* D21:3B

G43 /U, O, W/ *Quail chick.* D4:1

H. Parts of Birds

H6 /Maat/ *Feather; Maat, truth, justice, order.* D18:5T

H6 /Shu/ *Feather; with god or sun determinative, god Shu.* D18:10T

H8 /Sa, Si/ *Egg; son, also (silent) determinative for a goddess.* D18:2 , D19:8T /S/in Greco-Roman names and titles.

I. Reptiles, Parts of Reptiles

I3 *Crocodile, god Sobek,* /N/ in Greco-Roman names.

I4 /Sobek/ *Crocodile on shrine; god Sobek.* D13:12B

I5a /Sobek/ *Mummified crocodile, god Sobek.* D13:12B

I6 ☱ /Kem/ *Crocodile's tail; black.* D18:2B /S/ in Greco-Roman names.

I9 ∿ /F/ *Horned viper; he, his.* D4:1

I10 ∿ /Dj/ *Extended cobra* I10+X1, N17

∿ /Djet/ *(living) forever.* D12:2

I12 ∿ *Cobra with hood spread.* /K/ in Greco-Roman names.

I14 ∿ *Snake.* /R/ in Greco-Roman names.

K. Fish

K1 ⊂ /In/ *Tilapia fish.* D5:6B /Y/ in Greco-Roman names.

L. Insects

L1 ⚘ /Kheper/ *Dung beetle; become, come into being; manifestation.* D12:2T /T/, /D/ in Greco-Roman names.

L2 ⚘ /Bit/ *Bee; Lower Egypt.* D12:2B

M. Plants

M3 /Nakht/ ⊜ ⌒ *Stick, (M3) with phonetic complements; strong, victorious.*
D30:1B

M8 /Sh/ *Marsh, lotus blossoms and papyrus umbels.* D22:1B

M13 /Wadj/ *Papyrus stalk; green, flourishing.* D13:21T

M17 /I/ *Reed.* D5:3B

M17a /Y/ *Two reeds.* D6:1B

M18 /I/ *Reed with legs; come.* Queen Nefertiti, D18

M23 /Su/ *Sedge plant; Upper Egypt.* D12:2BT. /S/ in Greco-Roman names.

M26 /Shema/ *Flowering sedge plant; south, southern.* D18:12B

M29 /Nedjem/ *Carob pod; sweet, pleasant.* D21:7B

M85 (Petty) /R, L/ *Pomegranate (?) blossom.* D33:10B

N. Heavens and Earth, Water

N1 /Her, Pet/ *Heaven; chief, captain.* D20:11B. /P/ in Greco-Roman.
names

N5 ⊙ /Ra, Re/ *Sun, sun god Ra, Re.* D4:3. /R/ in Greco-Roman names.

N6   /Ra/ *Sun disk with protective cobra; god Ra (Re).* D33:10B
/R/ in Greco-Roman names.

N11   /Ah/ *Crescent moon, moon god Ah.* D18:1B

N12   /Ah/ *Crescent moon, moon god Ah.* D18:1B

N14   /Seba/ *Star.* D21:3B. /S/ in Greco-Roman names.

N16   /Ta/ *Land.* /T/ in Greco-Roman names.

N17   /Ta/ *Land.* /T/ in Greco-Roman names.

N18   /T/ *Land.* /T/ in Greco-Roman names.

N19   /Tawy/ *Sandy tract, repeated; two lands.* D12:2BT

N21 + N33A   , a combination of N33A, *grains of sand,* and two copies of
N21, *tongue of land.* /T/ in Greco-Roman names. See N16 above.

N27   /Akhet/ *Sun on the horizon.* D18:10T

N28   /Kha/ *Rising sun; appear, shine.* D4:4

N29   /Q/ *Hill.* D22:1B

N35   /N/ *Water; of* or *by.* D5:6T

N36 ⊏⊐ /Mer/ *Canal; love.* D19:3B /M/ in Greco-Roman names.

N37 ☐ /Sh/ *Pool.* Divine Adoratrice Shepenwepet, D25

N41 ♡ /Hem/ *Water well, pool; wife.* Queen Tiye, D18

Nx2 (**PAYNE**) 𓏤 *Winged sun disk.* /N/ in Greco-Roman names.

O. Architecture

O1 ☐ /Per/ *House* D33:6T

O4 ⌐☐ /H/ *Room.* D25:6B

O28 ⊔ /Iunu/ *Architectural column; Heliopolis.* D18:6B

O29 ⇐⊂ /Aa/ *Column; great.* D11:3B

O34 ⊸∞⊸ /S/ *Door bolt.* D5:8B

O49 ⊗ (silent, as a **DETERMINATIVE**, or /Niut/) *City, town, inhabited area.* D18:2

P. Parts of Ships

P5 𓏞 *Sail.* /T/ in Greco-Roman names.

P8 ⎪ /heru/ /hepet/ *Oar, voice.* D11:5T

Q. Domestic Furniture

Q1 ⌐/Eset/ *Throne, symbol of Isis or Osiris.* D33:4B

Q3 □/P/ *Woven stool,* seen from above. D6:3B

R. Temple furniture, cult objects

R4 ⚊/Hotep, hetep/ *Offering loaf on a mat; be pleased, satisfied.* D11:5B

R7 ⎈ /Ba/ *Incense bowl; Ba aspect of the soul.* Queen Bintanath, D19. /B/ in Greco-Roman names.

R8 |/Netjer/ *Temple banner; god, divine.* D12:2

R11 𝌆/Djed/ *Djed pillar; stability.* D4:3

R19 ᴪ /Waset/ *Was scepter with plume; Thebes (Luxor).* D18:6B

R24 ⋈, 𝍖/Net, Nit/ *Two bows; goddess Neith* Divine Adoratrice Nitocrit, D26. /N/ in Greco-Roman names and titles.

S. Scepters, clothing

S1 ⎨ /Hedj/ *White crown; shining.* D22:1T

S3 ⎨ /N/ *Red crown.* D18:4T

S12 𓋞 /Nub/ *Gold.* D20:3

S29 ⌐ /S/ *Piece of cloth.* D4:1.

S34 ☥ /Ankh/*A sacred knot; life, to live.* Queen Ankhnespepy, D6

S38 ⌐ /Heka/*Crook (scepter); ruler.* D18:6B

S40 ⌐ /Was/ *Was scepter; dominion.* D20:8B

S42 ⌐ /Sekhem/ *Sekhem scepter; powerful.* D13:21T

S81 ⌐ *Royal headdress.*/K/ in Greco-Roman names.

T. Weapons

T16 ⌐/Khepesh or Khopesh/ *Scimitar* D20:5B

T21 ⌐/Wa/ *Harpoon; unique one.* D18:10T

T23 ⌐ /Sen/*Arrow head; brother.* D33:3T

U. Tools

U1 ⟋ /Maa/ *Sickle.* D12:6T

U4 ⟋ /Maat/ Combination of *sickle and pedestal; truth, justice, order.* D12:6T

U6 ⟍ /Mer/ *Hoe; beloved.* D6:1

U7 ⊤ /Mer/ *Hoe; beloved.* D18:14B

U15 ⊨ /Tem/ *Sledge.* D25:6T

U21 ⌐ /Setep/ *Adze with block of wood; choose.* D18:14T

U22 ⌂ /Menkh/ *Chisel; beneficent.* D33:4T

U31 ⟵ /M/ *Baker's tool,* in Greco-Roman names and titles.

U33 ⌡ /Ti, T/ *Pestle.* Queen Tiye, D18

U36 ⌡ /Hem/ *Washerman's bat; servant* D20:11T

V. Fibers, Basketry

V4 ⟨glyph⟩ /U, O/ *Lasso.* D22:2B

V6 ⟨glyph⟩ *Clothing.* /S/ in Greco-Roman names.

V13 ⟨glyph⟩ /T, Ch/ *Hobble for cattle.* D11:5B

V28 ⟨glyph⟩ /H/ *Wick of twisted flax.* Princess Neferuptah, D12

V29 ⟨glyph⟩ /Wah/ *Fiber swab, to ward off.* D26:1T

V30 ⟨glyph⟩ /Neb/ *Basket; lord, master, all, every.* D11:5T

V31 ⟨glyph⟩ /K/ *Basket with handle.* D13:12B

V38 ⟨glyph⟩ /Tyet, Tit/ *Sacred knot or amulet.* D19:2B

W. Vessels

W3 ⟨glyph⟩ /Heb/ *Alabaster bowl used in feasts and purifications; festival.* D18:14B

W4 ⟨glyph⟩ /Heb/ *Alabaster bowl + pavilion, supported by a column.* D30:3B

W9 ⟨glyph⟩ /Khnem/ *Pitcher; united with.* D18:5B

W10 ⟨glyph⟩ /Itu?/ *Cup* /A/ in Greco-Roman names. D33:4T

W11 ⬜ /G/ *Jar stand.* /K/ in Greco-Roman names. D32:1B

W19 ⬯ /Mi/ *Milk jug carried in rope net; like. as.* D18:3B

W24 ⬤ /Nu/ *Pot.* D33:10B /N/ in Greco-Roman names.

W25 ⬆ /In/ *Pot with legs; bring, fetch.* D11 2 /N/ in Greco-Roman names.

X. Bread Loaves

X1 ◁ /T/ *Bread loaf.* D6:1

X2 ⬭ /T/ *Bread loaf.* D18:13B

X8 ◭ /Di/ *Conical loaf; give.* D12:6:

Y. Writing, Games

Y1 ⬯ /silent/ *Papyrus roll, wrapped and sealed; abstract ideas.* D13pB

Y3 ⬯ /Sesh/ *Scribe's outfit; a scribe.* D13 pB

Y5 ⬯ /Men/ *Game board and pieces; firm, established.* D4:6

Z. **Strokes**

Z1 | /silent/ Denotes that the object shown is just that, and not a symbolic or phonetic symbol. D13pB

Z2 | | | /U/ Plural marker. D13pT

Z3 | /U/ Plural marker. D18:5B

Z4 \\ /Y/ Dual marker—the item is doubled. Queen Ahmose Nefertari, D18

Z7 ℰ /U, W, V/ *Spiral.* D33:2B

Z9 × /silent/ crossed strokes; *to divide.* Divine Adoratrice Shepenwepet, D25

Z11 ✛ *Crossed planks* /M/ in Greco-Roman names.

Sign List by Pronunciation (English alphabet order)

Each entry shows the pronunciation of a sign as used in the cartouches in the *Field Guide,* the hieroglyph itself, the **GARDINER** number, definition, and where, namely with which pharaoh, the sign was introduced in the *Field Guide.* As a reminder: D4:2 refers to the second king in Dynasty 4. *B* and *T* refer to the **BIRTH NAME** and the **THRONE NAME** respectively. All possible pronunciations are *not* included.

/A, I/ M17 *Reed.* D5:3B

/A/ G1 *Egyptian vulture.* D32:1B

/A/ D36 *Elbow, forearm and hand.* (Hebrew *Ayin*, Arabic *Ain*), D13p:T

/A/ D6 D8 *Eye.* In Greco-Roman names.

/A?/ A17 *young, child.* In Greco-Roman names.

/A/ W10 *Cup.* In Greco-Roman names. D33:5T

/Aa/ O29 *Column; great.* D11:3

/Ah/ N11 *Crescent moon.* D18:1B

/Ah/ N12/Ah/ *Crescent moon.* D18:1B

/Akh/ G25 *Crested ibis; beneficial, beautiful.* D18:10B

/Akhet/ N27 *Sun on the horizon.* D18:10T

/Anhur/ Cx2 (**PAYNE**) *God Onouris.* D30:3B

/Ankh/ S34 *A sacred knot; life, to live.* Queen Ankhnespepy D6

/Amen/ C12, D12:1B; *God Amen (Amun).* D19:3B

/Amen-her-khepshef/ Cx8 (**PAYNE**) *Amen with his scimitar.* D21:5B

/B/ D58 *Leg or foot.* D13:12B

/Ba/ E10 *Ram; Ba aspect of the soul.* Queen Bintanath, D19. /B/ or /S/ in Roman names

/Ba/ G29 *Stork; Ba aspect of the soul.* /B/ in Greco-Roman names.

/Ba/ R7 *Incense bowl; Ba aspect of the soul.* Queen Bintanath, D19. /B/ in Roman names.

/Bit/ L2 *Bee; Lower Egypt.* D12:2

/D, T/ D46 D46 *Hand.* D33:13B

/D/ D53 *Male genitals emitting fluid* /D/ in Greco-Roman names.

/D/ 🪲 L1 *Dung beetle.* /D/in Greco-Roman names.

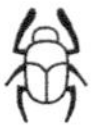

/Di/ △ X8 *Conical loaf; give.* D12:6

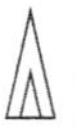

/Dj/ 〰 I10 *Extended cobra*

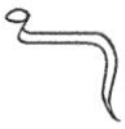

/Djed/ ☰ R11 *Djed pillar; stability.* D4:3

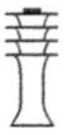

/Djet/ 🐍 I10(+X1, N17) *(Living) forever* D12:2

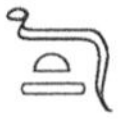

/Djehuty/ 🦅 G26 *Ibis on a standard; god Thoth.* D18:3B

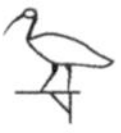

/Djeser/ 〰 D45 *Hand with nehbet wand; holy, clear.* D18:2T

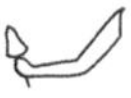

/Eset/ ⌐ Q1/Eset/ *Throne, symbol of Isis or Osiris.* D33:4B

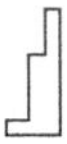

/F/ 〰 I9 *Horned viper, he, his.* D4:1

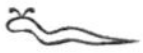

/G/ ⊍ W11/G/ *Jar stand.* D32:1B

/H/ ⊔ O4 *Room.* D25:6B

/H/ 𝓧 V28 *Wick of twisted flax.* Princess Neferuptah, D12

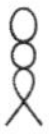

/Hat/ 🦁 F4 *Forepart of lion; in front.* D12:1B

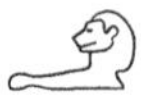

/Hathor/ 𓁜 C9 *Goddess Hathor*, or **DETERMINATIVE** for a *goddess*. D33:4B

/Heb/ 𓎱 W3 *Alabaster bowl used in feasts and purifications; festival.* D18:14B

/Heb/ 𓎳 W4 *Alabaster bowl + pavilion supported by a column; festival.* D30:3B

/Hedj/ 𓋔 S1 *White crown; shining.* D22:1T

/Hem/ 𓍃 U36 *Washerman's bat; servant.* D20:11T

/Heqa/ 𓋾 S38 *Crook (scepter); ruler.* D18:6B

/Hem/ 𓈔 N41 Hem/ *Water well, pool; wife.* Queen Tiye, D18

/Her/ 𓁷 D2 *Face; in, at, through, to.* D19:4B

/Her, Pet/ 𓇯 N1 *Heaven; chief, captain.* D20:11B.

/Hepet/,/Heru/ 𓊰 S8 *Oar; voice.* D11:5T

/Hor/ 𓅃 G5 *Falcon, god Horus.* D5:7BT

/Hotep/ or /Hetep/ 𓊵 R4 *Loaf on offering mat; satisfied.* D11:5B

/I/ 𓇋 M17 *Reed.* D5:3B

/I/ M18 *Reed with legs; come.* Queen Nefertiti, D18

/I or A/ D6; D8 In Greco-Roman names.

/Ib/ F34 *Heart.* D12:1T

/In/ K1 *Tilapia fish.* D5:6B.

/In/ W25 *Pot with legs; bring, fetch.* D11:2 /N/ in Greco-Roman names.

/Ir/ D4 *Eye; see, make, do.* D5:3T

/Itu/ W10 *Cup; father?* .D33:4T

/Iunu/ O28 *Architectural column; Heliopolis.* D18:6B

/Iwa/ F44 *Joint of meat; heir.* D33:3T

J (see DJ)

/K/ V31 *Basket with handle.* D13:12B

/K / A28 in Greco-Roman names.

/K/ ⬙ W11 *Jar stand.* In Greco-Roman names.

/K/ ⌢ S81 *Royal headdress.* In Greco-Roman names.

/K/ ⌇ I12 *Cobra.* In Greco-Roman names.

/Ka/ ⊔ D28 *Upraised arms; spirit, soul.* D4:6. /K/ in Greco-Roman names.

/Ka/ 🐂 E1 *Bull; Ka aspect of the soul.* D26:2B. /K/ in Greco-Roman names.

/Kem/ ⬿ I6 *Crocodile's tail; black.* D18:2B /S/ In Greco-Roman names.

/Kh/ ⊜ Aa1 Unidentified. D4:2

/Kha/ ⌂ N28 *Rising sun; appear, shine.* D4:4

/Khnem/ ⬹ W9 *Pitcher; united with.* D18:5B

/Kheper/ 🪲 L1 D*ung beetle; to become, come into being; manifestation.* D12:2T

/Khepesh/ ⟋⬓ F23 *Foreleg of bull, power, strength.* D18:6B

/Khepesh or Khopesh/ ⌇⬓ T16 *Scimitar.* D20:5B

/Khnem/ ⬹ W9 *Pitcher; united with.* D18:5B

/Khu/ 🐦 D43 *Protection.* Roman title /enty-khu/ ○ ◠ 🐦 is *Augustus.*

/L/ 🦁 E23 *Lion.* D25:6B

/M/ ⬭ Aa13 *Unknown object.* D18:10T

/M/ 🦉 G17 *Owl.* D12:1B

/M/ ⤚ U31 *Baker's tool.* In Greco-Roman names.

/M/ ✚ Z11 *Crossed planks.* In Greco-Roman names.

/Maa/ 🪝 U1 *Sickle.* D12:6T

/Maat/ 🪝 U4 Combination of *sickle and pedestal; truth, justice, order.* D12:6T

/Maat/ ⬭ Aa11 *Pedestal for a statue; Maat truth, virtue.* D12:6T

/Maat/ 𓆄 H6 *Feather; Maat, truth, justice, order.* D18:5T

/Maat/ 𓐩 C10 *Seated goddess Maat wearing a feather headdress; truth, justice, order.* D18:5T

/Men/ ⬚ Y5 *Game board and pieces; firm, established.* D4:6

/Menkh/ ♀ U22 *Chisel; beneficent.* D33:4T

/Mer/ ⟅▭⟆ N36 *Canal; love.* D12:3B /M/ in Greco-Roman names.

/Mer/ ⟋ U6 *Hoe; beloved.* D6:1B

/Mer/ ⟍ U7 *Hoe; beloved.* D18:14B

/Mi/ ♀ W19 *Milk jug in rope carrier; like, as.* D18:3B

/Mos/Mes/ 𓏠 F31 *Fox tail apron; give birth, be born.* D17:15B

/Mut/ 𓏠 (Not in Gardiner) *The goddess Mut.* D19:8B.

/Mut?/ ▱▭ D39 *Arm and hand offering jar of liquid, offer.* D33:9T

/Mut/ 𓄿 G14 *Vulture; goddess Mut, mother.* Queen Nefertari, D19

/N/ ⊢┬┤ Aa8 *Irrigation channels,* in Greco-Roman names.

/N/ 〰 N35 *Water; of or by.* D5:6B

/N/ G14 *Vulture; goddess Mut.* /N/ in one Roman name (Nervo).

/N/ I3 *Crocodile,* in Greco-Roman names.

/N/ S3 *Red crown.* D18:14B

/N/ Nx2 (**Petty**) *Winged sun disk.* In Greco-Roman names.

/Nakht/ D40 *Arm with stick; strong, victorious.* D20:1B

/Nakht/ D40 *Stick (M3), with phonetic complements; strong, victorious.* D30:1B

/Neb/ V30 *Basket; lord, master, all, every.* D11:5T

/Nedjet/ Aa27 Unknown object. D33:9B

/Nedjem/ M29 *Carob pod; sweet, pleasant.* D21:7B

/Nefer/ F35 *Heart and windpipe; good, beautiful, perfect.* D4:1

/Net, Nit/ , R24 *Two bows; goddess Neith* Divine Adoratrice Nitocrit, D26. /N/ in Greco-Roman names.

/Netjer /   ⚑ R8 *Temple banner; god, divine.* D12:2BT

/Nu/ ⬮ W24 *Pot.* D33:10B /N/ in Greco-Roman names.

/Nub/ 𓋞 S12 *Gold.* D20:3

/O/ 𓅱 G43 *Quail chick.* D4:1

/O/ 𓍿 V4 *Lasso.* D22:2B

/P/ ☐ Q3 *Woven stool, seen from above.* D6:3B

/Pa, Pi/ 𓅮 G40 *Flying duck; the, this.* D21:3B

/Pehty/ 𓄤 F9 *Leopard's head; strength.* D18:1T

/Per/ ⌷ O1 *House* D33:6T

/Pet/ ▭ N1 *Heaven; chief, captain.* D20:11B. /P/ in Greco-Roman names.

/Ptah/ 𓁰 , 𓁫 C19a *God Ptah.* D19:4B

/Q/ △ N29 *Hill.* D22:1B

/R/ ⬯ D21 *Mouth.* D4:1

/R/ ॠ I14 *Snake.* In Greco-Roman names.

/R/ ॠ E23 *Lion* in Greco-Roman names.

/R/ ॠ M85 (**Petty**) *Pomegranate(?) blossom,* D33:10B

/R/ ॠ F10 *Head and neck of bovine animal,* in Greco-Roman names.

/Ra/ ॠ C2 *Sun god Ra (Re).* D12:3B

/Ra/ ⊙ N5 *Sun, the sun god Ra (Re).* D4:3 /R/ in Greco-Roman names.

/Ra/ ॠ N6 *Sun disk with protective cobra; god Ra (Re).* D33:10B. /R/ in Roman names.

/Ra-Horakhti/ ॠ G9 *Falcon with sun disk; god Ra-Horakhti, Ra on the Horizon.* D18:10T

/S/ ॠ Aa18. *Unknown object,* in Greco-Roman and other foreign names. D22:2B

/S/ ★ N14 *Star.* D21:3B /S/ in Greco-Roman names.

/S/ ⊸ O34 *Door bolt.* D5:8B

/S/ ॥ S29 *Piece of cloth.* D4:1.

/S/ ⍭ V6 *Clothing.* In Greco-Roman names and titles.

/Sa/ 🦆 G39 *Pintail duck; son.* D5:9B

/Sa, Si/ ◯ H8 *Egg; son, also (silent) determinative for a goddess.* D18:2 , D19:8T /S/in Roman names and titles

/Seba/ ✳ N14 *Star.* D21:3B /S/ in Greco-Roman names.

/Sekhem/ ⍭ S42 *Sekhem scepter; powerful.* D13:21T

/Sah/ 𓂾 D61 *Toes; approach.* D5:2

/Sen/ ⍭ T23 *Arrow head; brother.* D33:3T

/Sesh/ 𓏞 Y3 *Scribe's kit; a scribe.* D13:pB

/Set/ 𓋴 C7 *God Set or Seth.* D19:2B

/Setep/ ⍭ U21 *Adze with block of wood; choose.* D18:14B

/Sh/ 𓇉 M8 *Marsh; lotus blossoms and papyrus umbels.* D22:1B

/Sh/ ▭ N37 *Pool.* Divine Adoratrice Shepenwepet, D25

/Shema/ 𓇗 M26 *Flowering sedge plant; south, southern.* D18:12B

/Sheps/ A50, A51 *Seated person holding flail; noble person.* D4:7; D18:5

/Sobek/ I4 *Crocodile on shrine; god Sobek.* D13:12B

/Sobek/ I5a *Crocodile mummified; god Sobek* D13:12B

/Shu/ H6 *Feather; with god or sun determinative, god Shu.* D18:10T

/Su/ M23 *Sedge plant; Upper Egypt, king.* D12:2BT
/S/ in Greco-Roman names.

/T/ A31 *Man averting face.* In Greco-Roman names.

/T/ D37 *Arm and hand offering a loaf,* in Greco-Roman names.

/T/ V13 *Hobble for cattle.* D11:5B

/T/ X1 *Bread loaf.* D6:1

/T/ X2 *Bread loaf.* D18:13B

/T/ L1 *Dung Beetle,* in Greco-Roman names.

/Ta/ N16 *Land.* /T/ in Greco-Roman names.

/Ta/ N17 *Land.* /T/ in Greco-Roman names.

/Ta/ ⬭ N18 *Land.* /T/ in Greco-Roman names.

/Ta/ ⌁°°°↘ (not in **Gardiner**)/T/ in Greco-Roman names.

/T/ ⛵ P5 *Sail,* in Greco-Roman names.

/Tawy/ ⩵ N19 *Sandy tract, repeated; two lands.* D12:2BT

/Tem/ 𓏴⊏⊏ U15 *Sledge.* D25:6T

/Tep/ 𓁶 D1 *Human head, first, principal.* D20:11T

/Thut/ 𓅝 G26 *Ibis on a standard; god Thoth.* D18:3B

/Ti, T/ 𓏏 U33 *Pestle.* Queen Tiye, D18

/Tyet, Tit/ 𓎬 V38 *Sacred knot or amulet.* D19:2B

/U/ 𓅱 G43 *Quail chick.* D4:1

/U/ ꝯ Z7 *Spiral.* D33:2B

/U/ | | | Z2 Denotes plural. D13:pB

/U/ ꞁ Z3 Plural marker. D18:5B

/Un/ 🐇 E34 *Desert hare; to be.* D5:9B

/User/ ⌇ F12 *Canine head on staff; strong, wealthy.* D5:1

/Usir/ 𓁹 (Not in Gardiner) *The god Osiris.* D19:2B

/V/ 𓍢 Z7 Spiral, in Greco-Roman names.

/V, W/ 𓅱 G43 *Quail chick.* D4:1 /V/ in Greco-Roman names.

/W/ 𓍢 Z7 *Spiral.* D33:2B

/Wadj/ 𓇅 M13 *Papyrus stalk; green, flourishing.* D13:21T

/Wa/ 𓏶 T21 *Harpoon; unique one.* D18:10T

/Wah/ 𓍅 V29 *Fiber swab; to ward off.* D26:1T

/Was/ 𓌀 S40 *Was scepter; dominion.* D12:3B

/Waset/ 𓋴 R19 *Was scepter with plume; Thebes (Luxor).* D18:6B

/Wehem/ 𓎗 F25 *leg and hoof of ox; repeat.* D26:2T

/Wen/ 🐇 E34 *Desert hare; exist.* D5:9B

/Wep/ ⛎ F13 *Bull horns; open.* Divine Adoratrice Shepenwepet, D25

/Wer/ 🐦 G36 *Swallow; great.* Queen Tiye, D18

/Y/ 🐟 K1 *Tilapia fish.* In Greco-Roman names.

/Y/ 𓏭 M17a *Two reeds.* D6:1B

/Y/ \\ M17a Dual marker—the item is doubled. Queen Ahmose Nefertari D18

Glossary

AMARNA PERIOD: The reign of Amenhotep IV (D18:10), who repudiated Amen and his priesthood in favor of the Aten Sun Disk. He changed his name to Akhenaten

ATEN: The Sun Disk, originally an aspect of the sun god Ra, worshiped by Akhenaten during the **AMARNA PERIOD.**

ANKH: This hieroglyph, meaning *life:* ⚲ Once said to represent a *sandal strap*, now fancifully described by enthusiastic souvenir hawkers as *The Key of Life!* I believe that it is a *sacred knot.*

ANTHROPOMORPHIC GODS: Hieroglyphs representing gods in human bodily form, seated on a throne, standing, striding, or sitting cross-legged or crouching on the ground. The heads may be those of animals, insects, or even objects, like the *Maat feather*. Up until the New Kingdom, most gods were depicted as objects or animals (sun, crocodile) or their names were spelled out phonetically.

BIRTH NAME: The name a future pharaoh was given at birth, enclosed in a cartouche upon his gaining the throne.

BREAKOUT: In this book only, the **BREAKOUT** is a chart showing all the hieroglyphs in a cartouche *in pronunciation order*, along with the **GARDINER NUMBER.**

CARTOUCHE: GARDINER (P 74) says it best: "This French word means an ornamented tablet of stone, wood or metal designed to receive an inscription." In this book it refers to the oval frameworks and the hieroglyphs inside that display a king's **BIRTH** and **THRONE NAMES.**

COGNATE: A word in one language that is related in form and meaning to a word in another language.

COMBINED CARTOUCHE: Occasionally a ruler's **THRONE NAME** and **BIRTH NAME**, and even royal titles, are combined into one cartouche. If a cartouche seems excessively long, try chopping it into smaller component parts. See D12:2

COPTIC: The last stage of the Egyptian language, written in an alphabet based on Greek. It is used now only in the liturgy of Egypt's Coptic Christian Church.

DEMOTIC: A cursive form of written Egyptian, and a late stage of Egyptian language written in this script.

DETERMINATIVE: Hieroglyphs that clarify the meaning of other signs or group of signs whose sense may otherwise be ambiguous, but which do not affect the pronunciation of a word or name.

DIVINE ADORATRICE/ADORER OF AMEN: Title of a High Priestess. The holders of this title had the most power starting about Dynasty 23.

DUAL GRAMMATICAL ENDING: An /Y (ee)/ sound at the end of a word, signifying that there are two of the objects in question, as in Neb Tawy, *Lord of the Two Lands.*

DYNASTY: Theoretically, a series of successive rulers belonging to the same family. **MANETHO** is the first person we know of to divide the rulers of Egypt into dynasties.

EFFACED NAMES: Rulers, or their "people," would sometimes hack out the names of an earlier pharaoh or god who was out of favor, and either leave the space empty or carve the current pharaoh's name in its place. Candidates for effacement were Queen Hatshepsut, the image of the god Set/Seth in the names of Sety I and II, and, during the **AMARNA PERIOD**, the name of the god Amen.

EPITHET: A group of signs added to the end of a ruler's name which serves to distinguish him or her from others of the same name. The geographical location of a cartouche can call for epithets, sometimes to honor local gods or to emphasize that the pharaoh is *Ruler of Thebes/Heliopolis*, or other location. See D18:6B

FIVE-FOLD TITULARY: The five names of each pharaoh.

GARDINER NUMBER: A letter and number assigned to a given hieroglyphic sign, according to **GARDINER'S** *Egyptian Grammar.*

GLYPH: A hieroglyph.

GOD'S FATHER: A priestly title held by Ay D18:13B, "perhaps indicating that he had acted as a tutor of the crown prince Amenhotep as a boy." **(Cooney p 169)**

GOD'S WIFE OF AMEN: Highest-ranking priestess of Amen, of most influence during Dynasties 25 and 26 **(Wikipedia, "God's Wife").**

GRECO-ROMAN: Refers to all rulers from Alexander the Great (D32:1) through the Roman emperors (D34).

GROUP WRITING: Sequences of two or three hieroglyphic signs that represent one sound. The combination of signs may have been a way to write sounds that in later Egyptian had changed from earlier stages of the language; commonly, but not exclusively, used with non-Egyptian words and names. (American Research Center in Egypt, https://www.arce.org/resource/demotic-history-development-and-techniques-ancient-egypts-popular-script).

HIERATIC: A cursive Egyptian writing system which was used throughout most of ancient Egyptian history.

HIEROGLYPH, HIEROGLYPHIC, HIEROGLYPHICS: Individual Ancient Egyptian signs are known as *hieroglyphs*; *hieroglyphic* is the adjective, as in "the *hieroglyphic* writing system." The use of hieroglyphics as a noun has a long history, but the use of hieroglyphics to describe the writing system does not seem to be favored in current Egyptology circles. "The document is written in *hieroglyphs,*" **not** *hieroglyphics*.

HONORIFIC TRANSPOSITION: When a cartouche contains the name of a god, the Egyptians almost always "bump the god up to first class," to the beginning of the cartouche, regardless of where the god's name is pronounced in the pharaoh's name.

HORUS NAME: One of the pharaoh's five names, featuring a Horus hawk sitting atop a **SEREKH**, with that name written inside.

HORUS OF GOLD: One of pharaoh's five names, accompanied by a Horus hawk atop the hieroglyph for gold.

IDEOGRAM: "A picture or symbol used in a system of writing to represent a thing or an idea but not a particular word or phrase for it, especially one that represents not the object pictured but some thing or idea that the object pictured is supposed to suggest." (Merriam-Webster).

LIGATURE: Three or four hieroglyphs that usually appear as an invariable unit, such as /Nakht/ in D31:B, /Amen/ and /Hotep/ in D18:2B. This is my usage of the word. Usually refers to a single word or name made up of two or more hieroglyphic signs.

LOGOGRAM: A hieroglyph that is a picture of something, and represents that thing. For example, a tree, fruit, animal or insect, where there is no symbolic meaning intended.

MANETHO: An Egyptian priest who lived during the early Ptolemaic Dynasty who, as far as we know, first divided the rulers of Egypt's long history into the supposed family groups, or **DYNASTIES**, that we reference today to identify the pharaohs and the time periods of their rule.

MODIUS: A short flat-topped crown favored by Egyptian queens and princesses.

NEBTY NAME: One of the king's five names, also known as the **TWO LADIES**.

NOME, NOMARCH: An Egyptian province and its governor.

NOMEN: A ruler's **BIRTH NAME**, usually the name by which he or she was known before coming to the throne. Usually preceded by *Son of Ra*, a duck and sun disk.

OBELISK: A four-sided column topped with a pyramidal point, covered in hieroglyphs and depictions of gods.

PAPYRUS: Marsh plant used by the ancient Egyptians to make a writing surface like paper, or the "paper" itself.

PHARAOH: A ruler of ancient Egypt. The term comes from /Per Aa/, *Great House*. See D34:1

PHONETIC COMPLEMENT: Optional, redundant consonant added to a hieroglyph to add clarity to the pronunciation. See examples in D4:1, D11:5B.

PRENOMEN: The **THRONE NAME** of a pharaoh, introduced by the signs for *the sedge and the bee,* adopted at the ruler's coronation.

PTOLEMIES: A dynasty of 15 rulers named Ptolemy, the first of whom was a general under Alexander the Great. The Cleopatras, including Cleopatra VII, *the* Cleopatra, were members of this dynasty

PTOLEMAIC WRITING: The latest stage of the hieroglyphic writing system, used on temple façades, characterized by a great increase in signs used and unusual readings of those hieroglyphs and combinations of signs.

PYLON: Monumental gateway to an ancient Egyptian temple, consisting of two tapering towers. Possibly representing the two hills between which the sun rises and sets. (Wikipedia)

ROSETTA STONE: A stone discovered by Napoleon's forces at Rashid (Rosetta) in the Nile Delta. It is inscribed in two versions of Ancient Egyptian and Greek, and provided a key to the deciphering of the **HIEROGLYPHIC** writing system.

SARCOPHAGUS: A stone box used for a burial. One or more coffins of more perishable material enclosed the body inside the sarcophagus.

SAVANTS: Napoleon's team of over 160 scholars and scientists. They produced a multi-volume set of oversized, illustrated books documenting all aspects of ancient and contemporary Egypt's architecture, flora, fauna, topography, and so on.

SCARAB, French **SCARABÉE:** An amulet, figurine or statue of a dung beetle, also known as a scarab beetle, which represents the progression of the sun god Ra through the heavens as it rolls its ball of *"excrementitious matter* in which the female encloses her eggs." (emphasis mine) **(NEWBERRY P 63)**.

SEREKH: A rectangular figure representing the façade of the palace.

SHEN RING: An amulet or painted figure of a circle of rope, bound at one end with the tips protruding. It means *to encircle,* and presumably represents *all that which is encircled by the sun.* **(GARDINER P 74)** The cartouche developed from this ring.

SIGN: A hieroglyph.

STANDARD: A long staff topped with an image representing a political division or military unit of ancient Egypt, as we use flags and banners today.

STELE or **STELA:** A flat inscribed stone slab, often with a rounded top like a modern gravestone, displaying royal decrees, boundaries, prayers to gods, and the like.

THRONE NAME: The name a pharaoh adopted upon becoming king, enclosed in a cartouche. One of a pharaoh's five names.

TWO LADIES NAME: One of the king's five names. Also **NEBTY NAME.**

TRANSLITERATION: In this book, a phonetic rendering of Ancient Egyptian words into the Latin (English) alphabet. There are more scientific types of transliteration where each Latin symbol represents one Egyptian symbol. Also called *romanization.*

URAEUS: Image of a rearing cobra on the brow of Egyptian royalty, a symbol of sovereignty and protection.

Illustration Credits

Unless otherwise noted, all photographs are mine; sketches of cartouches were produced by me from my own photographs.

Frontispiece: General Research Division, The New York Public Library. *Thèbes, Louqsor [Thebes, Luxor]. Rhamesséion, au fond d'une salle intérieure du palais.* New York Public Library Digital Collections. Accessed Febuary 20, 207, 2019. http://digitalcollections.nypl.org/items/c9ce1330-c5f8-012f-8b3a-58d385a7bc34

 "Essential Principles" binoculars icon: *Binoculars icon vector, filled flat sign, solid pictogram isolated on white.* ID 97328813 © Aleksey Vanin | Dreamstime.com

P 2: Front Courtyard of Egyptian Museum, Cairo, © Russel Johnson

P 2: *The ancient egyptian cairo museum from inside in egypt* on december 20 , 2015 ID 64054837 © Mohamed Ahmed Soliman | Dreamstime.com

P 9: (map cartouche) Schomburg Center for Research in Black Culture, Jean Blackwell Hutson Research and Reference Division, The New York Public Library. "Coste d'Afrique et les Isles comprises entre le Cap Rouge et la riviere de Nunho" New York Public Library Digital Collections. Accessed November 13, 2018. http://digitalcollections.nypl.org/items/418f1d70-fbb5-0131-5e5e-58d385a7b928

P 9: after *Cartouche papier à poudre noire type á la française du XVIIIᵉ siècle*, https://fr.wikipedia.org/wiki/Fichier:Cartouche_papier.JPG accessed November 2018

P 11: *Page of Hieroglyphs*, General Research Division, The New York Public Library. "Ibsamboul [Abu-Simbel]. Grande stèle." New York Public Library Digital Collections. Accessed February 20, 2017. http://digitalcollections.nypl.org/items/510d47e2-5d69-a3d9-e040-e00a18064a99

P 17: Souvenir hieroglyphs card distributed by many merchants in Cairo for many decades.

P 178: Ptolemy XII cartouches, *A close up of two pharoahs* (sic) *and their cartouches on a temple wall in Egypt* ID 12892353 © Robcsworld Dreamstime.com.

Annotated Bibliography
and Recommended Reading

The following are not only books cited in the text, but also works on the hieroglyphic writing system, kings' names, and ancient Egyptian history and culture:

ARDAGH, PHILIP. *The Hieroglyphs Handbook.* London: Faber, 1999.
> A cute 96-page book for young people who are serious about learning some basics of the Egyptian language. Not a bad introduction for adults, either.

BECKERATH, JÜRGEN VON. *Handbuch Der ägyptischen Königsnamen.* München: Deutscher Kunstverlag, 1984.
> Covers the main variants of the THRONE NAMES, BIRTH NAMES, HORUS NAMES, and sometimes TWO LADIES and GOLDEN HORUS names of over 400 kings, queens and ruling high priests from the Predynastic Period through the Roman emperors, with transliterations of (almost) each name. A disadvantage is that the text is in German, so names of kings are often quite different from those familiar to English speakers. Also, the transliterations and cartouches are in different sections of the book, leading to constant flipping of pages. The "scientific" transliteration system is also different from the ones used in English texts. The list is very complete and concise, as duplicates are not cited. Each king is given a number, by dynasty, and I have adopted these numbers in the *Field Guide.*

BETRÒ, MARIA C. *Hiéroglyphes: Les Mystères De L'écriture.* Paris: Flammarion, 2003. *Hieroglyphics: The Writings of Ancient Egypt.* New York: Abbeville Press Pub., 1996.
> I love this book. I first found it in French at the Egyptian Museum in Torino, Italy, and later acquired the English translation. The author devotes a paragraph or full page to each of 239 hieroglyphs, in roughly GARDINER order, including 15 gods not included in GARDINER, with photos and drawings. A fun addition is examples of HIERATIC and DEMOTIC versions of each sign.

BUDGE, E. A. WALLIS. *The Book of the Kings of Egypt.* Vol. 1, Dynasties I – XIX, Books on Egypt and Chaldea, volume XXIII, London: K. Paul, Trench, Truebner, 1908. http://dlib.nyu.edu/awdl/sites/dl-pa.home.nyu.edu.awdl/files/bookofkingsofegy02budg/bookofkingsofegy02budg.pdf.

> The incredibly productive E.A.Wallis Budge (1857–1934) has received a lot of bad press for many decades. His information and transliteration system are very dated, but I find value in the huge corpus of cartouches and titles, particularly of the Ptolemies and Romans. The cartouches are printed clearly, and oodles of variations are included.

CHING, FRANK. *A Visual Dictionary of Architecture.* Hoboken, NJ: Wiley, 2012.

CLAYTON, PETER A. *Chronicle of the Pharaohs, the Reign-by-Reign Record of the Rulers and Dynasties of Ancient Egypt.* London: Thames & Hudson, 1994.

> For those interested in the pharaohs and their cartouches, this wonderful resource is a must. It includes cartouches of 194 rulers, along with names (not cartouches) of family members, transliterations and even translations of most of the rulers' names. Contains plenty of history, maps, illustrations and chronologies.

COLE, JOANNA, and **BRUCE DEGEN.** *Ms. Frizzle's Adventures: Ancient Egypt.* New York: Scholastic, 2002.

> A delightful, whimsically illustrated children's book, a fantasy about Ms. Frizzle and her students visiting ancient Egypt. My only complaint is Ms. Frizzle's blithe oversimplification of how the hieroglyphic writing system works. I'm not asking for a complete treatise on the language. Just don't underestimate or shortchange third and fourth graders.

COONEY, KARA. *When Women Ruled the World: Six Queens of Egypt.* National Geographic Society, 2018.

> Dr. Cooney provides new insights into Egyptian cultural and political history, around the reigns of six queens who ruled as pharaohs.

COLLIER, MARK, and **BILL MANLEY.** *How to Read Egyptian Hieroglyphs: A Step-by-step Guide to Teach Yourself.* London: British Museum Press, 2008.

> Densely packed, for serious students of the language. As in the other works listed here, most of the examples are from monumental inscriptions.

DODSON, AIDAN, and **DYAN HILTON.** *The Complete Royal Families of Ancient Egypt.* Cairo: American University of Cairo Press, 2004.

> This book does not include cartouches or hieroglyphs except incidentally in the photographs, but is invaluable for teasing apart the convoluted family connections of the pharaohs. The book covers rulers up through the Ptolemies.

FAIRMAN, HERBERT W. *An introduction to the Ptolemaic signs and their values.* Cairo: Bulletin de l'Institut Français d'Archéologie Orientale 43, pp 51-138, 1943.

> I came across this source on the eve of my last proofreading of the *Field Guide*. I learned, not surprisingly, that the insane proliferation of hieroglyphs used in cartouches of the Roman emperors are a continuation of **PTOLEMAIC WRITING.** Happily, most, if not all, of the phonetic values I had deduced from studying the Roman cartouches in **VON BECKERATH** and **GAUTHER** were validated in **FAIRMAN's** paper. In addition to the information provided, the article is highly entertaining. **FAIRMAN** had shown his work to an associate, a Dr. Drioton, and claimed that the latter had badly misquoted him in defense of his own, Drioton's, theory of *acrophony,* namely, as I understand it, the idea that the new phonetic hieroglyphic readings of the Ptolemies were each based on the first sound of the word represented by the sign. The paper is full of juicy put-downs, along the lines of "I consider Dr. Drioton's attempted defense of the principle of Acrophony as the most damning attack on that principle that has yet appeared in print...", and "There is neither amusement nor profit in flogging a dead horse...it is clear that Acrophony is a very dead horse unwittingly killed by the hand of its creator." I have to say that I am glad that Fairman is no longer around to critique *my* work.

GARDINER, ALAN H. *Egyptian Grammar: Being an Introduction to the Study of Hieroglyphs.* Oxford: Griffith Institute, Ashmolean Museum, 1957.

> Sir Alan Gardiner's monumental work lays the foundation for virtually all modern books on hieroglyphs and the Egyptian language. He came up with the ingenious, in retrospect obvious, system of classifying and numbering hieroglyphs by subject matter. He was scrupulously detailed, listing the signs in the *Parts of the Human Body* section from top down, head and hair to feet and toes, and presents animals in order from most complex (mammals, birds) to the invertebrates. The 400-odd pages of grammar may have been displaced by more modern works, but there are still many insights in the body of the work that are worth reading.

> This work is available on line at https://www.academia.edu/35940356/07_A.H._Gardiner_-_Egyptian_Grammar.pdf

GAUDARD, FRANÇOIS. *Ptolemaic Hieroglyphs.* Oriental Institute, Chicago, 2010.

GAUTHIER, HENRI. *Livre des Rois d'Égypte: Recueil de Titres de Protocoles Royaux, Suivi d'un Index Alphabétique, vol 1-6;* Bulletin de l'Institut Français d'Archéologie Orientale du Caire, sous la Direction de M. George Foucart, vol 17-21, 1907-1917.

> This oversized, multi-volume opus is a real monster. I can't imagine the work that went into producing it. As far as I can tell, Gauthier cites *every instance,* including variations, of every cartouche or other name of the royal families from predynastic times through the Romans that was available to him as of 1917. While there are no photos or facsimiles, each name is printed out with associated titles and location information. Unfortunately, the index to each volume does *not* list all variations. The set is available electronically, but searching is difficult due to the French spellings and accents. A treasure, but hard to use.

GOLDSTEIN, PEGGY. *Long Is a Dragon: Chinese Writing for Children.* Berkeley, CA: Pacific View Press, 1991.

GRAJETZKI, WOLFRAM. *Ancient Egyptian Queens: A Hieroglyphic Dictionary*. London: Golden House, 2005
>   Much shorter (121 pages) and humbler (no illustrations, only printed hieroglyphs) than TYLDESLEY'S *Chronicle of the Queens of Egypt*, it was cited in the latter's bibliography. It gives the names of 193 queens

How to Read Hieroglyphs. Cairo: Lehnert & Landrock Succ., 1974.
>   Included here only because it was my first book on hieroglyphs. Inconsequential, but does take the pioneering step in a popular publication of breaking down 15 of the 30 cartouches cited, showing the pronunciation of each hieroglyph individually, a boon to the beginner.

JACQ, CHRISTIAN. *Fascinating Hieroglyphics*. New York: Sterling, 1999.
>   Not a text for Egyptian language or kings' names, but very humorous and engaging. JACQ looks at everything from an unexpected angle. I have to read this book again!

JOHNSON, KEVIN L., AND BILL PETTY. *The Names of the Kings of Egypt: The Serekh and Cartouches of Egypt's Pharaohs, along with Selected Queens*. Littleton (Colorado): Museum Tours Press, 2012.
>   A wonderful, pocket-sized work meant for people on tours of ancient sites or museums. In terms of numbers of kings it is much more complete than the *Field Guide*, including Horus names and most common variations ("over 300 kings and queens listed in chronological order…and 850 cartouches.") There is an index of all hieroglyphs seen in the text (excluding the Ptolemies and Romans!) with each sign followed by a reference to the names it is found in. Thus, you can look up every cartouche that includes the horned viper (50 cartouches) or the flag (36). Someone with experience would not choose these very common hieroglyphs to search on, but a certain amount of flipping between pages is unavoidable in any event. On the other hand, this type of index is invaluable for identifying cartouches that are broken or only partially legible.

A suggestion to JOHNSON and PETTY for another edition would be to include THRONE NAMES in the alphabetical index, as sometimes the THRONE NAME is the only cartouche available. Another would be to label the dynasty on each page of the book, again, to minimize page flipping.

KAMIL, JILL. *Luxor, a Guide to Ancient Thebes*. London: Longman, 1989.
———. *Sakkara: A Guide to the Necropolis and the Site of Memphis*.
London, Longman, 1982.
Jill Kamel's guides to major antiquities sites in ancient Egypt are very complete and detailed. Her books take you step-by-step through temples, tombs and other ancient sites.

KAMRIN, JANICE, and GUSTAVO CAMPS. *Ancient Egyptian Hieroglyphs: A Practical Guide*.
New York: Harry N. Abrams, 2004.
A very accessible introduction to hieroglyphs. Photographs of inscriptions, some color-coded to help you follow along, are grouped into such categories as *Royal Names and Titles* and *Offering Prayers*. Grammar and signs are explained and exercises (with keys) are provided. Inscriptions include an autobiography and a description of the Battle of Qadesh.

KAZHDAN, ALEXANDER, ed. (1991). *Oxford Dictionary of Byzantium*. Oxford University Press. (reference from Wikipedia)

KEMP, BARRY J. *100 Hieroglyphs: Think like an Egyptian*. New York: Penguin Group, 2005.
This book by Egyptologist Barry J Kemp is less a book for learning Egyptian than it is for learning about the Egyptian world view and material culture. For each of the 100 hieroglyphs, we get two or three pages of information. Under the header *Red*, for example, we see the hieroglyph for *flamingo*, meaning *red*; *red* to denote *otherness*; the use of red ink; the red crown; that doors and windows were painted red; and how the pigment was made. Very interesting, but not really a language book.

LAMBELET, EDOUARD. *Gods and Goddesses in Ancient Egypt.* Cairo: Lehnert & Landrock, 1986.

————. *How to Read Hieroglyphs,* Cairo, 977-481-026-0a 20-page pamphlet published by Lehnert & Landrock SUCC. Publishers, Nubar Pubishing House 1974

MÁLEK, JAROMÍR, and MARION COX. *ABC of Egyptian Hieroglyphs.* Oxford: Ashmolean Museum, 1994.

> Short and easy to read (48 pages) but very complete introduction to the ancient Egyptian writing system. **MÁLEK** walks the reader through hand-drawn facsimiles of 16 interesting artifacts. Includes exercises.

MANLEY, BILL. *Egyptian Hieroglyphs for Complete Beginners.* New York: Thames & Hudson, 2016.

> From the co-author of **COLLIER** and **MANLEY,** *How to Read Egyptian Hieroglyphs,* this is an actual textbook for those who wish to teach themselves the language. Not easy or quick, but well worth acquiring.

MCDERMOTT, BRIDGET. *Decoding Egyptian Hieroglyphs: How to Read the Secret Language of the Pharaohs.* London: Duncan Baird, 2002.

> An excellent book on Egyptian culture, with chapters on the order of *The Magical Dimension; Trades and Skills; Love and Family Life;* and *Celestial Worlds.* The actual hieroglyphs and Egyptian words presented serve more as illustrations to a lecture than part of a language-learning text.

MCDONALD, ANGELA. *Write Your Own Egyptian Hieroglyphs.* Berkeley: University of California Press, 2007.

> Large format but a manageable 80 glossy pages, a very engaging book for young people or any beginner. One section asks readers to make up their own "Egyptian" names, choosing from lists of adjectives and nouns. This instead of the slavish "translating" of names letter by letter seen in so many books and websites aimed at young people. The book is fun and educational, with lists of insults, names for pets, and the like. Recommended for everyone.

MERCER, SAMUEL A. B., and JANICE KAMRIN. *The Handbook of Egyptian Hieroglyphs: A Study of the Ancient Language.* New York: Hippocrene Books, 1998. Originally published in 1961.

> An actual grammar textbook. Rather dated style, but has useful English-Egyptian/Egyptian-English word lists and quite a few typed Egyptian texts, *without* translations or explanations.

MUDLOFF, THOMAS F., and RONALD E. FELLOWS. *Hieroglyphs for Travelers: What Do Those Little Pictures Mean?* Lemon Grove, CA: R.E. Fellows Publishing, 1999.

> This unique book takes the reader through 28 antiquities sites and points out cartouches to be found there and how to translate some texts, including how to read Hatshepsut's obelisk at Karnak.

NEWBERRY, PERCY E. *Egyptian Scarabs.* Mineola, NY: Dover Publications, 2002, original publication 1906.

> Covers the development of Egyptian scarabs and contains 49 plates of scarab inscriptions. Most interesting to me were illustrated explanations of how seals (on boxes, doors, and jars) actually worked. Also a precious quote on the dung beetle on p 63: "Scarabaeus sacer… remarkable… for its habit of rolling up *balls of excrementitious matter* in which the female encloses her eggs"(emphasis mine).

PAYNE, PHILIP BARTON, LaserHIEROGLYPHICS, Linguist's Software, Inc. Edmonds, Washington

> Though not technically a bibliography item, any typed hieroglyphic script in the *Field Guide* uses one or more of LaserHIEROGLYPHICS five fonts. Worth mentioning here because PAYNE'S fonts include several hieroglyphs not found in GARDINER, notably depicting gods and goddesses.

PETRIE, WILLIAM MATTHEW FLINDERS. *Scarabs and Cylinders with Names:* Illustrated by the Egyptian Collection in University College, London. London: British School of Archaeology in Egypt, 1917. (Nabu Public Domain Reprints, undated).

> Not for the faint of heart, this book contains hundreds (I didn't actually count!) of drawings and photographs of scarabs and seals, many of which include cartouches. Good for looking up specific kings and queens.

MURNANE, WILLIAM J. *The Penguin Guide to Ancient Egypt*. London: Penguin Books, 1983.

PETTY, BILL. *Egyptian Glyphary: A Sign List Based Hieroglyphic Dictionary of Middle Egyptian*. Littleton, Colorado.: Museum Tours Press, 2012.
This book is an Egyptian-English dictionary, relatively compact at 296 pages, listing common compound words in GARDINER order.

————. *Hieroglyphic Sign List: Based on the Work of Alan Gardiner*. Littleton, Col.: Museum Tours Press, 2013.
A companion volume to JOHNSON and PETTY's *The Names of the Kings of Egypt*, it distills the sign list portion of GARDINER'S *Egyptian Grammar* into a 134 page pocket-sized guide.

————. *Understanding Hieroglyphic Inscriptions, an Introductory Course to the Ancient Egyptian Language*. Littleton, Colorado.: Museum Tours Press, 2015.
Prolific Dr. Petty gives us a few pages of grammar basics, then nudges us right into translating texts, culminating in the 18 page, hand-transcribed (*not* facsimile) *Annals of Thutmose III* from Karnak Temple, all followed by answer keys.

QUIRKE, STEPHEN. *Who Were the Pharaohs? A History of Their Names with a List of Cartouches*. London: British Museum Press, 1996.
Complete history of royal naming conventions with cartouches of 145 rulers, including token Ptolemies, Roman emperors and Kushite kings. At 80 pages, more compact than CLAYTON, but special to me because it was my first real cartouche book, the one I dissected to make my first key.

RITNER, ROBERT, *Ptolemy IX (Soter)* Oriental Institute, Institute of Chicago. https://oi.uchicago.edu/research/individual-scholarship/ptolemy-ix-soter-ii-thebes

ROSE, JOHN. *The Sons of Re: Cartouches of the Kings of Egypt.* Warrington: Rose-Technology, 1985

> John Rose's background is similar to mine. He visited Egypt in 1978 (I first visited in 1974), and like me, was frustrated by the lack of a quick, portable reference for identifying cartouches, so decided to make his own. His book shows the cartouches and Horus names of an incredible 448 rulers and queens, including "contemporary kings of Nubia," in addition to 29 gods and goddesses. He states that the scope of the book ends with Dynasty 30, but he *does* give a nod to the Ptolemies. He names no Romans, but provides a few versions of the titles *Autocrator* and *Caesar*.

> Rose made a gallant effort at a cartouche identification key, but I, for one, find it incredibly difficult to use. Maybe it's because the print is so small. His first "discriminator" (my word) is the name of the god *Amen*, which is extremely common and optional in many cases as well. This is the opposite of the strategy used in the key in the *Field Guide*, which is to start with the more unique signs.

RUMFORD, JAMES. *Seeker of Knowledge: The Man Who Deciphered Egyptian Hieroglyphs.* Boston: Houghton Mifflin, 2000.
> A delightful children's biography of Champollion. The stunning watercolor illustrations alone are worth the price of the book.

SCARRE, CHRISTOPHER. *Chronicle of the Roman Emperors: The Reign-by-Reign Record of the Rulers of Imperial Rome.* New York: Thames and Hudson, 2007.
> Another in the Thames and Hudson series including *Chronicle of the Pharaohs* (CLAYTON) and *Chronicle of the Queens of Egypt* (TYLDESLEY). Well organized and illustrated, as you would expect. Indispensable for sorting out the emperors.

SILIOTTI, ALBERTO. *Guide to the Valley of the Kings.* Luxor, Egypt: A.A Gaddis and Sons, 1996
> A beautifully illustrated and useful, large format paperback guide to the Valley of the Kings as well as temples and tomb complexes in the area.

Tyldesley, Joyce Ann. *Chronicle of the Queens of Egypt: From Early Dynastic times to the Death of Cleopatra.* London: Thames & Hudson, 2006.
> A companion volume to Clayton's *Chronicle of the Pharaohs*, with all the beautiful photographs and drawings, cartouches, chronologies and family relationships you could wish, for this otherwise neglected demographic. 180 Queens, up through the Ptolemaic dynasty, are treated.

Von Beckerath, Jürgen, *See* Beckerath.

Weeks, Kent R., Araldo De Luca, Valerià Manferto De Fabianis, Laura Accomazzo, and Clara Zanotti. *The Treasures of the Valley of the Kings: Tombs and Temples of the Theban West Bank in Luxor.* Cairo: The American University in Cairo Press, 2001.
> Lavishly illustrated coffee-table-sized hardback. Nothing else like it.

Wehr, Hans, *A Dictionary of Modern Written Arabic.* Hans Wehr ; Edited by J. Milton Cowan. Cornell University Press, 1966.

Wilkinson, Richard H. *Reading Egyptian Art: A Hieroglyphic Guide to Ancient Egyptian Painting and Sculpture.* London: Thames and Hudson, 1994.
> One of my favorite books. It taught me that Egyptian art is made up of hieroglyphs, and hieroglyphs *are* Egyptian art. Wilkinson points out hidden (to the casual observer) hieroglyphs in wall paintings and sculpture, such as the sign for *sky* often placed at the top of a painting; hands and arms of deities and kings "spelling out" signs for *to embrace*, or *ka*, an aspect of the soul. He does this for 118 different signs. Read this book!

―――. *The Complete Gods and Goddesses of Ancient Egypt.* Cairo (Egypt): American University in Cairo Press, 2003.

WILLOCKX, SJEF, *The Cartouche Names of the New Kingdom. Ancient Egypt.* http;//www.egyptology.nl

    57 pages of kings' names and cartouches from Dynasties 18–20, and more importantly, all the **EPITHETS** that were used in that time period. New Kingdom names can be a nightmare since there are so many rulers with long and eventful reigns, and with so many duplicate **BIRTH NAMES**. A must-read! Thanks to SJEF WILLOCKX for making his studies freely available online.

WILSON, HILARY. *Understanding Hieroglyphs: A Complete Introductory Guide.* Lincolnwood, IL, USA: Passport Books, 1996.

    Illustrated with line drawings. You may learn less about the hieroglyphic writing system than you will about Egyptian culture, with sections on Royalty, Priesthood, and Numbers. Which is not a bad thing.

ZAUZICH, KARL-THEODOR. *Discovering Egyptian Hieroglyphs: A Practical Guide.* London: Thames & Hudson, 1992.

    Also published as *Hieroglyphs without Mystery*. A very reader-friendly book, it has a good explanation of the Egyptian writing system and explains the hieroglyphs and grammar of 13 artifacts depicted in color photos. Lists 20 **BIRTH NAME** cartouches of 20 pharaohs and names of 22 gods. Highly recommended.

Index